BELUGA DAYS

For Fred and Robin—
Thanks for caring about
our belugas—
Nancy

BELUGA DAYS

Tales of an Endangered White Whale

Nancy Lord

NANCY LORD

Alaska Oceans Festival
June 2, 2007

THE MOUNTAINEERS BOOKS

THE MOUNTAINEERS BOOKS
*is the nonprofit publishing arm of The Mountaineers Club, an organization
founded in 1906 and dedicated to the exploration, preservation, and
enjoyment of outdoor and wilderness areas.*

1001 SW Klickitat Way, Suite 201, Seattle, WA 98134

First trade paperback edition, 2007

Hardcover edition published in 2004 by Counterpoint, a member of the
Perseus Books Group

Manufactured in Canada

Cover photograph: *Beluga whale swimming in the St. Lawrence River* © Nick
Caloyianis/Getty Images

Library of Congress Cataloging-in-Publication Data
Lord, Nancy.
  Beluga days : tales of an endangered white whale / Nancy Lord.—1st
trade pbk. ed.
       p. cm.
  Includes bibliographical references.
  ISBN 1-59485-001-1
  1. White whale—Alaska—Cook Inlet. 2. Endangered species—Alaska—
Cook Inlet. I. Title.
QL737.C433L67 2007
599.5'42—dc22
                                          2006037546

♻ Printed on recycled paper

To Ken, again

COOK INLET

Map by Marilyn L. Perry, Seattle, Washington

SUMMER DISTRIBUTIONS
of ALASKA'S BELUGAS

ALL STOCKS EXCEPT COOK INLET
ARE THOUGHT TO OVERWINTER
IN THE BERING SEA.

RUSSIA

CHUKCHI
SEA

BERING
SEA

EASTERN
CHUKCHI

BEAUFORT

CANADA

BARROW

PT.
LAY

FAIRBANKS

ALASKA
U.S.A.

EASTERN
BERING

ANCHORAGE

COOK
INLET

BRISTOL
BAY

GULF
OF
ALASKA

Map by Marilyn L. Perry, Seattle, Washington

WORLDWIDE BELUGA POPULATIONS

Map by Marilyn L. Perry, Seattle, Washington

CONTENTS

PREFACE

Late this August reports began to flood my way: People were spotting beluga whales in Turnagain Arm, a branch of Cook Inlet south of Anchorage. The whales were feeding on late-run silver salmon in the waters just beyond the highway that hugs the Arm, and cars were pulling off the road all along the way to watch the activity. I heard there were dozens of whales, maybe a hundred or more, whales lined along the shoreline as far as anyone could see. I heard there were white whales (mature) and gray whales (immature) together. I heard excitement in the voices of parents and their children—that they had seen this phenomenon of whales, too seldom chanced-upon in recent years—and I heard relief that perhaps, in the numbers of young whales, there was hope for the future.

I was happy for the news. Many "beluga days" have passed since this book was first published two years ago, however days less full of actual belugas and more of concern about a diminished population and its ultimate fate. Today we understand a few more things about beluga whales and the unique, very small population that inhabits Alaska's Cook Inlet. Additional population surveys have been flown, tracking the whales' distribution and numbers. Government bureaucracy has creaked with excruciating slowness toward (but not to) the adoption of some sort of conservation plan and—possibly—a protective listing under the federal Endangered Species Act. But in August in Turnagain Arm, for the general public to see belugas in their natural environment and to enjoy them, to value them, to want them, to spread the word that belugas belong to this place—that was good, and necessary, news.

My purpose in writing this book was to share my particular experience with beluga whales and within the "culture"—the history, Native use, scientific study, and political context—that has surrounded them. I hoped that by telling an intriguing story about one species in one place, I might play a small role in saving the local population from extinction. But I also wanted to present a story about relationships between people and animals, using this one set of specifics to point up the more general questions we must answer if we are to live alongside other species in our modern, ever-more-crowded world.

At this writing, I admit I am not optimistic about the future of Cook Inlet belugas. This year's count is the lowest ever, suggesting a continuing decline in a population that numbers fewer than 300 individuals, involving factors that have not even been identified. Although Cook Inlet belugas were recently added to the Red List of the World Conservation Union as "critically endangered," and despite a new petition from environmental groups, neither the Alaska nor federal government has acted to list them as endangered or to protect their critical habitat areas. A conservation plan mandated years ago has never been completed, and research funds have been cut. Busy Cook Inlet gets busier, with several pending industrial developments related to oil and gas production, port expansion, bridge construction, and coal export—all scheduled to occur within the northern waters most essential to the belugas.

I am more optimistic about the larger picture. We humans may yet, by paying attention to Cook Inlet's wildlife management debacle and other examples of our poor behavior with animals, begin to demand better from ourselves and our institutions. We might still honor what history and Native knowledge systems can teach us. Already, we're beginning to understand that we needn't choose between economy and environment—that good economic choices can and should support environmental and community health.

The evidence of a tidal change is all around us, wherever we live. Increasingly, ordinary citizens who witness the results of human thoughtlessness and the squandering of our natural heritage are speaking up. Discussions of global warming have shifted dramatically just in recent months from "Is it real?" to "What can we do?" as individuals and local governments confront this life-altering (literally, altering the conditions for life) challenge of our age. I want to believe that we will decide to use our large brains and all our multiple talents and abilities to lift our heavy human hand from the earth and its systems. If we care for belugas, and for butterflies and bullfrogs, we must insist upon the worth of all our fellow creatures and what they need for their continuance.

What is essential now is that we love the world and act upon that love.

Nancy Lord
October 2006

PROLOGUE — WATCHING

West Foreland, Cook Inlet, Alaska

The sound got my attention first.

I was walking back along the beach, just after low tide, after having checked the "sets" where my partner Ken and I place our gill nets on fishing days. I'd tightened fixed lines and retrieved an extender line left tied to a buoy—standard tasks on the "off" days between fishing periods. I was, as usual, lost in thought, an occupational advantage of the kind of commercial salmon fishing I'd done for fifteen summers on the remote western shore of Alaska's Cook Inlet. For me, a favorite part of fishing—after hauling in nets full of shining fish, enough to fill the skiff bottom and stack toward the gunnels—is the quiet, meditative time spent walking the beach or rocking, waiting, in the open skiff.

If my mind had taken a Zen turn, that didn't mean I was oblivious to the world around me. I was that day carefully keyed to a few particular, and essential, points of awareness: the placement of my feet on rocks, the state of the tide (which rushes in and out of Cook Inlet in one of the world's greatest tidal exchanges), and any movement along the beach (which frequently enough turns out to be a bear absorbed in tasks of its own).

The sound of breathing brought my head up and turned me to the water. The exhalations were both familiar and distinctive: "poofing" percussions, blows with both liquid and airy dimensions. They're never much to see. Certainly not spouts, they're at most short mists. On this calm day, with the inlet as smooth as polished pewter, the whales' risings cut the surface like knife blades, and the whales' breaths were remarkable only—and sufficiently—by being audible.

18

For as far as I could see, a long stream of belugas was proceeding north with the tide, looking like a sudden swatch of whitewater along the shore. I stood just in from the water's edge, in gray mud among rounded cobbles, and they passed just beyond that border, through the element that was muddy gray water, across the same cobbled bottom. The closest ones weren't thirty feet offshore, and they couldn't have been in much more water than would cover them. They must have been nearly brushing bottom as they passed, dodging the boulders that lay within their paths.

My eyes swept the line of them, dozens at a time showing some slice of brilliant white skin. Up and under and up again: The belugas, troop-like, were rolling forward at a steady, traveling pace. In any snapshot of time I was catching sight of only a fraction—a fourth? a fifth?—of them; the whole pod had to number well over one hundred. I fixed my eyes on a particular whale, watched it arch through the water, its smooth back gleaming. It looked like nothing so much as a wheel, a round white disk churning the sea. It turned under and then, a few beats later, rose up again fifty yards ahead. The turn of another glistening wheel, and then I looked ahead, and there it rose again, and then it was too far from me, and I chose another nearer whale to follow. And then I looked across them all and marveled at the sea of them: white wheels turning. Some were larger, some were whiter, some were paired—swimming close and rising together. Some were young and smaller and gray, more difficult to see in the mud-colored water, above and beside and slightly behind the larger belugas that were their mothers. Like geese in a V-formation or bicyclists in a pack, those young were getting a ride, a hydrodynamic assist.

I looked more closely at individual rising whales, trying to catch them at the first break in the water's surface, trying to snatch a view of something other than that quick white arch. In other places where belugas live, and perhaps in other parts of the inlet when they're doing something other than traveling, these whales will lift their heads from the water as though looking around. They hang vertically in the water and bob upward—"spy-hopping," biologists and whale-watchers call it. They slap flippers and tails, float at the surface, and otherwise show themselves in more of their dimensions. But here, at this point of land between broad bays, the whales always seemed to pass back and forth without lingering and with frustratingly little show. Here, where the currents run fast, I'd at best seen an occasional fluke flip up into the air.

This time, I was close and the light was good, and when I was quick to set my eyes on a whale just beginning to surface, I could glimpse the bulbous swelling that was the back of the head, before the narrowing that makes a neck, and then—especially if the whale was turned slightly toward shore—the knobbiness of the vertebrae along its back. And again, I was looking at a wheel turning, those knobs like gear teeth.

I had, of course, seen photographs of belugas, and I knew they were nothing like that illusion of round, turning wheel. An entire beluga looks, in fact, something like the lumpy Pillsbury Doughboy. Belugas are not full-bodied like other whales, and they're certainly not streamlined, not sleek, not as beautiful as we imagine creatures that slide through the sea to be. I knew as I watched the whales pass along the beach that the ten- to sixteen-foot bodies I couldn't see were shaped more like poorly rolled cigars, bulging and gaunt in odd places, with small, bulbous heads and pathetically blunted, petal-shaped flippers. As whales go, belugas are not fast swimmers—one reason, where there are killer whales (as there sometimes are in Cook Inlet), that they travel so close to shore; they can't outswim their predators but they can swim in very shallow water. I knew, too, that those bulbous heads, if I could only see them, were famous for their expressiveness. Belugas have mouths that "smile."

Only once had I seen a beluga body in full—a dead one washed up on our beach the summer before. It was swollen and smelly, its skyward eye plucked out by birds, its mouth open to peg teeth, its skin sunburned pink and brown. It was not a lovely creature. Still, I looked hard at it there on the beach, filling my sight with the bulk of it so that when I saw, again, the mere crescent of a back, I might at least complete the idea of the whole to which it belonged. Ken and I briefly wondered what had caused the death—we saw nothing obvious—and were not concerned. Death was, we knew, natural enough. Bears came and ate the dead beluga, and then there were only greasy bones.

Later, however, we wondered a little more. Ken studied the teeth in the jaw and pulled one out when it loosened from its flesh. The teeth were many and fierce—not the worn-down stubs of an elderly animal that had reached the end of a long life. Some disease, maybe? Something it had eaten that it shouldn't have? Had it stranded and died on another beach before washing onto ours? Had it been caught in a fishing net and drowned? Had it been shot?

We knew that in the old days fishermen sometimes shot at belugas—because they didn't like them eating fish or because shooting was fun. But that had stopped twenty years before, with the passage of the federal Marine Mammal Protection Act in 1972. The penalties for "taking" or harassing whales and other marine mammals were severe, and aside from that, those old attitudes about whales being nuisance predators were, well, old.

One exception to marine mammal protection provided for subsistence hunting by Alaska Natives. That is, traditional hunting rights were also protected, and Alaska's Indians, Eskimos, and Aleuts could take from most marine mammal populations what they needed for food and crafts. Villagers throughout Alaska lived with the seasonal sequences of fishing, berrying, and hunting—providing their families with the foods they depended on for both nutrition and cultural value. Cook Inlet, the long estuary reaching up through southcentral Alaska, from the Gulf of Alaska to the city of Anchorage between two arms at its head, was home to most of Alaska's human population and much of its industry. Certainly belugas had been a source of food for the region's early people, but times had changed. Natives I knew—both along my fishing beach in the upper inlet and from villages near my winter home in Homer, in the lower inlet—hunted seals and otherwise depended to a great degree on the bounty of the sea, but they did not go after belugas. I thought the village of Tyonek, to our north, might still take an occasional one.

It was an extraordinary thing, when I stopped to think about it: that we should have whales in such a place, at such a point in time.

In 1992 nearly 400,000 people lived around Cook Inlet and up its streams and rivers. Elsewhere in the world, where you find people in such numbers, whales and other large (and small) creatures generally have a hard time of it, generally don't last. Why should Cook Inlet be different? For more than a century, commercial fishermen had been removing salmon and other fish from its waters. People cleared land and eroded riverbanks. Ships and barges traveled through the waters. From my spot on the beach, I looked across the inlet's narrowest part; on the far shore, a vaporous white plume rose and merged into the billows of cumulous clouds building over farther mountains. The plume, from an ammonia plant, was cleaner now than it used to be, when the spruce trees all around the plant were killed by its gases. Beside the plant, rows of huge tanks gleamed whitely, and a tanker, loading with liquefied gas, rested at the dock. To the north, oil platforms flared their orange flames. The inlet was a busy place, surrounded by and filled with competing uses, under enormous developmental pressures.

In Anchorage, office workers spotted belugas from their desks. In Kenai, just down the road from the ammonia plant and the tank farm, friends who lived by the river heard the breaths of belugas through their open windows. Down in Homer, families made a Mother's Day tradition out of driving out the Homer

Spit to watch lines of belugas swim past the hotel. We had all that contact, and still nobody seemed to know very much about Cook Inlet's beluga whales.

I probably knew as much about belugas as any ordinary citizen. I knew they were called "sea canaries" for the variety of sounds—clicks, whistles, chatterings, chirps, trills, buzzes, grunts, and pops—they made by blowing and vibrating air through passages around their larynxes and blowholes. Some sounds are associated with communication among themselves. Other sounds, principally the clicks, are used in echolocation—that is, the whales "bounce" the sounds they make off objects and then receive and process the echoes in the oil-filled structures of their heads to "see" what's in their environment. Mariners in wooden ships used to hear beluga songs resonating in the hulls, and some said that blowhole whistling carried clearly through the air. The fact that I'd never heard so much as a squeak was a disappointment to me— and something I attributed to the nature of beluga traveling behavior, which seemed a straight-ahead and silent business.

I knew as well that belugas had as their only close relatives the single-horned narwhals, which were as fantastic as unicorns, and that they were (generally speaking) Arctic whales—hence the lack of a dorsal fin, which could be a problem in ice, and the substitution of a hardened dorsal ridge. I'd seen the range of beluga coloration and knew the animals started out gray, gradually whitening into maturity. And I knew they had "necks," unfused vertebrae that allowed them to turn their heads.

My local museum had on display an articulated beluga skeleton, and the bones were a giveaway to the whale's evolutionary past as a land mammal: Inside the flipper the skeletal design looked very much like a hand, and back where a pelvis may once have been floated two small, unattached bones reduced to connecting muscles. The museum also owned a couple of rocks taken from a beluga stomach—suggesting that belugas did, at least sometimes, feed on the inlet's floor.

I'd been intrigued with the various names we humans have given belugas—names that remark one way or another on appearance. The scientific name, *Delphinapterus leucas,* had not been affixed until the late date of 1776; it means "white dolphin without a wing" ("wing" meaning, in this case, a dorsal fin). The common name "beluga" or as some prefer "belukha" comes from the Russian; I knew from studying Russian that *byeli* meant white and that names deriving from colors often have the ending *-kha*—thus, "white one." (The belukha spelling/pronunciation eliminates confusion with the completely unrelated beluga sturgeon, whence come the fish eggs valued as caviar.) The

English called the beluga the "white whale," a name often still used (and not to be confused with the white whale of *Moby-Dick,* which was an albino sperm whale). Most recently, I'd learned that in the Dena'ina Athabaskan language of Cook Inlet the name for beluga was *qunshi* or *quyushi,* which translates as "that which comes up."

Belugas in the world are not particularly rare. Relatively large numbers (perhaps 60,000) seasonally inhabit the waters of western Alaska. More than 100,000 form the worldwide circumpolar population. In the scientific arena, there is little urgency to study them, and work in Arctic waters has never been easy. Cook Inlet is one of a very few southerly regions where belugas are found, but our whales have never been given much attention. No one knows how many there are. No one knows where they go in winter when they seem to disappear. Scientists only speculate they are a stock separate from any other belugas—that they stay in Cook Inlet or in the Gulf of Alaska and do not intermix with any other belugas.

I liked that I lived with mystery whales.

The stream of whales reached its tailend, and I stepped back from the water's edge to watch the stragglers from atop a sun-warmed rock. Had they even known I was there?

Sometimes, when Ken and I were on the beach together, we'd call to one another to look at the whales, and even with us running back and forth and being boisterous, the whales seemed to pay no attention to us. Sometimes when we were fishing from the skiff, we'd look up to find whales passing nearby, again seemingly undisturbed by our presence or by the sound of our outboard, and always avoiding our nets. These were times we liked nothing better than to kill our motor and drift among the whales. It was as close as we ever got to their watery world, tossed by the same waves they were tossed by, and we felt, cradled there within our curved metal skin, almost like their reverse images—creatures of the dry side as they were of the wet.

But there were other times, when the whales passed the beach at low tide, that I would try to get close by rock-hopping out onto the reef in front of our camp, only to have the whales spook. One moment they were there, and then they were gone, headed wide or simply down and on, out of sight. I suspected the passing whales this day were aware of my standing, then sitting, at the water's edge and that they had not found me particularly threatening.

And then they were all by the point and around into Trading Bay, and I was left staring at the gray inlet that was flat and still except for the currents that swept past, rumbling around the giant, rounded rocks exposed by the tide.

Salmon—red salmon, sockeyes—were moving with the tide too, invisible in the murk unless one should throw itself clear in an acrobatic leap or, in water so smooth, crease the surface with its dorsal fin. They were, in any case, safe from our nets until the next fishing period two days off. Other unseen creatures shared the waters—starry flounder skimming the bottom, Dolly Varden trout, colorful red and green Christmas anemones flailing from the sides of rocks, a saucer-eyed seal that might at any moment bob its head clear. Upper Cook Inlet, with its load of sediment, is not the world's richest marine environment, but millions of salmon headed for their nascent streams and lakes pass through every summer. I was there because of salmon, and so were the belugas, the seals, the trout that follow the salmon to feed on their eggs and fry, the bottomfish, and the invertebrates that partake in what comes down to them.

Water was visibly flooding in over the flats, moving up the beach, surrounding the rock on which I perched. An eagle squawked. The breeze, warmed to tepid by its passage over sun-soaked mud and sand, brushed my bare arms and stirred the alders on the hillside. I ached as I do when the gifts of the place caught me unaware. The West Foreland and Cook Inlet are, in general, hard places, and a person has to be tough to live there, on the beach or water. I kill fish for a living. I am not generally given to sentiment, don't gush over animals, have no desire to pat whales on their heads. But I did like beluga whales, and I did appreciate living in a time and place that sustained fish, whales, and fishermen—all of us together.

It wasn't every day that belugas passed my door. But it was often enough throughout the summer months to remind me just how fortunate I was.

After all, I might have remained in New Hampshire. Growing up there, I'd never seen a whale—or an eagle—and my concept of "beach" had been Hampton, part of the tiny and excessively crowded New Hampshire coastline where on hot summer days it was nearly impossible to find a towel-sized square to call one's own.

Our first week in Alaska, Ken and I, paddling a kayak across Kachemak Bay in a late-night, dusky calm, found ourselves surrounded by circling black fins. In our ignorance, I'd thought them sharks, and Ken imagined killer whales. That our companions were only porpoises made the experience scarcely less memorable; here we would live with whales and other finned and flippered creatures.

And we did: killer whales alongside as we ran a salmon tender in Prince William Sound, humpbacks leaping into the light beyond a window where I wrote one winter in Sitka, gray whales slapping their enormous chins while a friend and I cut salmon at the end of the Alaska Peninsula. Minke whales sped around our bay, and once, walking behind our house in Homer, Ken and I spotted some much larger whale's tall blow, a mile off, fall back to sea. A dead fin whale washed up, and we hiked with friends to its lonely beach to look upon its length.

I learned, along the way, to divide whales into their two groupings of toothed and baleen, that the nearly exterminated right whales were called that because they were the "right" whales for whalers to go after (that is, they were loaded with oil and floated when dead), and that at least some biologists preferred to call killer whales "killer whales" instead of "orcas" because they wanted to acknowledge their predatory nature and not pretend that all whales were peaceable-kingdom pacifists. Our living room windowsill at home began to collect—among agates and glass fishing floats—odd chunks and strips of beach-combed baleen. At museums, I looked with sharpened interest at Native-made baleen baskets and at lonely sailor scrimshawing on sperm whale teeth. I read *Moby-Dick* for a first and a second time.

But it was belugas, small and relatively undramatic, that we lived with, summer after summer. When we crossed the inlet by plane, we were accustomed to seeing pods of them below us, looking like expanses of whitecaps in the middle of wide water. At camp, our skiff drifted among them, and I tried to cup my ear to the deck to listen for their "singing." When we got together with our neighbors on the beach, we talked about them: "Did you see…" and, "There were a lot of young ones," and "Yeah, there was a pilot whale [the local name for a porpoise] with them."

My rock had become an island, the eagle had sailed off, and the whales were long gone. Other chores beckoned from my cabin, up the beach, beside the creek, where our yellow Don't Tread on Me flag hung limply from its pole. I headed home.

Little did I know, that July day in 1992, that the whales I'd stopped to watch—that I'd unquestioningly assumed to be a constant in my life—were in trouble. In the summers to follow, fewer whales passed my beach on fewer occasions. Within a few years, I watched all season without seeing a single beluga.

Summer after summer after summer, I kept watch for belugas. On calm days at my camp, I tracked, without thinking, the tide changes, and I found myself looking toward the point the whales would round—if only they would—on the flood. On rougher days, my eyes caught on the tops of waves, tricking me into white illusions. On the quietest nights, when the water barely brushed the shoreline, I lay in bed and in half-consciousness heard that rhythmic wash as the exhalations of whales. I lifted my face to the window and looked out over the beach and the empty gray water, and then I lay down again and listened to the breathing in my dreams.

1

OLD TIME

Sweating from my mile-and-a-half walk up the beach, I arrived at my neighbor's fish camp to find its proprietor, George Hayden, paying bills at his kitchen table. At midsummer, George was looking leathery and relaxed, his white hair and beard curling around his ears.

"I'm on a mission," I announced, loudly. George is hard of hearing and doesn't like to wear his hearing aid at camp, where he's too likely to get water in his ears. I set my notebook on the table. The fewer belugas we saw, the more curious I was about them and the relationships people had had with them in the past. George had lived with belugas for sixty years and had more history than anyone else I knew. "Beluga Days," I said. "You've always talked about Beluga Days, but I don't think I understand what that was all about. They used to have, like, a beluga barbecue over in Kenai? And you had something to do with it? You used to kill a beluga for them?"

George poured me a glass of ice-cold well water, then hefted the world's largest bag of animal crackers from a side table and filled a bowl he placed between us. I could see him thinking, his mind shuffling through the stories he tells every time friends and neighbors gather in his kitchen. I know all about how he brought his young family up the Alaska Highway during World War II, how he worked as a cobbler for the military, how he ran a busline in Anchorage. George knew everyone in Anchorage, all the old-timers who built the place. He likes to joke about the fact that they all seemed to get rich and he didn't: "You know why I've got such sharp eyesight? I developed it from watching for my ship to come in."

Mostly, George has fished. His camp had been the Trading Bay Cannery, where salmon were hand-packed into cans as a premium product. George worked there first as a fisherman, then bought the place. But by the 1940s, the Cook Inlet salmon industry was declining, and it wasn't profitable to keep the necessary crews on site. Soon after he purchased the cannery and all its equipment, he stopped canning and settled for catching and selling fish to larger canneries, which sent fish-buying boats from Anchorage or the Kenai Peninsula. George still has the giant retort, once used for pressure canning, but for decades now he's used it as a locker for his sacks of flour and cases of motor oil. He winters in Nebraska but comes back to the beach every spring before the swallows.

"Beluga Days," I repeated. "What years are we talking about?" All I knew was that whatever the beluga event was, it had to have occurred before 1972, when the Marine Mammal Protection Act curtailed everything but Alaska Native subsistence hunting.

"I guess it was the 1960s," George said. "The druggist in Kenai had a lot to do with it. They had the Beluga Hunt Club."

That was the first I'd heard anything about a club.

"A hunting club?"

A promotional thing, George said. They took people beluga hunting and then presented them with both a certificate that said they'd been beluga hunt-ing and a little vial of beluga oil. "I might still have Charlotte's certificate. She was an honorary member." Charlotte, George's wife, looked down on us from a photo on the wall; when I knew her, she was already an old woman, not well, but in the photo she and George are both startlingly young and attractive. "I suppose," George said, "I must have been an honorary member too. I didn't belong, but I helped them out."

Beluga Days, George said, was sometime during the summer—he couldn't remember when. The town of Kenai held a parade, featuring the dead animal on a float, and then the whale was butchered and ground up, and everyone ate beluga burgers. As for the hunt club, on a few occasions its members had come across the inlet, and George took them hunting to show them how to do it. But when it came time to get a beluga for Beluga Days, the club wasn't always successful. "At least twice they asked us to get them one. One year they came over just the night before, and they didn't have a beluga. Buck and Ken got them one and towed it across."

Buck is George's son, and Ken Tapp was another fisherman who had worked for George—and who had been an unparalleled seal hunter and general marksman.

"They paid them a hundred dollars," George continued. "But belugas tow awful hard. That was the last one Buck and Ken caught for them, and maybe that was the last Beluga Days—I don't remember. It was a big deal then, though, just like the salmon derbies they have everywhere now."

George's clearest memory of that time is of a photo taken on the North Kenai beach. The beluga had been picked up by a crane and was hanging by its tail while one of the Beluga Club members hosed it off. That was the background. In the foreground, Buck was brushing his teeth, and the man with the hose turned and sprayed some water his way so he could rinse. "I always thought that picture should have been on the back page of *Life* magazine," George said.

He'd been able to help with Beluga Days, George said, because he'd learned how to hunt belugas, and he was pretty good at it—better than anyone in the hunt club, and better than any Natives he knew. He and Buck and whoever was around used to go out and chase around after belugas every now and then, for sport.

"What did you do with them?" I asked. "Did you eat them?"

"Just the liver. A chef at the Captain Cook wanted me to pickle the flukes. They wanted to serve them with cocktails. But I never sent him any." And no, he didn't like muktuk, the delicacy of skin and fat. George made a face. He gave the belugas, minus their livers, to two Native families who lived up the beach—Inupiat who had relocated to Cook Inlet from the Nome area.

It was another Eskimo, George said, who'd first given him a harpoon, and from that he'd designed and made his own. The one he'd been given was made by cutting the tip off a butcher knife and inserting it into a piece of moose horn. The harpoon handles were usually made of bamboo. George pointed to the clothes pole hung along one side of the room, on which hangers with shirts were arranged. The pole (I'd never noticed) was bamboo—a former or never-quite-become harpoon handle. I was reminded of the Spouter-Inn in *Moby-Dick:* Ishmael, when he stopped for the night, found the entryway decorated with old whaling lances and harpoons and in his room a sea chest in use as a table.

Like Ishmael, George must have learned just how to chase down and harpoon belugas from someone with prior knowledge—so I thought. But when I asked how he'd learned, he shrugged modestly and said, "I just figured it out from watching the movies in my youth."

"So it was sport, it was fun, to go out and kill a beluga now and then?"

"Well, and we wanted to get rid of them."

I was, for a moment, caught off-balance. It hadn't occurred to me that George would ever have wanted to "get rid of" belugas. Of course I knew about the competitive history between fishermen and fish-eating animals. And I knew that the 1960s had been the peak of bounty hunting for seals. But I hadn't thought that belugas in Cook Inlet had ever been so many or so visibly rapacious as to become a scourge to fishermen like George.

He said, "I tried to get the government to put a bounty on them. Once I found the remains of eighteen king salmon in one. I thought they would go for that, but they didn't."

George smiled, at the memory or, very possibly, because I might have been frowning. "I didn't want to get rid of all the belugas," he said. "I just wanted to get my share of fish." And the belugas, he added, were sometimes helpful. Sometimes they chased a school of king salmon from the deeper water inshore into a net. Once he found twenty-six king salmon in a net and was sure the belugas had driven them in.

Eighteen. Twenty-six. If George was sometimes vague about years, he was impressively exact with some numbers. He reached into the cracker dish for a handful of elephants, camels, giraffes, lions and tigers, monkeys eating bananas, and bears. There are no whales in the animal cracker kingdom.

"So," I asked, "were there many more belugas in those days?"

"Oh, yes! There were lots of belugas in those days." And this year—no, he hadn't seen a single one. The year before, he'd seen one pod, one time, but it was big—hundreds, he was sure. He was concerned about the belugas, but he was more concerned about the salmon runs, which weren't great, and salmon prices, which had fallen so low that it was hard even to begin to make a living fishing anymore. "The belugas, they follow the fish," he said. That's the reason he was always glad to see them, he said. Where there were belugas, he knew there were fish.

Salmon, belugas, people: They had a long Cook Inlet history together. Beluga hunting—or at least salvaging of stranded or dead whales—presumably goes back to the inlet's earliest human occupation, a few thousand years ago. Just a couple of miles from my fish camp, in the other direction from George's, lies an old Dena'ina Athabaskan village known as Kustatan. In 1930, shortly after it was abandoned, the anthropologist Frederica de Laguna explored the site and found it to be "of considerable area and respectable age." She identified beluga bones in a midden with clam and cockle shells.

De Laguna and other, later archaeologists also found beluga bones at older Eskimo-type Kachemak Bay sites, in the lower inlet. There, the bones were mixed with those of porpoises and harbor seals, indicating cultures that were clearly oriented toward marine mammal hunting. The importance of marine mammals to those early people is also supported by rock paintings from the period.

Once, years ago, I volunteered with a "salvage dig" at a site in Kachemak Bay. Someone preparing to build a house gave permission for the area, which had obvious shell middens, to be excavated first for its archaeological value. Our group, from Homer's Pratt Museum, divided the hillside into squares and scraped down layer by layer, cleaning and bagging and mapping as we went. Most of the work was plain and tedious bending and kneeling and moving buckets of earth, and most of the finds were bits of shell and bone, worked pieces of slate, and fire-cracked rocks, but we also uncovered riches of notched stones (used for sinking fishing nets), clay beads, and beautifully crafted spear points—materials radiocarbon dated to AD 36. My "personal best" find was a beluga tooth carved with many close rings. A groove near its base suggested that it may have been worn as a pendant. The tooth went to the museum, but I kept with me the idea of an ancient hunter wearing that tooth, a talisman for the beauty, or the strength, or the fishing ability of the whale that also fed him.

One thing we'll likely never know about Cook Inlet's prehistoric people— among many tantalizing questions—is just how large a part belugas played in their diets and lives. De Laguna and the anthropologists who followed her noted that the expected variety of beluga bones was not represented at sites and that few of the bones that were found were uncut. That is, most bones they examined had been used as tools. They speculated that the size of belugas generally discouraged anyone from hauling their bones to village or camping sites. Instead, skin, fat, organs, and meat would likely have been removed at the beach, with carcasses left to return to the sea. Only bones selected for some purpose made it to high ground and into the archaeological record.

We do know that early explorers of Cook Inlet found its inhabitants hunting belugas. Ferdinand Petrovich Von Wrangell, an Estonian German exploring for the Russians, reported in 1834 that Dena'ina in the upper inlet hunted belugas from platforms atop poles driven into shallow places near the shore. When a whale feeding on salmon drew near, the hunter threw a harpoon attached to a line and bladder, and then he and/or other hunters chased after the beluga in their skin boats to stab it with a lance. The same method of hunting is detailed in *Shem Pete's Alaska* by Pete, a Dena'ina man who died in 1989. Pete had heard about the *yuyqul,* or spearing tree, from elders, including a man thought to be the last to use one—before modern boats and weaponry made them obsolete. Anthropologists had seized upon the *yuyqul*—unique to the upper inlet Dena'ina—as a fascinating adaptation of a technique used by inland Athabaskan Indians to hunt bears from trees along salmon streams. The Dena'ina are the only Athabaskans to live at tidewater and to have developed marine technologies.

A beluga, butchered and brought back to a village by hunters, was well and thoroughly used. Numerous early accounts mention how valued the skin and fat layer was as food and how other fat was melted into oil, meat was dried for the winter, sinew was prized for its strength and used particularly for bow strings, and stomachs were used as containers. Beluga oil served as a preservative for other foods, such as clams and squirrel meat.

Cornelius Osgood, an ethnologist who studied the Dena'ina in the 1930s, wrote that some Dena'ina considered belugas better eating than seal and that the whales were "much sought after as they sport warily in the wide rivers." The people of Tyonek, he reported, built a weir across the Beluga River and trapped whales that followed salmon in with the tide.

Although belugas were never pursued commercially to the extent that large whales were, they were nonetheless the object of various commercial "fisheries," particularly in the late-nineteenth century. In the Canadian Arctic, visitors to Somerset Island can still find shorelines layered with bleached beluga bones—left from Scottish whaling ventures that trapped large numbers of the whales in shallow inlets. Between 1874 and 1898, whalers killed some 10,000 belugas there. The skin was said to be especially sought after for boot laces and coach covers. The high-quality oil was used with machinery. In Svalbard, islands north of Norway, commercial beluga whaling continued until 1955. The Soviet Union and Russia allowed and continue to allow commercial takes.

Early in the twentieth century, Americans tried to develop commercial beluga whaling in Alaska. Nome and Golovin, both in the northwest, were two places where whaling "stations" processed small numbers of belugas for oil and leather, with the meat sold locally for dog food. But perhaps the most successful commercial beluga whaling in Alaska took place in Cook Inlet between 1915 and 1920.

Joseph A. McGill was in the seafood business, operating fish traps and canneries at various places around Cook Inlet. He came north from Chicago or Seattle each summer and went south again in fall with shipments of canned and salted salmon and herring. In 1915, with his gas boat, he began to take belugas as well. The principal value was apparently in the hides, sought in this case as fine glove leather. In 1916 he incorporated the Beluga Whaling Company, which a year later had twelve employees.

In 1918 the Beluga Whaling Company took forty-one beluga hides valued at $1250. In 1919, at its plant six miles up the Beluga River, fifty-five beluga whales were processed.

The Anchorage Museum of History and Art holds a collection of photos from 1919 of Joe McGill, his Beluga River plant and employees, and some of their catch. In some photos, four or five dead whales, with lines around their flukes, lie beached. In others, two men carry a pole between them, and a baby beluga hangs from the pole. We see substantial frame buildings, one with a dormer window, on pilings atop the riverbank, and a wooden ramp up which a beluga is being winched. There's Joe McGill himself, standing on the deck of a boat and watching stranded belugas thrash in a foot of water. There are nets laid out on a net rack to dry and identified as "nets used to block entrance to channel after whales enter."

A 1921 article, "A Remarkable Whaling Development," describes McGill's genius in catching belugas. "Notwithstanding the desirability of taking belugas, both for these valuable products [leather and oil] and for the conservation of salmon, little has formerly been done in this direction because of the difficulty of capturing them, as the beluga is an exceptionally wary animal." McGill's technique involved a heavy net made from cotton seine twine, 1,550 feet long. The net's lead (weighted) line was lashed to stakes near the mouth of the river, and a hose attached to the corkline connected to a pipeline that, in turn, ran to a compressor and tank some distance away, out of sight and hearing of any belugas that entered the river. The net, lying on the bottom, was invisible. The whales, as the (24-foot) tide came in, crossed it and proceeded up the river to eat salmon. Then, the hose was inflated, bringing it to the surface and cutting off the belugas' escape. Keg buoys were attached at intervals to hold the corkline high and to prevent whales pushing on the net from pulling it under. As the tide fell, the trapped whales were driven to strand and were then shot. When the tide rose again, they were towed up the river to the rendering plant.

At the end of the 1920 season, McGill, then managing J. A. McGill & Co., Inc. (successor to the Beluga Whaling Company, which went bankrupt), reportedly shipped south "several car loads" of beluga whale oil and hides from its most successful season yet, one in which one hundred belugas were taken. The "Remarkable Whaling" article says that the McGill plant at that time had three large rendering tanks for the blubber oil. Two other, higher grades of oil—from jaw and head—were rendered by the heat of the sun.

McGill had bigger plans yet. For the next season, he planned to operate on three rivers in the vicinity and to take one thousand belugas. He planned, as well, to add a fertilizer plant to process the meat, bones, and other waste.

After that, press references to McGill identify him as "trap owner and fish packer," "trap owner and salmon salter," and "the well-known Cook Inlet fishery operator," but they no longer mention beluga products. In September of 1929, "Anchorage canner" Joseph McGill committed suicide.

I have in my files a 1957 beluga hunting story from *The Alaska Sportsman,* "Gunning for White Whales," by Jim Rearden. At the top of the first page, under a photo of a hip-booted man leaning over a dead beluga in shallow water, the caption reads, "Hunting belugas is food-gathering to Eskimos, a salmon conservation measure to commercial fishermen, an exciting sport to the few white persons who have discovered it. To James W. Brooks, marine mammal biologist, it was all in a summer's work."

Brooks worked for the Alaska Department of Fish and Game when Alaska was a territory and in the mid-1950s directed the Division of Predator Investigation and Control. (He would shortly be promoted to head Alaska's Division of Game and would later, after Alaska's statehood, serve as commissioner of the Department of Fish and Game.) In his role overseeing predators (those pesky eagles, seals, and wolves) he'd taken on a study of beluga food habits. The study entailed killing, during a two-year period, 150 Bristol Bay belugas and examining their stomach contents for data about the effect of belugas on salmon fisheries. Commercial fishermen in the area—on the other side of the Alaska Peninsula from Cook Inlet—had been complaining for years, the article says, about the depredations of belugas on salmon, and the study was intended to determine how significant the problem was.

Just how many beluga stomachs would a person need to examine to figure out what they were eating? Could it possibly be necessary to kill 150 belugas to get useful data? How does someone justify killing such a large fraction of a population—the entire Bristol Bay population was thought to be about one thousand—in order to learn about some aspect of its life? When I read about Brooks's study, I was uncomfortably reminded of the "research" whaling now being done by some countries in order, so they say, to find out what minke and other whale species eat. After the "research" on stomach contents, the whale meat is sold, and everybody involved winks; everyone understands that the point is to get around the International Whaling Commission's ban on commercial whaling. In the beluga/salmon situation, it seems that the study was effectively meeting an unstated goal of predator control.

Predator control was, of course, a foundation of wildlife management at the time—hence the devotion of a governmental agency to it—and bounties were paid to those good citizens who went out and blasted seals, wolves, wolverines, and coyotes. (Bald eagles had only just been removed from the bounty program.) In Bristol Bay, there'd been a cry for help with the belugas; salmon runs were declining, and fishermen were hurting.

Like an adventure story, the *Alaska Sportsman* article details one of its author's "most thrilling hunts" and includes numerous documenting photos: Brooks ready with the harpoon in the boat's bow, the bucket-float at the end of the line careening after the harpooned whale, the dead whale and its stomachful of salmon. The language is full of the swagger of old-time sportsmen, as though the beluga were just another big fish. The whale is "quarry" and "a flash of white" before the harpoon "slammed" into it and "a huge white fluke erupted furiously." After a series of misplaced shots and laughter, the whale—"a fourteen-foot chuck of red-stained meat and blubber"—eventually "wilted." Much is made of the necessity of firing into the beluga's brain, from a foot behind the blowhole, "because a beluga hit anywhere except in the brain will continue to swim and fight seemingly forever... until it looked about like a colander." The killing of whales to look at their stomach contents was not wasteful, the author tells us, because the animals were given to local Eskimos to eat.

This particular hunting may have been, ostensibly, "scientific research," but the author—no doubt mindful of his audience—comments twice about beluga sport hunting. After telling us how popular beluga hunting was with Eskimos, he says, "With more and more people visiting Alaska, travelers and sportsmen are getting acquainted with the sport of beluga hunting, and each year more white men hunt them. I'm sure if more visitors to Alaska knew about them, the beluga would become one of the most popular big game species in the Territory." At the end, he adds his personal testimony: "...I became a real beluga-hunting enthusiast. I predict that the sport will grow in popularity, and that big game hunters will soon be including a beluga hunt in their Alaska itinerary." There were no restrictions, he reminds readers, except the territorial law against wanton waste; all animals killed had to be utilized, but that was no problem as long as there were Eskimos.

The article, published two years after the study was completed, doesn't mention results. I rounded up old Fish and Game reports. The conclusions were—surprise!—that belugas ate salmon. In May in Bristol Bay they largely fed on smelt (small oily fish), but once young red salmon (smolts) began to flood out of the river systems, they turned to them, and then, from mid-June through August, they fed on mature salmon returning to spawn. During the weeks belugas feasted on smolts, the average stomach contained 685 of the young salmon. Brooks calculated that the beluga population was taking nearly 3 million smolt salmon (of which, without the predation, five percent may have eventually returned as 150,000 adult salmon) and between 100,000 and 200,000 adult salmon, less than half of which were the valuable red salmon. Percentage-wise, the take of adult fish represented one to three percent of the red salmon runs—an amount the report labeled "of little practical importance." The department decided that the greater problem was the beluga take of outmigrating smolts. In subsequent years, it instituted harassment techniques consisting of chasing belugas with a high-speed skiff and setting off small charges of dynamite; it also tried to frighten the belugas by broadcasting killer whale calls.

I eventually discovered that there was never anything—ever, anywhere—called Beluga Days, except by George Hayden. Kenai's summer celebration was called, unimaginatively enough, Kenai Days.

In a newspaper clipping from 1965, I found a schedule of Saturday and Sunday events (in August that year): Marathon Race (ten-mile course), Children's Decorated Parade, Gala Float Parade, Army Band Concert, Fairground Food Booths and Carnival, Children's Races, Fashion Show Luncheon, Air Force Band, Skydivers, Air Force Drill Team, Softball, Circus Acts, Coronation Ball (of, naturally, the Kenai Days Queen), Pancake Eating Contest, and Square Dancing. Beluga Whale Butchering and Broiling was scheduled for noon on Sunday, in between the Fly-in Breakfast and the Children's Pet Show. Special and continuing events on both days included Russian Church Tours, Art Show, Hand and Needle Crafts, Air Tours over Kenai and Oilfields, Amusement Rides, and Beluga Whale Hunts.

Kenai Days organizer Peggy McBride praised the food: "Kenai Days is noted for the variety of local, excellent, taste-bud tantalizing foods served at this annual celebration... Not to be overlooked—by either eyes or nose—are the Beluga burgers which will be dispensed under the supervision of Beluga Whale Wrangler, John Hulien."

Hulien, the pharmacist, I found in a photo in another newspaper—standing in his white coat before shelves of cigarettes and holding out cans of beluga meat. The eight-ounce cans, described as "collectors' items," were sold by the Beluga Whale Hunt Club for a dollar each. The same article said that the club was selling a booklet prepared by Kenai resident Lance Petersen—"an informational booklet on requirements of Beluga Whale Hunting," which was "a complete guide on how to get there, what to wear, and the kind of trophy to expect from a Beluga Whale."

Trophy? I had a momentary vision of a stuffed fifteen-foot beluga hanging on some hunter's living room wall.

Lance Petersen, now a humanities professor at Kenai Peninsula College, had just graduated from college the year he wrote the beluga booklet. A primer, it was called: four double-spaced, typewritten pages subtitled "Basic Information on Requirements for the Hunter and the Hunt." It told how to get to Kenai and that there was a 28-foot cabin dory as a "mother ship" for the whaling, with a smaller "catcher" boat in tow for the actual hunt. It said the hunts were ideal for women because they took place from a boat ("no hills to climb, no packs to carry"). Costs were $200 for the one-day hunt and $900 for the four-day, either of which could be split by up to four hunters. All meals and accommodations, and of course the boats and guides, were covered, but hunters had to bring their own high-powered rifles and "plenty of ammunition. Hunters have used over one hundred rounds of ammunition on a single whale.... Whales are hard to hit, showing very little above water, and can absorb many shots without weakening."

The brochure solved the trophy mystery for me: "Whales taken during the hunt become the property of the Beluga Whale Hunt Club. A successful hunter will receive a case of whale meat canned by an inspected and approved cannery. Each tin will bear a personalized label with the hunter's name and the date the whale was taken. Another trophy for the whale hunter is the lower jaw with teeth. The jaw bones are approximately two feet long and when cleaned are quite suitable for mounting. The teeth can be set in the jaw or kept seperate [sic] and used for pendants, key chains, watch fobs, necklaces, or bracelets." There was also the certificate and the kind of hardware trophy that a high-scoring bowler might be awarded. "At the end of the season, the hunter bagging each of the three largest whales will receive a trophy stating the name of the hunter, the date, and whether his whale was first, second, or third largest for the season."

Lance, when I spoke to him, had sky-bright memories of Kenai Days. His family had moved to Kenai in 1953, and already, he said, there was a long tradition of summer celebration in the town, when everyone got together for contests and games, dancing, and eating. "A big part of every celebration was eating beluga. Someone would get a beluga, and they'd cook it. They'd cut off chunks of fins and make steaks and burgers." Lance's family owned a winch truck, which brought them into the proceedings. "In the 1960s there was always a parade. Everybody in town shined up their cars—it was that kind of thing. And part of the parade was hauling the beluga through town. We went out to Arness Dock and winched it up and paraded it through town." At parade's end, the beluga was brought to the civic center grounds in the middle of town, where there was a ten-foot-square barbecue pit. As Lance remembered it, everybody liked eating beluga meat. "It was kind of like buffalo—stronger than beef, but red meat like that, and not fatty."

It's Lance's business to think about cultural contexts. So I asked him what he thought about the beluga's place in Kenai Days—if the parading and barbecue may have evolved out of some earlier tradition, if Native people had been involved, if there was some meaning to the event aside from the novelty of eating a whale.

In those days, Lance reminded me, Natives in the area didn't identify themselves as such and didn't go public with their traditions. "There was no advantage in being Native. Most of them were just interested in being folks." No, it wasn't cultural in that sense. But it was, he suspected, "an older deal. This was the centerpiece of *stuff*. Beluga eating had a kind of sacramental feel. It wasn't just that a sports club went and blasted a beluga. There was something more enduring and significant to it. Everybody ate of the whale." The tradition, Lance felt, was rooted in the cycle of life of which people who lived on Cook Inlet—no matter where they may have come from, or when—were a part. There was a sense of, here we are again, another summer, bounty from the sea, it's time to eat of the whale as a way of honoring the cycle that continues to provide.

Lance had gone out with the hunt club a couple or a few times, never with any success. The hunts he described, involving a lot of high-speed chasing and shooting along the west side of the inlet, sounded Keystone Cop–ish. "We fired an enormous number of shots and never hit a whale." (The image of a colander came to mind.) "Once we were in pursuit, the whales rose rarely and briefly. When they did surface, everyone fired, whether we were in range or not." The rifles were what they normally used for moose hunting, and no one had a harpoon. "It was mostly sport," Lance said. In addition to amusing themselves, the hunt club organizers hoped to attract big game hunters from around the world.

Lance showed me his certificate and vial of whale oil, both still in the mailing tube they'd come in from the Kenai Chamber of Commerce. The top of the parchment-like certificate was illustrated with a drawing of four Eskimo-style men in what looks like a skin boat. Each figure is holding a lance or harpoon while in front a beluga slaps its tail on the water.

CERTIFICATE OF MEMBERSHIP
KENAI, ALASKA
BELUGA WHALE HUNT CLUB

This is to certify that *Lance Petersen*
Is a member in good standing of the Kenai Beluga Whale Hunt Club and is entitled to all of the prerogatives of said exalted organization, which shall include the right to a flask of whale oil and the inscription of his name on the official hunt club scroll located at Kenai, Alaska

Witness our hand and seal this *16th* day of *August 1964*

I held the little vial of oil, about a quarter of a cup's worth, to the light. In color and transparency, it might have been mistaken for an amber beer. I tipped the vial back and forth, and the oil moved easily, like a light cooking oil; it didn't cling to the glass. Tiny bits of white sediment swirled up from the bottom. I tried the cap, but it didn't turn easily, and I didn't force it. "It was touted as the finest oil," Lance said. "Better than sperm oil."

While the beluga steaks and burgers had cooked, the blubber had been cut up and rendered in vats at the same barbecue pit. I wondered to myself who had taken it home for cooking or for oiling machinery. In those days, who in Kenai would have claimed a genuine taste for beluga oil, as opposed to dividing it up into tiny souvenir jars?

The jar's pink and blue label, designed by the same artist as the certificate, showed two Eskimos with a harpoon in the bow of a boat and a beluga (head and tail lifting from the water) before them. It stated: "PURE WHALE OIL from Kenai Alaska."

Later, I found magazine and newspaper stories about the hunt club and Kenai Days. In December 1963, the *Alaska Sportsman* reported that because of blustery weather, the "newly organized Beluga Whale Hunt Club" had been kept on the beach during Kenai Days, but that a previous practice hunt had provided about 300 pounds of whale meat, which entirely sold out as beluga burgers. The magazine opined that the whale hunts were "a great idea publicity-wise" and touted the rights and privileges of becoming a hunt club member. For three dollars, you got the certificate, the bottle of oil, your name "burned into a six-by-six-foot whale hide on display at the city center," and the chance to participate in a whale hunt if you "happen to be in Kenai when one is on."

In June 1965 *The Cook Inlet Courier* ran a story, "Whale Hunting Is New Big Game Sport," that told about John Hulien and Ken Tapp, "head guide from Trading Bay," taking a couple of army men on a whale hunt near Big River (just south of my fish camp). For four hours one day and six hours the next, they chased belugas. They fired 250 rounds of ammunition and ended up with zero belugas. Apparently undaunted, Hulien explained that it was early in the season and that, later, the belugas would be in shallower water to eat salmon and would be easier to "bag." Hulien was nothing if not a promoter. The article ends, "John is enthusiastic about the sport for the entire family because there's no 'roughing it'—you're either in the whale hunting boat or back home. He said that Ken Tapp has excellent camps on the West side of the Inlet and the Beluga Whale Hunt Club is pleased to answer inquires. 'The Army thinks it's a wonderful sport,' said John." A later issue included a photo of the men and the dory and a few lines about the enthusiasm of the army men. "'Even though we didn't bag a whale,' they said, 'the excitement of the chase was well worth it.'" Guide Tapp was praised for his skills in "the chase for the elusive beluga."

Today Ken Tapp lives in Oklahoma, where he earns a living as a professional sharpshooter. The day I reached him by telephone he'd just returned from the Action Pistols Championships.

"The Beluga Hunt Club never did get off the ground," he said. "We took out those military guys—they were sick the whole time. They were supposed to write it up for *The Stars and Stripes,* but I don't know if they did. Those guys couldn't shoot anything."

Hulien was behind the whole business, according to Ken. "Hulien thought it would be the greatest thing since sliced bread." He intended to put camps all along the west side. Ken bought a couple of tents to use in the camps. But the two military reporters were all they ever took out. Hulien got a Norwegian whale gun, but "it went right through belugas. It was designed for something larger." Hulien had a beluga skin tanned, but it shrank up and didn't amount to much. (This was, I believe, the "scroll" upon which club members had, or would have had, their names inscribed.) A few years later, Hulien got cancer and committed suicide.

But aside from his involvement with the hunt club, Ken had hunted belugas with George and Buck Hayden and visitors to their camp. "We had a tradition that we'd go beluga hunting on the Fourth of July." Ken's voice, over the phone, slipped into youthful exuberance. "It's pretty exciting, really. We'd get them in shallow water and they'd splash around and hit the motor, and everyone would be hanging on for dear life."

And belugas were smart. "When you lost them, they'd always go into the sun slick where you couldn't see them. They did that every time."

Ken remembered a few times towing belugas across to the Kenai River, although he never went to Kenai Days. "It's a long drag with 25 horsepower," he said. There was a Native at the cannery in Ninilchik who canned beluga and paid him a hundred dollars per whale. "When we towed one into the river, all the Natives would come out and sample the flukes." He never tried any of the canned meat, but he sampled various fresh parts. "What I ate wouldn't be popular with the Caucasian crowd."

How many belugas did he think he'd shot, altogether, in those years?

He paused to calculate. "Maybe twenty-five or thirty? There were thousands of those doggone things. I've seen it look like whitecaps. There were tens of thousands. They were as thick as snowgeese on the flats."

Starting as a toddler and until he'd paid his way through college, Buck Hayden spent every summer fishing with his family at Trading Bay. Later, he came back every summer to visit. Now, it's not every summer, but he's been back often enough to have noticed and worried over the beluga decline.

From southern California, where Buck now lives by another piece of ocean and manufactures precast concrete forms, he told me that the original idea of developing beluga hunting as a big-game sport had been his father's.

"Like so many of his things, it just never got going," he said. In any case, he and his dad and Ken Tapp and whatever friends they had visiting had been doing it for a couple of years before the Beluga Hunt Club got started. He thought that they might have taken a dozen whales altogether over the years.

The hunt club, he confirmed, was short-lived. "They couldn't seem to capture a beluga, and that's how they ended up getting hooked up with us." He remembered they put out a poster; they wanted someone to bring them a beluga for a hundred dollars. "I literally tore one of those posters off a wall, and we went down and got a beluga and towed it across the inlet." He remembered the photo his father had mentioned—of him brushing his teeth, of the beluga hanging from the boom on Lance Petersen's stepfather's truck.

When Buck was in college, he wrote an article, published in the Anchorage paper, about fishing and hunting at his family's fish camp. With photos of him playing with a baby seal and pushing a dory full of salmon off the beach was another of Ken Tapp and a second man cutting a harpoon head out of a beluga. Buck described the rigors and pleasures of setnet fishing and the mechanics of seal and beluga hunting. Once a beluga was separated from its pod and herded into shallow water where its wake could be followed, "it's an hour or two of fast shooting and fancy boat work," with the whale eventually tiring enough that the boat could close in with the harpoon. Buck wrote at the end: "The ribs will end up in the smoke house, the fluke in the pickling barrel and the liver on the supper table. There may be some liver left over."

Buck has always had a sly sense of humor—and a kind heart. He told me about the time in 1965 when his father contracted with a marine park to catch a beluga for their display. They had been led to believe that, if they succeeded, they would be the first to live-capture a beluga.

In truth, the first captures—in Canada's St. Lawrence River, for short-lived display at the P. T. Barnum Museum in New York—had been made a full century before. Then in 1958 five young belugas were captured in Alaska's Bristol Bay. The three flown to New York all died en route or within a few days, but the two that went to California were trained to do tricks. And in the early 1960s more belugas—from the St. Lawrence and from Alaska—were sent to the New York Aquarium, where one survived for twenty years. A *National Geographic* article about the beluga expedition in Bristol Bay in 1961 was filled with photos of the capture and the transfer of belugas from water to skiff to sled to pond to fishing boat to converted bomber to tank at New York's Coney Island. Alaska Fish and Game reports also detailed techniques of

Bristol Bay captures. (They ranged from lightly harpooning the beluga before slipping a choke collar over its head to entangling it in a salmon gill net laid around it by a fast boat to—the "preferred method"—jumping onto the beluga from a boat and wrangling a collar over its head.)

Buck and his father, unaware of the earlier captures, adapted their hunting techniques. They separated a chosen whale from its pod and chased it into shallow water where, instead of harpooning or shooting it, they tried to surround it with a gill net normally used for king salmon—that is, their sturdiest fishing gear, with the heaviest twine and largest web. I'd heard about this from George before, and I recalled his saying that the target whale had to be a certain size—not too big or it would be too hard to handle and to transport in the coffin-like container supplied by the park, and not so small that it would still be dependent on its mother. George had told me that he and Buck tried for a long time—chasing and netting, catching too-big mothers and too-small calves—and never did get the job done.

But now Buck had a different story. They'd finally caught a six-foot-long gray beluga, one they rolled into the dory as a keeper. "We were bringing him home, and I was wetting him down. But I just couldn't do it. It was one thing—hunting them for sport—but this going in there and capturing this young whale away from its mother—I just couldn't do it. I told Dad to shut down the motors, that we were going to put him over. He never said a word. I've always been grateful to him for not arguing with me. I know it meant a great deal to him—the fame and all that goes with it, for capturing the first beluga. Maybe he was feeling a little bit like I was, too—that we'd crossed a line. I know that sounds funny, that we could shoot the mothers without batting an eye, but that we couldn't do—stealing the baby."

Buck was turning philosophical about the whole business of hunting belugas. "That was a wonderful time in our history when we didn't have to think about things. The belugas were predators to the salmon, just like the seals." There weren't consequences to killing belugas, he said—or the consequences were only positive. "The worst that would happen was we eliminated a few animals that just devastated salmon, that just went through them and ate them by the thousands. The idea of them becoming extinct never occurred to us. We were the only ones shooting them—there were thousands. Sometimes you could see them from one horizon to the other coming up the inlet."

That was a long time ago, and Buck could no longer imagine hunting belugas for fun. The old Alaska, he said, was gone. "It was a time in our lives and in the history of Alaska that will never be again. I feel fortunate to have been able to experience what were probably the last days in this country when we were still living that close to the land, without a lot of rules and regulations. But of course we need the rules and regulations today or we wouldn't have anything left.

2

THE WHALE IN THE ROOM

By 1995, two things were beginning to obsess me. No one knew how many belugas lived in Cook Inlet, but however many there were, they weren't as numerous as most people seemed to think they used to be. I certainly wasn't seeing as many as I had a decade earlier. Was something happening to the population? And, it seemed that Cook Inlet's belugas belonged solely to the inlet—or perhaps to the Gulf of Alaska at its mouth as well. They weren't spotted beyond those waters, didn't mix with other beluga stocks. There were implications to that: If something happened to the inlet's resident belugas, they wouldn't be replenished from elsewhere.

I pored over beluga counts. Had there ever been thousands? The Cook inlet stock hadn't even been identified in the scientific literature until the 1960s, when the first aerial surveys were flown. Simple surveys that decade and the next, by plane and boat, were really only looks to see where belugas were. The counts associated with them—generally 300 to 500—weren't meant to be population estimates or even minimums. Belugas are notoriously hard to spot in Cook Inlet's silty water, where anything half an inch below the surface disappears from sight, and young animals even at the surface match their gray backgrounds.

In 1989, when the Alaska Department of Fish and Game came up with its best estimate of Cook Inlet belugas, the number was 1,293. Despite that number's exactness, little confidence was attached to it. It was based on an aerial survey conducted in 1979, in which several key areas—most of the areas where belugas are found today—were missed.

The best estimate in 1995—the National Marine Fisheries Service administrator in Anchorage, Ron Morris, told me—was 1,150. Or maybe not. Researchers who worked for NMFS at the National Marine Mammal Lab in Seattle put the number at 747. Then they tweaked their "correction factors"—for missed whales, those underwater, or those simply not seen—and came up with 653. The population was "stable," Morris told me.

If the Cook Inlet belugas belonged to Cook Inlet and nowhere else, that meant they didn't swim down past Kodiak and along the Alaska Peninsula to pass through into Bristol Bay. Belugas are capable of swimming such distances, but no belugas had ever been spotted along the Alaska Peninsula south of Kodiak. Only very infrequently were single belugas or small groups seen outside the inlet, in the Gulf of Alaska. Based on these spotting records, researchers had come to believe that the Cook Inlet whales had been separated from all other belugas since the last Ice-Age jumbling of land masses and water levels 10,000 years ago. The Cook Inlet population was thus a "remnant" one, cut off from the species' more usual Arctic environment and comparable to another small, isolated population in Quebec's St. Lawrence River. After such a period of isolation, the population had presumably adapted to its particular environment.

Hot on this theory in the 1970s, University of Alaska researcher Francis "Bud" Fay and a graduate student began a comparative study of the skulls of Cook Inlet and Bering Sea belugas. In a paper presented in 1979, they concluded from the small number of craniums they'd measured that "some morphological differentiation may have taken place" as a result of evolution in the years the inlet whales had been isolated. Funding for the study ran out, but in a 1985 newspaper article Fay gave his opinion that a more complete study would have confirmed the uniqueness of the Cook Inlet whales and supported giving them special protection. He died before he was able to continue the work.

I thought about whale skulls and what they held in their bigness—not necessarily "intelligence" as we know it, but the radar-like equipment that allows whales both to navigate through oceans and to communicate among themselves. Belugas are thought to have the most sophisticated echolocation system of any whales—of any marine mammals—to help them maneuver and find food in the dark Arctic waters and the shallow channels that make up their homes. The Cook Inlet environment, with its extreme turbidity and tidal range, had to offer them particular challenges. Might our belugas have evolved skulls to support larger melons with particularly acute abilities? Might they have other differences we wouldn't want to lose?

A local killer whale biologist, Craig Matkin, told me that a geneticist in California was crunching up pieces of beluga DNA and finding out amazing things. "You ought to talk to him," Craig said.

Greg O'Corry-Crowe, at the Southwest Fisheries Science Center in La Jolla, was happy to talk to me about his work. In an utterly charming Irish accent, he told me that for two years he'd been working with tissue samples to analyze the molecular genetics of various beluga stocks in Alaska and Canada. His investigation so far had shown the Cook Inlet whales to be genetically "quite different" from other Alaska belugas, which did indeed support the hypothesis that they had been isolated for several thousand years.

"Does that mean," I asked, "the Cook Inlet belugas could be considered a subspecies?"

He hesitated. "Well, we don't use that word anymore. It doesn't have an exact meaning, scientifically." He went on with more explanation of mitochondrial DNA analysis than I could follow, but I gathered that the Cook Inlet belugas, yes, were significantly distinct from other belugas, at least in terms of what could be seen in their genes.

I asked, now that we had the science of genetics to work for us, whether the kind of skull measuring abandoned earlier would still be useful.

"Indeed," he said. "That would be very useful. It's always good to have a supportive data set. And then, it could demonstrate morphological differences—as distinct from genetic ones." Physical changes, he pointed out, can be traced through genetics, but they can also result from environmental factors. For example, a smaller body size may result from "genetic drift" over time as a population adapts to the specifics of its environment—or it may be determined by a poorer diet available to a population.

The main use of all this, O'Corry-Crowe said, was to apply to management decisions. That is, you'd want to be careful with any small population that wasn't receiving new members or genetic material from a larger pool.

Cook Inlet belugas, then, weren't just any old belugas, exchangeable or replaceable. They belonged to their place in the same way that the lunker king salmon of the Kenai River belonged to the depth, the current, the temperature and cool blue color, the holes and protective snags and rocky bottom of their perfect-for-them river. Except that, compared to prolific salmon, which run upriver by the tens of thousands every year to deposit their eggs by the multi-millions (giving them some safety in numbers as well as reproductive speed), a beluga population can grow only very, very slowly. Individual belugas may live a long time (into their thirties), but females don't give birth until age five or six and then normally bear only one calf every three years during their prime.

Bad things can happen to well-loved whales, I thought, and I began to imagine the ways in which a population like Cook Inlet's was vulnerable. Belugas as a rule tend to congregate in dense pods, and a single event like an oil spill or a disturbance that forced whales to strand on a hot day could devastate a small population. So could an outbreak of disease. So could interference with a critical part of their habitat—anything that may increase their stress levels or put more demand on their energy resources or affect their abilities to communicate, navigate, feed, or reproduce successfully. Even genetics could be a problem—if the population were too small to have a variable gene pool.

There were a lot of things happening in Cook Inlet. All those people on its shores and up its rivers were building homes, roads, parking lots, and delivering their waste, one way or another and in one form or another, to the inlet. The oil industry had its wells, pipelines, tankers, and occasional leaks and spills. Fishermen set and drifted and circled their nets. All that boat traffic came and went, and growing numbers of recreationalists took to the water.

Hunting was one sure, intentionally lethal way of removing belugas from a population. I went back to Ron Morris, the National Marine Fisheries Service administrator in Anchorage, to find out how many were being taken by Natives for subsistence purposes. Again, no one knew for sure. The best estimates, from interviews done by the state's Fish and Game subsistence division, were that sixteen belugas were taken in 1993 and nineteen in 1994. Additional animals—perhaps twenty-five percent of what were taken—were killed but not recovered, a condition known as "struck and lost." Fatally wounded animals sometimes get away to die later, or dead ones sink and can't be found if they haven't been secured with a harpoon, line, and buoy.

A newspaper article mentioned that the state, through its subsistence division, was only beginning to get a handle on who was hunting Cook Inlet belugas, and to what extent. No reporting was required, so the only information came voluntarily from people who were asked. Federal officials—in charge of beluga management since taking it over from the state in 1972—had only recently begun to talk to hunters. The article quoted Morris: "I haven't gone out to the camp and said 'Give me your name and rank and what are you doing?' I don't think that's what we should be doing. On the other hand, it's hard to get information because the hunters, until now, haven't been very organized.... All in all, the hunters haven't really been willing to talk with us."

From the newspaper article, I gathered that there were beluga hunting "camps" along the Susitna River west of Anchorage. I gathered that some of the hunters were from Anchorage. And, from what was said and not said, I gathered that the people in charge of managing the belugas—keeping track of their numbers, learning about their life histories, protecting habitat and prey species, and making sure they weren't harassed by non-Natives or overhunted by Natives—weren't doing much of a job.

"Will you be at the conference?" Greg O'Corry-Crowe, the geneticist, asked me at the end of our phone conversation.

"What conference?"

"Don't you know about it? The big beluga conference in Anchorage next month." I heard him rummage through some papers. He read me the dates. "It's open to the public, I'm pretty sure. It'll be presentations on all the latest research, for all the belugas in Alaska. I'll be giving a version of what I just told you."

I was becoming pretty darned interested in belugas, and the idea of getting a tutorial from the experts, just up the road, was very appealing. I called the person who would surely know about it—NMFS's Ron Morris. Yes, he allowed, there was "something" scheduled, but no, he didn't know details, including whether or not members of the public could attend, and no, he couldn't suggest who I might call to find out more.

A little detective work on my part turned up an agenda, with the information that the three-day beluga "science workshop," co-sponsored by NMFS and a group made up of beluga hunters and researchers, was explicitly "open to the public." The goals of the workshop were to review the status of beluga stocks throughout Alaska, to identify critical information needs, and to prioritize future research.

But what was with co-sponsor NMFS? Or Morris? If something is open to the public and the public doesn't know, does the public learn anything? If the public were to learn something, might that something be something someone doesn't want it to know? Was I right to feel not just put out by being denied information but also suspicious of a certain administrator's motives—or other answers he'd given me?

At the conference, I seemed to be the only person who might be considered a member of the public. The core in attendance, I came to see, were the members of the Alaska Beluga Whale Committee, an organization of hunters and researchers "dedicated to the conservation of beluga whales and their habitat, and to preserve traditional beluga whale hunting."

The committee had formed a few years earlier to collect and share beluga data and to develop a management plan. The thinking was that responsible self-management by those closest to the ground and most dependent on the resource could forestall distant regulators like the International Whaling Commission from involving themselves. Earlier experience with the IWC had been traumatic for bowhead whalers. In that case, whalers had disagreed with the IWC's low estimate of the bowhead population and its assertion that their take threatened the bowhead with extinction; they knew (correctly, it turned out) that the whales traveled not just in open leads but under the ice, where they went uncounted. The whalers eventually organized as something called the Alaska Eskimo Whaling Commission to wrest back some control of traditional rights and responsibilities. The beluga committee was modeled along similar lines and included hunters from all the areas in Alaska in which belugas were hunted—that is, Yupik and Inupiat Eskimo villages along the western and northern coasts, which hunted the four western beluga stocks. Cook Inlet was a different case, and its hunters were less involved.

I liked what I saw. Perhaps twenty muscled beluga hunters in T-shirts and ball caps sat side by side with nearly as many buttoned-down biologists, all of them attentive to the data, all of them involved in asking questions and making suggestions. If researchers and local resource managers presented most of the reports, hunters were always acknowledged as essential participants in the research. The hunters had been partners in deciding what should be studied; they'd conducted harvest monitoring and sampling; they'd added to the knowledge base what they'd been accumulating over lifetimes and generations of living intimately with belugas. When explanations strayed into technical jargon, someone was always sure to draw the language back to "plain English" in a way that was, amazingly, neither reductive nor condescending.

For three days, I absorbed lessons in stock assessments, harvest monitoring, biological sampling techniques, genetic analysis, ovarian analysis, contaminant analysis, population modeling, the conduct of aerial surveys, the development of correction factors, and the prospects of satellite tagging. Toward the end, sessions were devoted to explaining and discussing "co-management," a provision newly added to the Marine Mammal Protection Act and designed so that organizations like the beluga committee could fully participate in re-source management decisions. The process was just beginning, but the goal was for the committee eventually to negotiate a "co-management agreement" with NMFS not only to supply data but to make decisions about harvest levels and hunting techniques. Then, Native marine mammal hunters would essentially be self-regulating, within conservation guidelines.

One day, a gallon jar of beluga muktuk appeared on the refreshment table beside the coffee urn. The gift of the whale, brought by an Inupiat hunter who lived in Anchorage, was quickly surrounded by those who were far from home and their traditional foods, who had been feeding from the less satisfying fare of coffee shops and restaurants. As though they were canapés, chunks were scooped onto little paper plates.

I had never sampled muktuk before and was glad for the chance. The young man, in turn, was pleased to tell me how it had been prepared: in the usual way, by boiling the chunks of skin and fat. The bite-sized pieces consisted of a quarter inch or so of white skin attached to another inch of gelatinous, cloudy fat.

As I chewed, I tried to make comparisons to the texture and taste. The texture was the easier of the two; muktuk reminded me of those square candies that sandwich layers of caramel around sugary pink concoctions that them-selves surround soft marshmallow. The skin was chewy without being tough; whale skin, I was eventually to learn, tends to be soft and is easily (when on the whale) damaged. The fat was—well, not really like fat, not like what one would expect from eating the fat of other animals. It was firmer, maybe like very firm tofu. Taste was tougher to compare. It wasn't fishy, as I would have expected from an animal that feeds on fish. It didn't bear the remotest resem-blance to the flavor of beef or pork fat or to a spoonful of Crisco. It was neither sweet nor sour, nor exactly greasy. Although it was not unpleasant, it seemed to me the kind of thing for which a person may need to acquire a taste and of which a little bit might go a very long way. It was, I could say, "rich."

"In spring we hunt in Kachemak Bay," the hunter told me.

"You drive all the way down from Anchorage?" I asked. "You trailer a boat down?" Kachemak Bay, where my town of Homer is located, lies 250 curvy road miles from Anchorage. The bay wasn't exactly a beluga hot spot. Sure, in spring small groups sometimes circled through—although I hadn't heard of many sightings in recent years. I didn't know that belugas were hunted there. But now, I could see the logic. Spring came sooner to the lower inlet than to the waters around Anchorage. People hungry for a fresh supply of muktuk—people with mobility—apparently were building the necessary travel into their seasonal subsistence cycles.

"We come for seals too—seals and belugas both at the head of the bay," the hunter said, happy to be sharing and to see so many people enjoying what he'd brought.

The young man with the muktuk was one of only a few locals attending the conference. The relationship between the beluga committee and the Cook Inlet hunters appeared to be ambiguous, strained. There had been a rift, and a new group known as the Cook Inlet Marine Mammal Council had organized as a regional alternative. That council, with funding from NMFS, was trying to start its own harvest monitoring and tissue sampling program.

Cook Inlet's belugas were not a focus of the workshop, but they kept getting mentioned. The state subsistence representative confirmed that efforts to document Native beluga use in Cook Inlet and to determine how many people might be hunting were relatively new and not very thorough. Active hunters, he emphasized, included both those with a tradition in Cook Inlet—like the Dena'ina Athabaskans from the village of Tyonek—and Natives—mostly Inupiat—who had relocated to the Anchorage area from other places in which belugas were hunted and who had brought their traditions with them. Sometimes those hunters from outside the region sent muktuk home to their village relatives. Sometimes their relatives and friends came to Anchorage, and they all went hunting together. Cook Inlet had become a popular beluga hunting place because it was easy; the whales stayed in shallow water close to the port of Anchorage from May until October.

Those who hunted belugas in Cook Inlet were not organized among themselves. Maybe that would change with the new marine mammal council. For now, the best estimate the state had, from information gathered in interviews, was that about thirty households in the Anchorage area were actively participating in hunts and that about thirty whales were being taken per year.

We heard as well about how the Cook Inlet belugas had been surveyed from a plane flying transects and how a population estimate of 747 had been reached. In the summer of 1995, there would be another Cook Inlet survey, plus an effort with telemetry. The telemetry would include both suction-cup tags ("stuck" for a matter of minutes or hours to get a better idea of how much time the whales spent beneath the surface) and satellite tags (surgically attached, to track movements for weeks and months, until the attachments pulled loose). Cook Inlet hunters were invited to help with the surveys and tagging. During the co-management discussion, speakers recognized that the Cook Inlet situation was unique because of the fact that hunters were from everywhere—and that that posed special challenges.

The National Marine Fisheries Service, it was said, was not going to regulate the Cook Inlet harvest. Indeed, NMFS officials—not Morris, who was there, but others from more distant offices—said more than once that the agency had no authority to limit Native hunting unless the stock was first found to be depleted under the Marine Mammal Protection Act or to be threatened or endangered under the Endangered Species Act.

In the conference's three days, there was one word I don't think I ever heard: *overhunting*. Later, when I looked at my notes from the presentations, I contemplated three numbers: a population estimate of 747 Cook Inlet belugas, a population modeling explanation that concluded that the maximum sustained yield for any of the Alaska stocks would be two to four percent, and the Department of Fish and Game estimate that perhaps thirty Cook Inlet whales were being taken per year (with nothing said about a number for struck-and-lost whales).

It doesn't take a scientist to calculate that thirty whales are four percent of 747, but no one at the meeting did the math for the others, and no one said the word that no one wanted to hear.

In many families, there's some overarching issue, like a member's alcoholism, that others, weaving and dodging, manage to ignore. In 1995, all those beluga experts were squeezed in around, not an elephant, but—more appropriate to our case—a very large whale in the room.

∽

A year passed, and then another. Summers, from my fish camp, I witnessed changes in the inlet. Sandbars were building up south of us, and the salmon were running wider past our beach. Series of fall storms and high tides eroded the coastline, rounding off our point. We found new seaweed, and sharks, in our nets—results, perhaps, of warming waters. Seismic ships, in long transects and with small explosions, were exploring for oil. There could be many reasons for belugas to be elsewhere, for us simply to miss seeing them. I knew they were being studied; I trusted that, with so many people looking after them, some kind of progress in understanding and managing was being made.

And then, in the fall of 1998, the Anchorage newspaper ran a front-page article: "Cook Inlet belugas declining: Hunters may be killing too many, experts say."

There were quotes from Ross Schaeffer, the Inupiat chair of the Alaska Beluga Whale Committee, that something needed to change before the next hunting season. There was mention of Lloyd Lowry, chair of a scientific committee that advises NMFS on marine mammal issues, who had written in official correspondence, "It is critical...that the number of belugas being killed by hunters in Cook Inlet is reduced substantially and soon."

Lee Stephan, the chair of the Cook Inlet Marine Mammal Council—the hunter group organized to help with research—was also quoted, saying, "Nobody needs to get as excited as they are." Local hunters, he said, could take care of the situation.

That was the beginning, for me, of a new compulsion—attendance at beluga meetings. The beluga committee met, the Cook Inlet hunter group met, the scientific review group met. The National Marine Fisheries Service held a "status review," with series of meetings designed to share research information and to solicit public comment. There were proposals for rule-making and regulating, all with their meetings. There were scoping meetings and the preparation of environmental impact statements. There were lawsuits and judicial hearings, and more meetings.

More thorough interviewing, involving more active hunters, had determined that beluga hunters were taking more than a few belugas each year from the small Cook Inlet population. In 1998 hunters killed an estimated eighty-eight belugas—of a population drawn down to perhaps 350. "We know that more people are hunting in recent years than before," Barbara Mahoney, the biologist from NMFS's Anchorage office, said. Ron Morris from that office, who'd been so reluctant to discuss hunting, had retired.

Doug DeMaster, whose staff at the National Marine Mammal Lab in Seattle had done the population surveys and other studies, went before the hunters and warned, "If that level of hunting keeps up, the Cook Inlet belugas will be extinct in ten years."

Native leaders cried the alarm in a slightly different way. The chair of the beluga committee put into a letter to all beluga hunters: "The beluga population is declining so fast right now that unless something is done soon, NMFS has no alternative except to place the Cook Inlet belugas on the **Endangered Species List.** If this should happen, it will be the first time ever that a species becomes endangered because it is **over harvested by Alaska Natives."**

The emphasized words were very much the point. Alaska Natives, who were in a much bigger battle over subsistence rights generally, absolutely did not want to be blamed for putting an animal on the Endangered Species List. Native subsistence use of marine mammals might be well protected under federal law, but similar use of other wild foods, such as moose and salmon, was not. For two decades Natives had been fighting on the state level for subsistence rights. Once assured a "rural priority" to fish and game resources, rural—mostly Native—residents had lost out to lawsuits over "special" rights and the expanding appetites of urban sporting interests. Anything interpreted as misuse of current rights would hurt their cause. Tribal efforts to gain greater self-governance, including more responsibility for resource management, could also be set back by any appearance that Native stewardship had failed.

There were other politics to consider as well. Alaska's congressional delegation, opposed to anything that got in the way of economic development, wasn't shy about threatening agencies. I imagined the NMFS people shaking in their shoes at the thought of Alaska's Senator Ted Stevens, peeved to hear that another animal was endangered, drawing a zero on their budget line.

And then there was the international level. Although the International Whaling Commission didn't control the take of small cetaceans, they did periodically consider whether there might be a need for them to do so, and in 1999 they would be reviewing belugas. At the IWC, the United States had aggressively opposed commercial whaling while supporting limited aboriginal whaling. Could the United States speak with any credibility to other nations about whaling excesses while allowing the destruction of a whale population under its own jurisdiction?

What was to be done? The beluga committee asked that Cook Inlet hunters restrict their hunting and that hunters from outside Cook Inlet cease beluga hunting there altogether. As its leadership saw the problem, just a few hunters had caused it, and those same few could go a long way to fixing it. They wanted everyone to agree that there would be no hunting for commercial markets—that is, no commercial sale of beluga muktuk, either directly or through a Native store in Anchorage, to other Natives.

Commercial sale of whale parts? Average citizens—who may not have noticed pick-ups parked around Anchorage, with plastic coolers in the backs and Natives visiting around them as they handed off hunks of white skin and fat—were shocked. Hadn't the United States outlawed commercial whaling a long time ago? Yes, sort of. No, not exactly. Although federal law prohibited the commercial take of whales, the Native subsistence exemption was interpreted, broadly, to allow for the sale of edible marine mammal parts between Natives in Native villages. The intent of the framers of the exemption to the Marine Mammal Protection Act was to accommodate exchange in a village situation where, for example, one person might offer a tank of gas to a hunter, or might instead give money to pay for gas, in return for a share of whatever was hunted. The National Marine Fisheries Service, in an effort to cover as many people and circumstances as may be warranted, had defined Anchorage as a village. In Anchorage, the desires of 20,000 Native people for traditional foods˙had stretched the provision into the legal (sometimes expressed as "not illegal") business of providing food for money. Some Native hunters could be said to be, in fact, engaged in commercial whaling.

Officials with the National Marine Fisheries Service claimed they had no authority to stop commercial sales. They had, they repeated, no way to control Cook Inlet beluga hunting at all—not unless and not until the belugas were found to be either depleted or threatened/endangered. Either one of those findings would take time and documentation—an entire lengthy process of determination and adjudication. In the short term, hunting controls would have to come from the hunters themselves. "Help yourselves," one of the administrators pled.

In an early meeting, designed to bring everyone to a common understanding of the problem, the government researchers presented their data. They went through all the methodology used in the aerial surveys and to calculate population estimates and ranges of reliability; since systematic surveys had been instituted in 1994, the trend was downward, to the new 1998 estimate of only 350 belugas. They covered genetics; there was no intermixing of the Cook Inlet whales with other stocks. They reported on distribution; in summer months the entire population was holding together in estuaries at the head of Cook Inlet, adjacent to Anchorage. It was clear—clear—clear that here was a small population rapidly getting smaller, a population that would not be replenished from anywhere else, a population that had reduced its range to the very area where it was most vulnerable to hunting.

Clear to me, anyway. But then, although I'm not particularly trained in science, I do understand its principles and accept its methods. It hadn't occurred to me that there may be other ways of looking at the situation, or that the principles and methods may be rejected altogether.

Why, someone asked, hadn't they counted the whales earlier or later, when there might have been more? How were they so sure they were counting the whales that were underwater? What about the whales one of them had seen at the mouth of the Kenai River—did they count those? Why didn't they consider that it was tour boats that were scaring the belugas, or that the whales were poisoned by pollution? The objections from hunters and tribal people seemed to consist of two main ones: the government people hadn't proved that there was a decline in Cook Inlet belugas because their numbers were not to be trusted, and if there was a decline, it was not the fault of hunting but of any number of other causes, including pollution, disturbance, a lack of food, fishermen shooting them, or simply that the whales went somewhere else.

The researchers responded patiently, explaining again how studies had been designed, correction factors developed, results interpreted. If the population estimates weren't exact, at least the trends were apparent, and they were sharply downward.

When the reports were finished and the agenda listed a number of discussion items aimed at reaching some agreement on reducing hunting pressure, the chair of the Cook Inlet Marine Mammal Council, Lee Stephan, instead presented a letter stating the group's position. The letter, read in a flurry of emotion and emphasizing tribal authority, asked questions I thought had already been answered, and it praised hunters for not providing harvest data "to be used against them." Stephan, who was also the CEO of the Native Village of Eklutna, on Cook Inlet's Knik Arm, asserted that the beluga whales of Cook Inlet were not being overhunted. Sometimes there would be more animals and sometimes there would be less, he said; they were like rabbits, he said, and the scientists were at fault for not knowing whether the population was at a natural high or low.

After that, there was less to discuss. A government policy man, his face pinkening, suggested that Stephan's group hire its own scientists to review the data it questioned. A Native leader warned, "Once it becomes a public process, Native people will be blamed." A hunter said, "I don't think there's much decline. I'm out there every day. I know the whale. They go out of the inlet, they follow the fish." Someone else demanded "proof beyond a reasonable doubt." Doug DeMaster, head of the research lab, emphasized how supportive NMFS was of subsistence use, "but our obligation is to prevent extinction. The key issue is, is there a mechanism in place to prevent overexploitation? We don't have much time."

How could it happen that a population of animals—animals that everyone involved with valued and wanted to prosper—could be so seriously reduced without protections going into place? What were our protective laws for if not to respond to dangers before they became crises, before we would begin to use the word "extinction"? On the one hand, we had two conservation laws—the Marine Mammal Protection Act and the Endangered Species Act. On the other hand, we had the Native hunting exemption to the MMPA. Did Native rights trump conservation, and if so, how did that benefit anyone? What about the grand theme of Native stewardship and the ideals of co-management? These questions surrounded me like a net being pursed ever smaller.

In fisheries, I well knew of Garrett Hardin's "tragedy of the commons." When there's a common property—the field where all cattle graze, the ocean and all its fish—from which anyone can take, and not taking only means you get less and someone else gets more, Hardin argued that the result is always and inevitably overexploitation. Laws regarding ownership, shares, and quotas are designed to avoid that tragedy. There exist, as well, community-based management systems—such as, in fact, the beluga committee's system of village whale hunting—that can support sustainability. The key to the latter seemed to lie with dual community controls—over the resource and over social behavior.

People, half in jest, liked to refer to Anchorage as "Alaska's largest Native village." But Alaska's largest city was not, by any definition most of us understand, a village, and it did not have a village's traditional system of controls over its residents. If the tribally charted Cook Inlet Marine Mammal Council might exert some influence over the seven villages in the region—only one of which included active whale hunters—it had little to none with other Natives who were, by virtue of having left their home places to live in Anchorage, largely independent operators living outside of any tribal structures.

And our government, which exists to represent us all and to protect our common interests from our individual ones—what had it been doing? The National Marine Fisheries Service was not known for moving quickly to avert crises, whether from fear, timidity, or its own bureaucratic inertia. It had, it seemed, been quietly building its case for overhunting but, now that it had made it, was throwing up its hands and passing off the responsibility to "do something" to others—others without the power, except individually, to do anything.

After that early meeting, I walked Anchorage's grim, gray streets and tried to puzzle out what I'd seen of colliding worlds. There were subtexts to what had been said—to the resistance and denial I'd heard—but my grasp of them was sketchy. Surely, Lee Stephan and other Native critics had been speaking to the white world of science and regulation, warning that its messengers weren't the only source of authority and that they wanted more respect. Some of the rhetoric had also been inter-Native skirmishing, embarrassment of local tribes that their resources, in their territory, had been mismanaged, at least in part by other Natives who had come into the area without, perhaps, paying the proper respect.

As a minority in the state (sixteen percent of the overall population), Alaska Natives try to present a united front. In reality, they belong to eleven distinct cultural groups, and their history with one another before Europeans and Americans arrived included wars, raids, and enslavement. If Indians and Eskimos weren't exactly Serbs and Croats, there was something of that ancient tribalism at work, and I didn't know quite how much of what I'd witnessed was ethnic enmity, how much was standing together, and how much was complicated by family relationships, political expediency, personal histories, or business interests. On the business end of things, the villages—with corporate structures embedded since the Alaska Native Claims Settlement Act of 1971—depended upon various financial enterprises, including logging and mining. Bottom lines might well suffer if developmental activities faced increased regulation necessary for the protection of belugas or their habitat.

I stopped at downtown crosswalks and waited, dutifully, for the walk signals. I stood with other pedestrians, all of us breathing steam in frigid air, all of us part of the stew pot that was Alaska citizenry. Since 1973, when I'd moved to Alaska, the human population of the state had about doubled—and so had the number of people who identified themselves as Natives. I understood why half the state's population ended up in Anchorage, and why so many Natives also lived in urban areas; there were jobs there, and medical facilities, and other support systems absent from villages and small towns.

I also knew that Native people who moved to Anchorage didn't stop being Native. Even when they had other jobs, they generally continued their ways of hunting, gathering, sharing, and eating Native foods. Even in urban Alaska, even in 1998, gathering and preparing food was central to Native life. Salmon, caribou, seal, berries, clams, ducks, wild celery—these foods still, throughout Alaska, made up a sizeable portion of most Natives' diets. When Native people travel, they carry with them packages of dried fish, or walrus meat, or herring eggs. They share their gifts. For a long time, until health regulations stopped the practice, the Alaska Native Medical Center in Anchorage served its patients wild foods, including moose and beluga muktuk, purchased from hunters. People like foods to which they're accustomed, but, more important, Native people know they are, in a very real sense, the foods they eat.

I knew all this, and I knew the things I'd read—the anthropology that considered not just economic value but the whole cloth of social relationships and cultural identity. There was status to being a hunter; there was respect to be earned and to pay; there were responsibilities to family and to elders. It meant something to be a hunter—something more than bringing home food, which was, in itself, not a small accomplishment.

That way of life had resided largely outside the view of most of us. But the state was a smaller place now, as the world and all we shared was smaller. Alaska's Natives were more visible in part because they were more empowered—with the business resources of their regional and village corporations, federal recognition of tribal authority and rights, and pride of heritage and identity. Where they used to fall silent, they now spoke up, questioned, demanded. And still, they were frustrated. They were worn down by battles over subsistence and self-determination, by the chippings away of cultural worth. Losing the right to hunt beluga whales freely in Cook Inlet was going to be one more thing, one more loss of who they were and what they valued—even for those who didn't hunt. They didn't want to lose the opportunity. They knew the pattern; when Natives lost rights, they didn't get them back again.

One of the questions Stephan had asked stayed with me—that day, the next, and for weeks after. "How many belugas are needed to feed one family for a year?" I'd heard the question and dismissed it as more denial of the problem that needed to be addressed. Obviously, if the Cook Inlet belugas were about to be wiped out by overhunting, they could not continue to feed everyone who wanted or needed them. But later, the question suggested something else, something about traditional use. In a land where a failed salmon run or a late migration of caribou could mean starvation, meeting a family's and a community's needs was the first order of business. Waste was not abided, but use was expected, even required. If a plant were harvested for food and its unused parts respectfully returned to the earth, the old Dena'ina believed, the plant would grow in greater numbers. But if the plant were not used, its numbers would diminish.

In that context, asking how many belugas were needed to feed a family didn't seem quite so off-the-wall. An ethic of "take what you need" and "share what you have" served small, subsistence-based communities well. Elders and community pressure enforced behavioral standards against waste and misuse, and those who behaved badly faced sanctions. People did sometimes starve, or they moved to new locations; both reset the balance with food supplies.

The old beliefs weren't followed as completely or as literally as they once were, but it seemed to me that the underlying attitudes were still profoundly present in Native life. Food, from the plants and animals that "give" themselves to hunters and gatherers, is meant to be eaten. It's meant to be shared. If treated with respect, it will continue to provide. To think about limiting your take not because you have enough, but because there may not *be* enough, is a radical shift in perspective.

The National Marine Fisheries Service moved glacially. To list or not to list: That was the question. Its people announced they didn't want to be heavy-handed. As one administrator put it to me, "We need the Native community on board. If we ever lose that, then we have an enforcement problem." The agency proposed a "sealing and tagging" program that would require all Cook Inlet beluga hunters to report their kills and to turn in jawbones. This program would provide better information about who was hunting and how many belugas they were taking. It would be, hunters were warned, "more than voluntary." I shook my head over the feebleness of the suggestion. Once, such gathering of information would have been a helpful step. Now, it seemed far too little and far too late.

Listing choices were discussed. Which protective act would be invoked— Endangered Species or Marine Mammal Protection? Would the belugas be declared threatened/endangered or depleted? The distinctions, however significant, were no doubt lost on the general public. Under either designation, after more "process," hunting could be controlled—either limited or stopped. To qualify as "endangered," a species (or population) had to meet at least one of a set of five criteria; once listed, a recovery plan would be implemented, critical habitat would be identified, and federally funded actions that might negatively affect the species or its habitat would require consultation regarding possible effects and mitigation. A depleted designation under the MMPA, on the other hand, would be limited to controlling hunting and the development of a conservation plan—similar to a recovery plan but less well defined. A depleted designation was, moreover, quantitative; the species (or population) had to decline to less than fifty percent of its historical abundance. The National Marine Fisheries Service hesitated to say what the Cook Inlet beluga's historical abundance may have been. Their statisticians didn't have the proof.

Seven environmental organizations and one individual—Joel Blatchford, an Inupiat who had grown up in Anchorage and only recently stopped hunting belugas—faced no such indecision. They filed a formal petition with NMFS, asking that the Cook Inlet belugas be listed as endangered under the Endangered Species Act—immediately, on an emergency basis. The group held that the Cook Inlet belugas met every one of the criteria to be considered in judging the threat of extinction and that only the Endangered Species Act provided for the range of measures necessary to protect the small population and allow it to recover. It was not fair, they said, to place the whole blame and burden on hunters when nobody knew if other factors had contributed to the population decline, and surely additional protective measures were now called for. For one thing, critical habitat around river mouths should be protected—not open to new oil drilling, as state plans proposed.

All that year, 1998 and 1999, there were meetings. Moments stuck with me like sea lice to the side of a salmon:

John Burns, the highly respected granddaddy of Alaska's beluga research, flew down from Fairbanks "as a very concerned private citizen" to lead a quick seminar detailing the reproductive cycle of the beluga—the very long gestation, the nursing that lasted more than a year. In spring, two-thirds of reproductive-age female belugas would be pregnant—either newly so or near-term—and killing a female at that time usually meant killing a pregnant one. Killing a nursing one meant the loss of her calf. From a population as small as Cook Inlet's had become, taking even one female was going to hurt.

Discussions had progressed to a possible quota system—how many belugas might be taken and who would decide who would get them. "You haven't got a pie to divide," Burns concluded, with a sharp look around the room. "My recommendation would be—no hunting for three years. See what's going on. Then figure out what a safe level of hunting is. Protect the resource first, then talk about the pie."

The director of an environmental organization asked if hunters wouldn't consider, instead of hunting, taking out paying tourists on whale-watching excursions. That way, as he saw it, they could use their boats and skills to make money.

Among the hunters and other Natives present, feet shifted. Heads lowered. I knew what was coming because I'd heard it before, the uneasiness of subsistence users with other people "looking at our food."

It was Joel Blatchford, the former hunter who joined the endangered species petition—and who was always among the most outspoken at meetings—who answered. "People want to love our food to death," he said. Within Inupiat culture—within Native cultures generally—to bother whales for no good reason was without justification, in the same way that catch-and-release fishing was without justification. Such activities offended the animals, which did not exist to be toyed with. If you don't need to eat the animal, Joel suggested, then please just leave it alone.

A member of the Makah tribe, from Washington state, was in town, and someone brought him by to share his experience with the beluga hunters. The Makahs voluntarily stopped their subsistence hunting of gray whales some seventy years ago when commercial whaling brought the whales close to extinction, and now that the grays had recovered and some tribe members wanted to reinstate the tradition, they were being opposed by antiwhaling activists. Clifford Johnson, a short man with a seamed face, stood in front of the room and said, "It hurts me inside to see our people having to conform with non-Native rules and regulations.... You have a wonderful fight you can win. The non-Indian people don't want to understand where you're coming from. If the white man can keep us apart, the white man wins. They'll make you suffer. You'll lose and lose and pretty soon you won't be able to do anything." The man was cheered.

A toxicologist presented data on contaminant levels in Cook Inlet's belugas compared to belugas elsewhere. His bar graphs showed Cook Inlet belugas lowest in PCBs and DDT, and low as well in heavy metals. At the top of the food chain and long-lived, belugas have the potential to accumulate relatively high concentrations of contaminants in their tissues. Atmospheric transport of contaminants, which "deposit out" in cold air, meant that contamination was present in remote northern areas far from the source, and Arctic belugas appeared to harbor more chemicals than those of Cook Inlet. The most heavily contaminated belugas in the world were those in Quebec's St. Lawrence

River; they had one hundred times more PCBs and DDT residuals than the Cook Inlet whales.

The toxicologist's point was that industrial hazards, from the oil industry or elsewhere, did not appear to be a significant problem for the Cook Inlet belugas. There was no reason to think that contaminants played a role in the population decline.

Joel Blatchford spoke from the audience. "The Cook Inlet whales are sick," he said. He had, he said, personally thrown away four or five that had runny, yellow fat.

Among those who turned out for the beluga meetings, there weren't to my mind any "bad guys." It was hard not to like the Native men who, blustery one moment in public, later chatted amiably over coffee in the hall. Even the mostly silent figure who, we knew, was one of the "commercial" hunters, was known as a good man who took care of a large extended family. The woman in the Eskimo kuspuk who cried for the belugas she believed were full of oil-industry chemicals was kindhearted and committed to keeping Native culture strong. The oil representative in the dark suit was only looking out for the best interests of his industry and the people who worked in it.

The NMFS scientists and managers were also, I thought, doing the best they could within the system they had. I liked Doug DeMaster, who headed the marine mammal lab and maneuvered between science and frank talk in a way I admired. He promised me that the belugas would not disappear, "not on my watch," and I knew that wasn't ego talking—or not solely ego—but a genuine commitment. Certainly no one in a position of responsibility would want his career memorialized with an extinction, but with Doug—and others from his staff—I'd sensed a true devotion to the whales and their survival. Beluga study was not an academic exercise for them, and the data gathering and reports were not ends in themselves.

Still, there were limits. Neither Doug nor his staff of perhaps seventy—only ten of whom worked on beluga issues, only part-time—were decision-makers. As scientists, their jobs were to present their data, the hard science—not to interpret beyond what was scientifically established; not to speculate; not to warn; admonish, or advocate; not to determine what should be done with what they knew. Decisions were made by other people at NMFS, those who weighed politics and economics along with science. Those people, in turn, were appointed and influenced by decision-makers further up the NMFS, National Oceanic and Atmospheric Administration (NOAA), and Department of

Commerce ladders, and by members of Congress, each of whom was further and further removed from the science and the ground-truth of the situation.

One of the marine mammal lab biologists put it to me bluntly: "It's frustrating. We do the science, then policy decisions are made for political reasons. The fact that we're mandated to manage for 'multiple use' makes us a very schizophrenic organization."

The months leading up to the 1999 hunting season brought painfully slow, painfully achieved progress. The National Marine Fisheries Service declined to act on an emergency basis to restrict hunting and left decisions about hunting to the hunters. Meanwhile—privately—agency people expressed fears that, with no restrictions in place and the likelihood that 1999 would be the last year there would be none, hunters might hunt even more aggressively.

Behind the scenes, agency people, hunter groups, and tribal leaders continued to talk. Some of these talks—billed as "co-management negotiations"—ended with a declaration by hunters that they would stand down (not hunt) during the 1999 season while more surveys and more discussion of a quota system were conducted. There was still no structure—no group that represented all hunters, no regulatory or enforcement mechanism. There were just individual hunters, joining together, promising to stand down for a year and then see what was what.

Meanwhile, visits were made to the nation's capital. Alaska's Senator Ted Stevens—although first declaring that there was no such thing as a Cook Inlet beluga separate from other belugas—attached a last-minute rider to a congressional appropriations bill. The rider prohibited for two years the hunting of any Cook Inlet belugas except as provided for in an agreement between NMFS and "affected Alaskan Native organizations."

No known hunting took place that summer, although there was little monitoring effort. A plan to hire hunters to patrol fell apart when NMFS decided that could lead to dangerous confrontations.

I felt as though I spent the summer holding my breath. My sympathies were everywhere. Everywhere except with whomever—maybe the system itself—was responsible for the dithering that had led to, and perhaps past, the eleventh hour. I couldn't see that there was much choice anymore short of an endangered species listing and a longer-than-my lifetime recovery period.

But then, there were more meetings, and more waiting. It wasn't until the following May that NMFS finally designated the Cook Inlet belugas depleted under the Marine Mammal Protection Act, beginning more process on an environmental impact statement and harvest rules before any controls would actually be implemented. The agency missed its one-year deadline to act on the endangered species petition from the environmental groups; the groups sued to make the agency respond, and in midsummer 2000 NMFS declared that the belugas were not endangered. The environmental coalition sued again, arguing that they were, by every definition of the law. Their attorney, with clenched jaw, told me, "We have to sue them to get them to do their job."

In between the congressional rider and the depletion ruling, I saw Doug DeMaster in Seattle and, mindful of his "not on my watch" promise, asked him for a prediction. What kind of story was the Cook Inlet beluga one? Would it have a happy ending, or would it flatline out as an obituary?

Doug smiled, and I knew he must have been asking himself something very similar. *"If,"* he emphasized, "the Natives stay on board, and *if* the fisheries stay healthy so food is not an issue for the whales, and *if* we don't have a major oil spill, then I think this population can recover." The most recent population estimate of 369 whales, twenty-two more than the estimate for the previous year, had, he said, given him a bit more hope. And then he paused. "I tend to be an optimist."

3

THE SCIENTIFIC METHOD

Early on a September Saturday, I drove through downtown Anchorage to a place I'd never been before—its port. Anchorage is an odd kind of coastal city—one that looks inward rather than outward, that tends not to recognize its connection to the sea. At the top of Cook Inlet, between two arms that are the scoured trenches left by glaciers, the water sucks in and out in a tidal exchange among the world's most extreme. With new and full moons, the tides can rise and fall as much as thirty-five vertical feet.

Anchorage has no real waterfront, no harbor, no seaside businesses selling fresh seafood or boat charters or seascape art. Instead there are wide expanses of mudflats, the port with giant cranes for unloading the barges that bring much of Alaska's material goods from Seattle, and—nearly overlooked in the old, industrialized part of town by Ship Creek—a boat launch consisting of a wooden ramp and finger. This was where the city's few adventurous boaters—Native hunters among them—brought their skiffs to access the inlet.

At the boat launch, I would be joining a team of researchers attempting to catch belugas. If they could catch some, they would fit them with saddle-like attachments holding transmitters that reported to satellites. Then—through the magic of science and technology—the researchers could find where, day by day, those belugas went about their business.

In 2000 there were still plenty of mysteries about the whales. Where did they go in the fall and winter? What did they eat? What, beyond Native hunting, may have contributed to the population drop or may influence the recovery? What actions might be required to protect habitats, food supplies, social structures? So much depended on first knowing where the whales went during the non-summer months when they seemed to disperse from feeding at the head of the inlet.

It had been a year and several months since beluga hunting was stopped by congressional rider, four months since the National Marine Fisheries Service had finally designated the Cook Inlet whales as depleted, and three months since the agency had ruled that they were not also endangered. In another month, the law that had halted the hunting would expire, but the depleted listing was only a first step toward any regulation to replace the temporary law. Meanwhile, basic research continued. For the tagging operation, a dozen people from all points of the compass had gathered for ten days. They had shipped up a specially outfitted boat from Seattle, brought in another three inflatables, and chartered a plane.

It was a big effort—and an expensive one. No one thought it would be easy to capture Cook Inlet whales in the shallow, silty, current-driven water that made them hard to approach and follow. No one thought it was a good thing to subject a population already under stress to chases and captures. But everyone seemed to agree that the results—if they could get satellite tags on one or more whales—would be worthwhile.

Telemetry—the science of recording instrument readings and transmitting them by radio—has made it possible to spy on wildlife as never before. From its first use with animals—strapping on radio transmitters and following along within signal range—telemetry had leaped into science fiction dimensions. In the 1970s grizzly bears in Yellowstone National Park were the first to wear satellite-linked transmitters, allowing their travels to be tracked without anyone leaving the office. Whereas those early "packages" worn as collars were the size of shoeboxes and weighed ten pounds, transmitters and battery packs were rapidly reduced in both size and weight until even birds could carry some version of a satellite tag.

Amazing discoveries were made: Laysan albatrosses in the North Pacific flew 4,000-mile round-trip flights to bring home a single liter of fish oil for their chicks. Salmon sharks tagged in Alaska swam south to waters off California. Leatherback turtles nested in the tropics, then swam thousands of miles to reach subpolar feeding grounds, and along the way regularly made straight-down dives of more than 3,000 feet. Knowing all this fostered decision-making to manage and conserve those species and the habitat upon which they depended.

For belugas, the first use of telemetry took place in Alaska's Bristol Bay, where biologists in 1983 attached VHF radios to the dorsal ridges of two animals and trailed them for two weeks to record their movements and dive behavior. The dive behavior was particularly useful in establishing correction factors for aerial surveys—that is, figuring the number of whales below the surface and thus out of sight compared to those actually seen and counted.

Researchers in Arctic Canada, where chasing around with signal receivers was less agreeable, were the first to try satellite-linked transmitters on belugas, beginning in 1987. They tracked belugas for longer distances and time periods and demonstrated how much could be learned about beluga movements, stock separations, and behaviors. By the year 2000 more than one hundred belugas throughout the north had been fitted with satellite tags. Belugas had become the most "instrumented" of cetacean species.

The Canadian experience of beluga capture and tagging in the Mackenzie River delta, just east of the boundary with northern Alaska, had been shared with Alaskans at the beluga conference I'd attended in 1995. The Canadian capture method was referred to as the "Arctic" or "cowboy" way; it involved herding a whale into shallow water, close enough for someone to jump out of a boat and throw a large padded hoop net over the animal's head. Once the beluga was quieted with the hoop and a rope around its tail, the tag was attached with Teflon pins pushed through the skin and blubber of the dorsal ridge, to sit atop the whale like a small backpack. Over the next several weeks—until the pins worked themselves loose—the Canadian researchers were astonished to find the whales traveling farther north and west than they'd ever suspected, through seas covered with pack ice.

At that same meeting—or perhaps it was a later one—a transmitter was passed around the table. A box the size of a thickened TV remote, it was mostly battery pack encased in clear plastic, sprouting a wire antenna. Less obvious were the sensors, the microprocessor, and the circuitry—all the "stuff" that made it an expensive little item, valued at more than $4,000. (The satellite time for collecting the data is additional.) A simple pressure sensor on the side recorded the depth of dives when the weight of the water, greater with depth, pressed against it. Each time the antenna poked above water, it sent location and other information to a satellite system. How much time the whales spent at the surface, how much time below and at what depths, swim speed—it could all be collected and connected to behavior in whatever places, near and far, a beluga traveled. In Canada, researchers found belugas diving to 1,780 feet, and in Greenland to 3,300 feet—much deeper than anyone had guessed and the first suggestion that Arctic belugas weren't necessarily feeding in coastal waters but depended on food sources deep under pack ice.

That was all very exciting, but still, there were issues with putting tags on belugas. It was both difficult and expensive to work in northern waters, and it was quite an operation to capture belugas and surgically attach the transmitters—which was the only way they could be held on. There was also an ethical dimension to chasing, capturing, and attaching gadgetry to animals. Native people, in particular, have sometimes objected to the indignity and danger to the animals, and the Alaska Beluga Whale Committee had always sought the approval and cooperation of hunters in regions where such research was proposed. So far, hunters had agreed the information gained was worth the trauma to individual animals. At meetings, I'd heard the scientists say that the insertion of pins through a beluga's dorsal ridge, where there were few nerve endings, didn't cause any visible reaction from the animal. The closest thing to an objection came from beluga expert John Burns, who called the tags primitive, barbaric, and hurtful—but also necessary to learn what needed to be learned in order to manage and protect the animals best.

In Alaska, the first successful use of satellite tags was at Point Lay, an Arctic village southwest of Barrow. Once every summer, hunters there drive belugas migrating along the coast into a shallow lagoon and take what they need for the village's subsistence—usually about thirty animals. Researchers, working with hunters to collect samples, had already established themselves as a yearly presence in Point Lay. Hunters understood the value of knowing where the belugas went after passing their village. They wanted to know who else might be hunting them and what areas and prey might need protection—and they wanted to be sure the animals they ate weren't feeding in contaminated places.

At Point Lay in 1998 and 1999, five whales were tagged each year—a total of nine large males and one small female captured mostly by driving them into stationary nets. Like those across the border in Canada, the belugas tagged at Point Lay destroyed assumptions that they would summer along the coast. The female spent most of the summer near the edge of the pack ice, but the males shot far up into the Arctic Ocean, under the ice. They traveled halfway to the North Pole, more than 600 miles from land, and both years followed the same route over a bottom thought to lack significant features. Some of the waters they traversed were more than 10,000 feet deep.

Neither scientists nor hunters had ever considered that belugas hunted at Point Lay would travel so far north under ice. Robert Suydam, a wildlife biologist with the North Slope Borough, was in charge of the project. He told me, "Satellite telemetry has really revolutionized how scientists and hunters look at the biology of whales. We now know belugas are capable of doing a lot more than what we'd dreamed they could." The discoveries raised a plethora of new questions: How did the whales navigate under pack ice and find enough breathing room without getting trapped? How did they navigate so precisely? Why did they travel so far north, and what did they do when they got there? "We were all a little bit boggled about what they were doing there," Robert said. Perhaps there was food up there—Arctic cod under the ice? And, apparently, the ice wasn't a barrier. Pack ice is always moving and shifting under the clockwise pull of the Arctic currents, and in spring and summer there's always some open water. Using their echolocation abilities, and perhaps also relying on the light that shone into open water, belugas could apparently make their way through the pack ice, never leaving the safety of one breathing area until the next one was established. New ice would not be forming in summer, so there was little chance of getting trapped in a breathing hole with no place to go.

Robert told me: "Canadian researchers have speculated that the deep diving observed in belugas is part of their traveling behavior. They may dive down so they can 'look up' to find the next breathing hole." This action would be similar, in mirror image, to the way an airplane pilot trying to descend through clouds gains altitude to look for a hole in the clouds.

Cook Inlet was a different kind of place than the Arctic—more compact, and with less ice cover. Still, everyone seemed to expect satellite tags to bust open some of the unique mysteries of its whales.

The day I joined the Cook Inlet taggers was their fourth day out, and they had not yet claimed any success. The day before, they'd managed to get a net around a whale, but when they found it was only nine feet long and had a less-than-distinguished dorsal ridge, they let it go. Now, at the boat launch, I zipped into a dry suit and took my assigned place on the big boat—the 21-foot Boston Whaler outfitted with a netbox on its stern. The idea was that our boat would try to spill a small, specially designed seine net (15 feet deep and 800 feet long) around a beluga in shallow water. The other three boats—more maneuverable inflatables—would do the whale tracking and herding and, once there was a whale trapped and tangled in the net, secure it safely with a hoop net over its head and a line around its tail so that it could be towed to shallower water for tagging.

That morning gave us the kind of crisp, clear September day that comes like a gift, with high cirrus clouds streaking the sky and a sharpened scent to the air. New snow dusted the mountaintops, and the long slopes down from the mountains were softening to pale yellows and burnt reds. Most important, the water was as flat as a paved prairie road.

Rod Hobbs, from the National Marine Mammal Lab in Seattle and leader of the tagging project, gathered everyone for a quick review of procedures and safety and the sharing of ideas on what might be done differently, or better. Try to push the whales into shallower water. After capture, be very careful not to hold a whale's tail up; if it can't push down with its tail to lift its head, it can drown. The chartered plane had gone out to look for whales and would be reporting soon.

And then we were off, north into Knik Arm. The city immediately disappeared behind us. For all we could see around and ahead of us, Anchorage might not have existed at all; we might have been entering a world as wild as when Captain Cook first laid eyes upon it. We saw no other boats, no buoys, no floating debris, nothing humanmade along the shore, no air pollution. The flats and beaches alongside ran to clay bluffs that rose to mixed woods—alder and birch and stunted spruce. Much of the east side of Knik is a peculiar kind of uninhabited wilderness—military property—and one of the participants among us was an army biologist charged with making sure no one trespassed. Far to the north but nevertheless looming ahead stood the brilliant peaks of Denali, the Big One, and its fellow mountains Foraker and Hunter. Fog patches rose and swirled like smoke from the water.

It was late in the year for such benevolence. September in south-central Alaska is known for rain and wind, but there was a reason for our timing. No one had yet figured out how to keep a satellite transmitter on a beluga for more than three or four months. It wasn't that the batteries ran out; it was that the attachment devices—the nylon rods stuck through the dorsal ridge and held in place with washers and nuts—would gradually work through and out of the skin and blubber holding them. The pull of water against the tag as the whale swam, and perhaps the beluga's own rubbing, must exert a considerable force. Once lost, the tag would no longer be heard from; its antenna can only signal above water, when the beluga's back rolls into air.

This year was the fourth one during which satellite tagging had been attempted in Cook Inlet, and so far the result was one tagged beluga, total. Despite the precedents of Arctic beluga tagging, and help from Arctic taggers, researchers had found that Cook Inlet was another kettle of whales. In 1995 they'd tried the "cowboy" way—that is, herding whales into the shallows and jumping out with a hoop. But Cook Inlet has turbid rather than clear water, a soft mud rather than a gravel bottom, and other differences that made the technique unworkable. In 1997 researchers tried to drive belugas into a net, and they learned that Cook Inlet belugas are highly skilled at avoiding nets.

Not until 1999 did they try to surround whales with a net. That year, it took a team of seven biologists and two Native hunters twelve days of camping out by the Susitna River and chasing whales as often as the weather and tides allowed to capture and tag one whale, a young male. The tag stayed on from the last day of May until mid-September, as the animal made its rounds of the upper inlet.

This time, the hope was that the "encirclement approach" would again prove successful, for multiple captures, and that September tags would stay on into the winter months and help solve the where-do-they-go mystery.

Our group of wannabe-taggers passed one beluga in deep water and kept going. After a few miles we stopped and rafted up while Barbara Mahoney, the biologist from the Anchorage office, called to find what the plane had spotted. Gathered together, the collective was serious and single-minded—whalers nearly as obsessed with their white-whale quest as Ahab had been with his. They brought together, from various quarters, considerable boat, beluga, and capture expertise. In addition to Rod Hobbs, two young women doing graduate studies, Laura Litsky and Kristin Laidre, had come from the marine mammal lab. Dan Vos and Matt Eagleton were NMFS biologists—mostly committed to fish—from Anchorage. Dana Seagars represented the U.S. Fish and Wildlife Service. Charles Saccheus, an Inupiat hunter with tagging experience, had come all the way from Elim, in Norton Sound on the Arctic coast, as a boat driver and representative of the Alaska Beluga Whale Committee. Greg O'Corry-Crowe, the geneticist, was up from California and would be taking skin samples from any captured whales. Bill Walker, from Washington state, had once specialized in capture work for what he referred to as the "live display industry" and was now, as a private contractor, conducting life history research for NMFS. The other Bill—Gossweiler, the army biologist—was set with a video camera to record the capture and tagging procedure.

Barbara talked by cell phone to yet another team member, a NMFS policy person from Washington, D.C., who was with the plane. I listened to a language of absent and occasionally added Rs: Barb's Boston accent that fifteen years in Alaska had done nothing to diminish. Yes, a *shot* time ago they'd *sportted belugers*—six in the Eagle River, sixteen to twenty in Eagle Bay.

We headed for the bay, about ten miles from Anchorage, and found the whales, white backs rising, then disappearing. The inflatables tracked them, following wakes and the flat, glassy spots—called "footprints"—made on the water by up-and-down underwater fluke movements. The water was too deep, however, and the boat drivers were unable to maneuver the belugas into shallows. The white whales dove and were gone, and we were left among smaller gray ones, some of which, unabashed, surfaced repeatedly beside us.

Many of the whales we'd spotted were cow-calf pairs, which surface often and move slowly. Females with calves may be easier to catch than males but are to be avoided; it would not be a good thing to tangle—and possibly drown—a calf while trying to tag its mother, or to separate the two and have either panic.

We anchored up again, waiting for the water to run out on this day of 25-foot tides. It was nearly noon, and we hadn't gotten anywhere close to catching a whale.

The sun grew hot. Hats and gloves came off, and dry suits were peeled away, sleeves tied at waists. We ate Barbara's chocolate chip cookies and Bill Gossweiler's smoked salmon. Harbor seals bobbed past. Greg had everyone laughing at the story of Captain Boycott, the Irishman behind the lowercase boycott, and the trouble he had with a family named (pause) Mahoney.

I studied the equipment in two of the inflatables—hoop nets six feet across that would be placed over the heads of captured belugas and loops made from thick soft nylon line to hold their tails. Someone had been talking about tail-holding, and the name for the place the line would circle stuck in my mind, repeating like a two-word poem: *caudal peduncle*. Packed away in our boat we had the tagging kits—like large tackle boxes—supplied with the transmitters and the tools and parts for attaching them.

The sound of gunshots came to us over the water. It was duck hunting season, and hunters were out there, somewhere.

Near low water, we got on the move again, following a channel sometimes only two or three feet deep. Downstream, the inflatables tracked various whales and groups of whales, breaking off as soon as they saw calves. They were having trouble finding anything but cows with calves. Finally they called on the radio; they had a small group, coming our way.

After that, things happened fast. We had a whale among us. When directed, I threw the buoy attached to one end of the net, then got out of the way as Dan goosed our boat around the spot where we'd last seen the whale. The net flew off the back end and settled into the water in something resembling a circular fence—the buoyant top line floating, the weighted leadline sinking to the mud. We hoped there was a whale within it. The smaller boats zoomed in to cut off the opening and to pull the ends together.

But there was no splash of water, no ripple or wake, no tugging of the net. We had nothing but water inside the net and no sign of belugas anywhere around.

We pulled the net back into the boat, untangling it as we went, restacking it in its box. The net was made of soft, tough, large-sized mesh—suitable for snagging a beluga by its head, flipper, or fluke without harming it. It was also made up of panels that could be "unzipped" to wrap around a whale, or more important, to free a whale that might be underwater and in danger of drowning. The metal panel attachments were a problem; they caught on web and bunched it up. Moreover, the lightness of the leadline combined with the speed of the boat caused the leadline to fly up and cross the float line, leaving gaping holes in the enclosure once the lines and web settled in the water. The leadline, I was told, needed to be light to keep the net from presenting too much resistance; too heavy, and a whale would punch through taut web instead of tangling.

All afternoon, we saw only one other boat. When we spotted it, it was beached, with men leaning over a smoking outboard. The crew in one of our inflatables went to see if they needed help and was told they were okay. Later, the boat was back on the water, and the men were firing rifles less than a mile from us, near a group of belugas.

I stared at the speck of boat, disbelieving, then turned to Barb, rafted beside us. "Do you think they're shooting at belugas?" I hadn't seen any ducks on the arm, and I couldn't think of anything else they could be legally hunting.

The others were concerned too, but someone said, "We told them who we were and what we're doing. There's no way they'd be shooting at whales."

Maybe not, but what impressed me was the impossibility of enforcing either the old law against any take, including harassment, of marine mammals by non-Natives or the new prohibition against Native beluga hunting. If we couldn't even tell what was going on right next to us, how—in an area as large and remote and unpatrolled as Cook Inlet—could there be any protection of belugas? Cook Inlet, at roughly 20,000 square kilometers, is only slightly smaller than the whole of my home state of New Hampshire. It seemed to me that anyone who wanted to shoot at whales, for any reason, could pretty much do so with impunity.

We found more whales and made another set. This time, the net went out with less fouling. We were pretty sure we'd gotten around a whale. But again, the water inside was still. The net lay calm. We pulled the net back in and found a whale-sized hole in one section. Dan stitched it closed.

One of the whales we'd spotted had a fresh injury to its back—as though it might have collided with a boat. The researchers had noticed it now several times over the past few days—one identified whale among how many? Talk drifted to the idea of a photo-identification program. Other whale species—killer whales and humpbacks—were distinctively marked, and catalogs of individual whales helped researchers learn about their travels and relationships to one another, even how many made up different groupings. Could such a thing be done for Cook Inlet's belugas? What would such an effort take?

The water was flooding in. Soon there'd be too much of it—depth and breadth both. But belugas were coming in with the tide, too. We decided to try to set from the beach. Laura waded to shore with the buoy and held that end of the net onshore. When belugas neared us in the channel, Dan started the engine, preparing to run out and block them with the net, then zip around and close behind them. But the net immediately caught on a panel attachment and tumbled out in a big snarl, and then the whales were past us.

We tried something else, similar to what salmon seiners call "holding a hook." We laid out some net from shore, across the channel, then had the small boats get behind a group of belugas and drive them toward us. On the radio, Rod, sounding tired, said, "You guys are in pretty deep water. We've never been able to drive them in deep water. I think it's time to hang it up."

A long line of belugas—maybe fifty white animals—was coming our way. They were coming. Coming. Coming. They were down and gone. We didn't see them again.

Three days later, on a more typical fall day of wind and threatening clouds, I joined the researchers again. It was day seven for them, and they had yet to catch a whale. Weary and disheartened, the crew assembled slowly at the dock. While I waited, I looked around more closely at what a sign said was Ship Creek Waterfront Development Project—less a project than someone's idea for the future. For now, there was the boat ramp, an old dock on creosoted pilings, a gravel parking lot, and a locked restroom. The wind carried the cries of gulls and the snap of an Alaska flag that flew from a tugboat at the dock. A very few weathered wooden skiffs, sans outboards, perched on the mudflats.

I read another sign by the ramp, one with a drawing of a beluga. "HELP PROTECT BELUGA WHALES. It is illegal to hunt or harass Cook Inlet beluga whales. Help us prevent unlawful harassment, chasing, hunting, or killing of these whales to aid recovery of this depleted population. This will ensure their presence in Cook Inlet for future generations." The sign specified a reward of up to $2,500 "for information leading to the conviction" of anyone who violated the Marine Mammal Protection Act.

The plane, going out ahead of us, reported a group of belugas in Knik Arm, near where we'd been before. We headed up, with a stiff wind at our backs, and anchored near the top of a narrow channel to wait for the tide to drop and the whales to move down the arm. Whitecaps broke steadily over the bar. It would be hard to work in the wind, or to spot calves, but the forecast called for the wind to turn around and diminish.

We waited. The group talked about the cow-and-calf problem. It had not been anticipated. In the previous tagging operation, in May, they hadn't had to deal with it; calving usually occurred in June. It was also possible that Knik was a nursery area, but they hadn't observed the Susitna and other areas in the same close way and didn't know if they were similar or not. The aerial surveys couldn't spot calves well enough even to begin to identify birthing and nursery areas—although such places were assumed to exist.

Hail—the first of three poundings that day—bounced all over us and the boats. Someone said, "The worst day in the field is better than the best day in the office."

Finally, a group of large whales came down the channel, and we loosed our net around them. We were in eight feet of water and had four whales inside the net, but the small boats weren't quick enough to close the opening, and the whales were gone. Slowly, we pulled the net back to the boat and restacked. On the military lands just to our north, exercises banged off explosions with puffs of smoke. Practicing paratroopers drifted across the sky like fluff-topped dandelion seeds carried in the wind.

We went ashore and sat on the beach while awaiting another report from the plane. I picked highbush cranberries and shared them with Charles, the soft-spoken boat driver from Elim, who said he knew them as "Indian berries." Charles had managed tagging efforts in the Arctic and was, in fact, the first nonscientist authorized to conduct capture-tagging. At the beluga committee meeting that fall, Charles would be honored with the recognition that

NMFS had, for the first time, "granted authority to people in this room to do their own research," and everyone would cheer the chair's pronouncement, "Charles, you are now a scientist."

In mid-afternoon, we got the report from the plane. A few whales had been spotted, coming our way on the flood. Thinking to get behind them and trap them upstream, we kept quiet in the anchored boats while the first two swam past. Where the others that had been spotted went to, we didn't know. For the next couple of hours our little fleet of boats chased sightings—some of which may have been only the tops of waves—all around the upper reaches of Knik Arm, but we never even got close to tracking a whale into shallows where we might have a chance of netting it. Each of our approaches only sent the whales under, and long minutes passed before our binoculars caught another spot of white. Belugas can stay underwater, without surfacing to breathe, for as long as thirty minutes, and hunters say they will lie on the bottom for that long, hiding.

I felt sorry for the researchers, whose dedication to the effort was not in question. This outing was no joyride, no pleasure boating at taxpayer expense, but an intense—approaching desperate—attempt at obtaining critical information about the Cook Inlet belugas. I was feeling equally sorry for the whales, which had been subjected now to day after day of chase—what, if anyone other than researchers were doing it, would be considered harassment and would be firmly prohibited. Escaping from us was, obviously, interrupting their normal behavior—presumably feeding—in their preferred locations and was not desirable from a conservation point of view.

It was some comfort to remember that earlier studies, conducted in Cook Inlet and elsewhere, had shown that disturbances by researchers and hunters did not have long-term or serious effects on belugas. Belugas, known for their "site fidelity," seldom leave an area; if they do, temporarily, they quickly return to it and to patterns of normal behavior. For all I knew, the whales might even enjoy the games of hide-and-seek, at which they were obviously so superior.

Back at the boat ramp at the end of the day, Rod tried to find something positive to emphasize. With a weak smile—or was it a grimace?—he said, "We're having a lot of learning opportunities."

The very next day, in two different sets in Eagle Bay, the crew caught and tagged two belugas. One, a small female, they called Paul. (Not having sexed it at the time, they had to wait for the genetic analysis to determine they'd goofed on the name.) The other, a male almost 14 feet long, they called Ringo. They never did catch up with John and George.

When I spoke with Barbara a few days later, she was ecstatic. "We got them tagged real good," she said, hopeful that the tags would stay on through the fall and into winter. "It was easier on the incoming tide." Everything had gone smoothly. It had taken time—an hour for the small one—to tow the netted whales gently into shallow water where the researchers could ground them and stand knee-deep to work. The actual tagging had taken about forty minutes each. Immediately after the small one's release, it had shot ten miles down the arm, near Anchorage, before turning around and returning to Eagle Bay.

The movements of the small beluga they knew immediately because they'd fitted it with a second, temporary tag just forward of the satellite tag. The smaller "time depth recorder," or TDR, was attached with a suction cup and could be tracked by radio signal. Suction cup tags are designed to be slapped on from the end of a pole after getting close to a whale, and the chance to press one carefully and firmly onto Paul resulted in a new, ninety-hour record for length of attachment. For the first fifty-five hours, the TDR recorded every second—essentially detailing the whale's pattern of moving, surfacing, and diving.

In the months that followed, one of my most-referenced computer bookmarks was the site that posted the travels of Paul and Ringo. Making the website hit was like tuning in to a favorite soap opera; what were Paul and Ringo up to now?

The two were very seldom together. Paul tended to move around more and to cover greater distances than Ringo, perhaps befitting her juvenile status—less sure of where to find what she needed (food?), more curious and exploratory in general, less settled in her ways. At the start, in September, Paul zipped around Knik Arm. Ringo left the area and roamed the other arm—Turnagain—and the bay—Chickaloon—just outside it. In mid-October, Paul left Knik and traveled down the west side of the inlet, past my fish camp, and then was back and forth between the two bays on either side of my camp, always close to shore. Ringo, during the same period, pulled out of Turnagain and moved a short distance down the inlet's east side, then stuck around Chickaloon Bay. But at the end of October—surprise!—Paul moved back up the inlet, to the Susitna delta, and on November 6 both whales were back in Knik Arm.

Throughout November and early December, the two belugas continued to frequent the upper reaches of the inlet—Knik, Chickaloon, the Susitna delta—the same areas where belugas gathered to feed in summer. The notable difference was that the fish runs that fed them in summer were long gone from those areas. Later in December, the two whales left the iced-over arms and bays but remained well up in the inlet's northern reach. In January, when their tags stopped transmitting, they were still frequenting the upper inlet.

Barbara and the other researchers were just as surprised as their colleagues had been, earlier, to find Arctic belugas in unexpected places. Was the Cook Inlet population wintering in the upper inlet? If so, why didn't anyone see more than the occasional glimpse of one or two? How did 300-plus whales hide so well? Were these two whales truly representative, traveling with others? Or were they rogue whales, a rare pair that stayed behind while the rest headed south?

Or had the particular winter of 2000–2001 presented unusual conditions that allowed the whales to stay north when normally they would have gone south? It was true that it had been a mild winter, with air temperatures averaging ten to twelve degrees warmer than usual and light icing. I was teaching in Anchorage, every week flying over Turnagain's open water and looking down from the commuter plane at scattered ice pans among which, presumably, some belugas were conducting their winter lives.

∞∞

Throughout that winter, Barbara Mahoney chartered occasional flights to look for belugas. She and her NMFS colleagues looked in areas from which Paul and Ringo signaled, and they looked through the arms and along the coasts southward. They never spotted more than a few whales. In spring, I arranged to ride along.

The weather was nasty for weeks, with winds that tore roofs off buildings, and Barbara repeatedly scheduled, canceled, and rescheduled flights. Finally, on April 19, we caught a bluebird day. Brad Smith, another biologist from Barb's office, brought the Mustang (dry) suits—just in case: We would be flying at 800 feet over the water, far lower than what's recommended for a wheel plane, which can use a little more height from which to coast to land in the (unlikely) event of a problem in its single engine. At Merrill Field—Anchorage's small-plane airfield—Barbara, Brad, and I loaded into a four-seat Cessna 207 with our pilot, Merle. Brad sat in the front as principal spotter, Barb behind him on the right with notebook, watch, and handheld GPS. I had the least advantageous seat, which would always be facing outward—the deeper inlet waters—rather than looking toward the shoreline, across the half-mile of water where belugas were most likely to be found.

Very quickly, we were over the shopping center at the end of the field (where an electronic clock blinked the time: 9:24), then over downtown Anchorage, past the Hilton Hotel towers, over the port, over the inlet, and heading west. The water below us was a flat brown with a grainy texture like leather. I pressed my forehead to the window, wanting to display my whale-spotting ability, to be the first to call out with a beluga. There were ice chunks still washing around—looking like belugas. There were seagulls sitting on the water—looking like belugas. There were lots of exposed shoals.

"One whale here, Barb," Brad said calmly into his headphone mike. "Just under us now."

We were off the Susitna River, a favorite beluga area. The plane circled.

"Both sides now," Brad said.

As the plane banked around, I saw one beluga, then a second. The white backs were almost crescents, fingernail parings. Wet, they glowed brightly, that white that always seems whiter-than-white against Cook Inlet's mud-colored water. They were easily separated from bits of ice not only by shape and shine but also by their flash—now there, now gone.

"I counted twelve," Brad said. "Not a very good count, though, Barb." Barbara wrote down the count, time, location.

In the old days, a survey like this was as good as it got. Now, as we continued following the shoreline's bend south, I contrasted the primitive-ness of what we were doing to the systematic summer surveys conducted since 1994 to establish the abundance estimates: 653 in 1994, then 491, 594, 440, 347, 369, and 435 in 2000. During fair-weather days every June, when the belugas congregated most densely in the inlet, a specially outfitted airplane with a crew of four flew over the inlet in a precise pattern. At 800 feet—the same altitude I was flying with Barbara and Brad—the plane fol-lowed the coast of the entire inlet as well as offshore transects in a sawtooth pattern, back and forth, back and forth. After fifty or more flight hours, each survey covered one hundred percent of the coastal waters and lower reaches of rivers and about thirty percent of the entire inlet. Many areas were covered multiple times.

When belugas were spotted during those surveys, the plane circled while observers—separated from one another to assure independence—counted and shot videotape. At least four counts of each whale group were made by each observer. Later, each observer's mean count was used to calculate the number of whales observed in each group, and the videotapes were analyzed for *their* counts.

Once, when I visited the National Marine Mammal Lab in Seattle, a biologist showed me how the videotapes were used. Janice Waite sat me down at a computer monitor and selected a video from the previous summer, a portion that showed perhaps a dozen white beluga backs. The drill was to stop the video every half second, put a plastic sheet over it, and mark the whales seen. The next half-second showed the same whales, although some, more exposed at the surface, were easier to see, and others, beginning dives, were less clear, and the pale shadow beside another now appeared as a gray calf. Half-second by half-second, each still photo was recorded on a plastic sheet.

I offered to Janice, in a way I hoped was admiring, that the video work seemed enormously time-consuming. It was tedious, she agreed. It was so tedious that it was shared by a number of assistants in turns, so that no one went crazy or, perhaps more important, applied less than the most careful attention and accuracy to each half-second of record.

On a second monitor, Janice showed me how the count was further checked against the second videotape, taken by the camera with the telephoto lens. Studying the zoomed version, I picked out two whales that had blended into one in the first video.

The video counts, once compared to the observer counts, helped to adjust for over- or undercounting. Additional correction factors were applied to account for whales missed because they were underwater or outside the survey areas. The end result each year was an abundance estimate important less for its numerical accuracy than for establishing the population trend. The trend had been downward until hunting was stopped. With two years of no hunting, the numbers suggested that the population might be at least stabilizing.

Down the west side of the inlet now, we flew over more ice chunks, strung out in lines by the currents. Snow still covered the land to tidewater, and volcanic peaks formed giant snowcones against the sky. On my side of the plane, I looked out on the inlet's oil rigs, one with a badly smoking flare; ahead of us, I counted twelve, including the new, southernmost one located just off my fishing sites. Through Barb's window, I spotted the log dock near the village of Tyonek, then a cluster of onshore oil facilities. We curved in along Trading Bay, past my neighbor George's snowed-in, boarded-up camp. We swung the other way to clear the Foreland, and I pointed out my cabins, looking small and cold, their white and gray hard to pick out but for the rectangular shapes. A single barge was making its way up the inlet—the only boat traffic we'd seen.

Brad said, "I wonder if the Susitna water is warmer this time of year than these streams that are closer to glaciers. Why would they be hanging out there, where there's no food?" The question was one he was throwing out to the universe.

We reached Harriet Point, halfway down the inlet, gained altitude, and crossed the inlet, passing over Kalgin Island. We'd left the cloudless skies and now flew under a high overcast, ideal for cutting glare. "What a perfect day," Barbara said.

Brad turned in his seat. "Seems like it would be hard to miss a whale."

I thought so too. I'd been keeping a close watch from my side of the plane and was pretty sure I would have seen any sliver of white within a couple of miles.

When we reached the east side, green water from the Kenai River plumed into the inlet. Slow to mix in the calm sea, it held a sharp edge against the brown for a long way out into its tide-pulled northern twist. Barbara asked Merle to fly us a short way up the Kenai River. "We've had some reports of whales up the river." We dropped low over the river, saw the white heads of eagles, flocks of gulls, and what I thought were swans. No whales. At Kenai we were past low-tide (the best time for spotting belugas, when they tend to be more concentrated) by two hours, but we had another hour until the waters around Anchorage would hit low.

The inlet, of course, extended much farther south, but we wouldn't be checking beyond the Kenai River. While people still chose to argue over the numbers of Cook Inlet belugas, nearly everyone agreed that the distribution of the whales had changed dramatically over the years. The summer surveys consistently found belugas only in the upper inlet—in shallow water, mostly around river mouths. Since 1995, those surveys had found only a single beluga outside the northernmost areas.

Earlier summer surveys, back to the 1970s, also found large concentrations of belugas around the Susitna River, but they also found many belugas in other parts of the inlet—upper, middle, and lower. Whales were seen in various bays, around other river mouths, in the lower portions of rivers, and offshore—well out into the center of the inlet. During vessel operations in Cook Inlet in June and July 1974–1979, exactly fifty percent of the belugas sighted were in the lower inlet, and in the 1980s thirty percent were. A map drawn by university researchers in 1979, based on both aerial and shipboard sightings in all seasons from 1975 to 1978, placed belugas throughout the central inlet, in coastal areas of the lower inlet, and even out into the Gulf of Alaska, to Kodiak Island, Prince William Sound, and Yakutat Bay. According to that map, the West Foreland, where I fish, lay smack in the middle of the heaviest concentrations of sightings.

What did it mean that the summer distribution had changed so much, from such a broad (and more southerly) inhabitation of the inlet to an intense concentration around the Susitna River, and from largely offshore areas to almost entirely shallow waters within a ten-fathom line? When I'd asked Rod Hobbs, he answered with a question: "Is Big Su–Little Su [the Susitna River area] the best place to be?"

That may be it. In summer, the easiest way for a group of whales to get food may be to gather at the mouth of a major river that enjoys a steady sequence of fish runs. The steadiness, or the ease, of fishing there may be greater than around other rivers. The water may be warmer or cooler, better as a nursery for young whales, or have some other attributes. It is certainly more protected from killer whales, the principal beluga predator aside from humans. Killer whales live in the Gulf of Alaska but rarely venture up the inlet very far or into shallows.

When there were more belugas, perhaps they had to disperse, to travel elsewhere and to pursue other food sources; perhaps there wasn't room enough for them to all be in the same, most desirable place.

Now, we were headed north along the inlet's east side: past the oil industry plants and docking facilities at Nikiski and the tanker filling at the dock. Brad and Merle talked about bear hunting and silver salmon fishing. We were under clear skies again, over more chunks of ice.

Then, just off Point Possession (where Captain Cook had planted his flag back in 1778), we began to circle.

"Just off the wingtip," Merle said. "See where it dived?"

Brad studied the water. "I see a little mud trail, I think. Might just be a single."

I strained to see past Barbara but never saw anything except water and sky and a line of trees on the shore. The wingtip on my side pointed up.

"Yeah, just one," Brad said.

We straightened again and continued across Chickaloon Bay into Turnagain Arm. Turnagain was less wintry than the west side of the inlet had been; the south-facing mountains were clear of snow partway up their sides, even higher on steep slopes. Cars glinted from the highway pasted to its north shore. Beyond Bird Point, there were only mudflats, and we turned back toward Anchorage.

The last area to survey was Knik Arm. To get there and to cover it was complicated by the day's landing pattern at the international airport and by the military's airspace. Instead of following the coast, we had to fly across

Anchorage, then down a drainage that emptied into Knik. Black military jets shot past us. "Bad timing," Merle said. "The fighters are coming in for lunch." Knik was mostly mudflats, but we flew up one side and down the other, back to the port at Ship Creek, back over Anchorage to Merrill Field.

That was it, then. A group of maybe a dozen off the Susitna, a single by Point Possession. It was the same small count—the same group—they'd seen in October, November, and December. No more, no different. Brad said, "We may have had the bad luck to have tagged two of that small group."

As we were finishing up in the air charter office, I asked them both, "Where do you think they are then, the three or four hundred belugas, in winter?"

Brad said, "I've always thought they went down to Shelikof [in the Gulf of Alaska, the strait west of Kodiak]. If they do deep dive intervals, they'd be hard to spot, and there's no one there to see them."

Barbara said, "I used to think they wintered in the gulf. But after the tagging..." Her voice trailed off.

Back home, I studied scientific papers. I read about philopatry, site tenacity, site fidelity—all ways of saying that belugas are attached to particular areas, return to them, and are loath to leave even when disturbed or hunted. I read a U.S. Geological Survey report that suggested that the change in Cook Inlet beluga distribution may have resulted from habitat changes—that different areas had become more or less attractive because of declines in prey species, or increases in vessel traffic, or changing sea temperatures. I studied everything related to the Cook Inlet surveys and abundance estimates. I learned a new language. *Regression formulas. Monte Carlo simulations. Correction factors. Probabilities. Confidence intervals. Coefficients of variation. Bayesian analyses.* I had only the grossest understanding of how these were applied and what they meant for the belugas.

I thought about Rod Hobbs and a meeting where, armed with overhead charts and graphs, he'd tried to explain how the researchers had come up with abundance estimates lower than anyone wanted them to be. Questions came out of another world, hurled like harpoons—questions that disputed any count that didn't accept that whales weren't there to be counted because they were "somewhere else" (following the fish, or maybe resting on the bottom), questions that asserted that statistics were all a bunch of hooey used to support lies. The scientific conclusion—that aerial surveys indicated the belugas were depleted—might have been clear enough, but the proof was so far beyond most people's ability to understand that it came down to this: We're the scientists, and you just have to trust us.

Which I did. I trusted the scientists because I knew them to be educated in what they did. I knew them to be professionals, with a commitment to objectivity. I knew how the system worked, with peer review of methods and systems and published papers. I knew that Rod and his colleagues were smart and good people and that they had no reason to "cook" the numbers, to make a false case. I knew all that because, although I wasn't one of them, I still lived in their world. Not everyone does, and I remembered again the bowhead situation, in which the scientists knew one thing, and the hunters knew something else. The scientists themselves still shook their heads over that. One had told me, defensively, "Looking back, we recognize how primitive our surveying techniques were then. But now they're very sophisticated."

Twenty years ago Edward Abbey wrote, "The face of science as currently construed is a face that only a mathematician could love. The root meaning of 'science' is 'knowledge'; to see and to see truly, a qualitative, not merely quantitative understanding.... That which today calls itself science gives us more and more information, an indigestible glut of information, and less and less understanding."

Paul and Ringo, it turned out, weren't rogue whales. In subsequent years additional Cook Inlet belugas were successfully instrumented and tracked into and through winters. The tagged whales—eighteen of them by 2002—remained in the upper portions of the inlet, building a solid case for resident whales behaviorally different from belugas in other parts of Alaska and the world, where they migrate seasonally over considerable distances.

Later, too, we would have more surveys and more counts. The population estimate, after spiking at 435 in 2000, fell to 386 in 2001 and 313, the lowest estimate ever, in 2002. Rod Hobbs was quick to point out that the low number didn't necessarily mean that the population had dropped, just as the high number two years earlier hadn't meant it had increased. "The new figure is not statistically different from previous years," he told a newspaper reporter. The population in 2002 likely ranged somewhere between 248 and 396.

Three hundred beluga whales—give or take some dozens—seemed, to me, a frighteningly small number.

4

BELUGA LOVE

"*What?* You live with wild whales, and you're going to an *aquarium* to look at them?"

I hadn't, until seeing my friend's disbelieving look, considered the irony of the situation. There I was, in Chicago, and if there was some advantage to being in the city beyond wandering the Native American collections in the Field Museum, it was surely to see beluga whales at the Shedd Aquarium. There were maybe fifty belugas living in captivity in 1998, and five of them swam at the Shedd. I had never seen a living, swimming beluga that I could really see.

But, Maureen protested, didn't I know what a turnabout that was? The only live whales most people would ever see would be behind glass. That was the ordinary experience. The extraordinary one was mine. Other people could only dream of seeing belugas in the wild.

That was true, but the ordinary was something I wanted to know about too. I wanted to see other people seeing belugas, and I wanted to know what they made of that experience. One thing I understood was that there were many ways to love belugas. Some of those ways involved watching gleams of white from a distance, of rising and falling on the same swells of the same sea that kept beluga secrets. Some involved following "footprints" and admiring evasive abilities, or counting, or working out statistical probabilities. Some involved testing one's self against the whale, and taking part of it, as food, into one's own body. Most people's beluga love was of a simpler kind, less intimate perhaps—or maybe not. Maybe love was never simple. Who was to say that the millions of children raised on the Raffi song "Baby Beluga," who might never have any knowledge of belugas beyond the song itself—or the cover of the tape or CD from which it played, or maybe the book that went with it, with the smiling baby beluga, the "little white whale on the go"—didn't still love belugas with a kind of passion?

I had, I admitted, doubts about the propriety of confining wild animals to—essentially—cages. Could I justify entering the kind of place I had always disparaged as a "whale jail"? Did I really want to lend my support, with my admission fee and my presence, to the captivity of animals that had once kicked their flukes freely in icy Hudson Bay? The Shedd's belugas, after all, had neither been born in captivity nor rescued from some disaster that might otherwise have caused their deaths. They had been healthy wild animals pursuing normal whale lives until they were jumped on or tangled in nets, then hauled away to an entirely new environment. On the other hand, both aquariums and zoos—the good, responsible ones—serve educational and scientific purposes; the public and researchers learn things that will benefit wildlife in the long run. Intellectually, I knew that, but I also believed that putting animals on display is generally degrading to them and to the relationships that we ought to have with fellow species.

I was also a person who had lived long and happily among the many mysteries of whales, salmon, and ocean, and I wasn't entirely sure I wanted to replace some of that mystery with something that might, in its factuality, shake my equilibrium.

John Steinbeck wrote that there were three ways of seeing actual marine creatures (as opposed to photographic images of them): dead and preserved, in their own habitats for short times, and in an aquarium for long periods. He'd been referring specifically to the kinds of intertidal animals he encountered on his collecting trip to the Sea of Cortez, but this seemed a general truism. There weren't too many whales bottled in formaldehyde, but I had studied the dead beluga washed up on my beach as well as the articulated skeleton at my local museum. I had all those brief, silt-obscured Cook Inlet glimpses. Now I was going to add Steinbeck's third way. Seeing belugas in an aquarium would be, I thought, like adding a third dimension to the two-dimensional world I had inhabited so far. My picture would be, if not complete, at least fuller.

And there I was, at the door with money in hand, like any other dupe.

Once inside the Shedd, I skirted the main building devoted to fish and continued straight past the penguins, otters, seals, and white-sided dolphins to the beluga tanks. And there they were, such a long, long way from home, backed up to picture windows on Lake Michigan as though there were some connection between the freshwater lake and their own deep and dark distant ocean.

I stood frozen at the rail, as I might have on my beach, looking, and looking, and looking. While blowhole spray drizzled over me, three whales, three shades of white, sluggishly circled in clear water. But this—this—is what, above all, I saw: folds of fat bunched like double, triple, quadruple chins as the one vertically poised white whale bent forward, as if to look down its length to where some phantom toes may have been. Then the other way: Its doughy head lifted, the neck stretched smooth in front, and the back of its head stood out from the creases like a small globe held in place with loose wraps of sheeting. That huge, long body—three times my height—and then the little head perched almost at right angles to it: It was different, and more, than anything I had previously imagined.

I had known for many years that belugas turn their heads. I knew for a fact that they were the only cetaceans (aside from a couple of small dolphins) with unfused neck vertebrae—to have, in short, necks. I had carried with me a mental picture of them turning their heads sideways as they swam, like a human swimmer doing the crawl (except without the breath-taking). I thought of them suspended in the water, facing left or right, with all the mechanics of their neck and back bones well buried in the smooth rounded blubber of their bodies.

In all my years of beluga watching on Cook Inlet, I'd never seen more of the whales than the arcs of their backs rising above gray water, the misty blows of their breaths, and, very rarely, a flipping fluke. I'd never seen so much as a clear head, never mind a turning one. The one dead whale that washed ashore had been bloated to grotesquerie.

For all their detail, none of the photographs I'd studied had ever conveyed to me much more than a cartoonish shape stiffly floating.

I must have looked like a nutcase, standing in amazement beside the beluga pool. Up, down, around: Heads kept turning as the three animals engaged with one another, with the walls, the surface of the water, the rest of their surroundings. Other people came by. "Oh, look," they said. "Belugas." And then they were gone, while I was still watching heads turn, still adjusting what I thought I knew to be true. I couldn't get over those necks. I couldn't get enough of watching blowholes snap open and closed like mechanical valves. I was tantalized by textures and imperfections—the many scars and scrapes and rough patches, the distinctive wrinkles, a small notch in a fluke.

Where were those sleek segments of white wheels I thought I knew? They had always been illusions, I knew, but even knowing that had not prepared me for the bulbous little heads and blunt, petal-shaped flippers. These belugas were alternately lumpy and hollow and curiously contoured, as though their creator had been very unhandy in his application of modeling clay. They reminded me not even of whales but of manatees, of the extinct Steller sea cow.

And how was I to reconcile the very awkward shape with its most graceful of maneuvering? Because graceful is what they surely were, the three of them circling and swerving and brushing up against one another, bending and curving like the most flexible of ballerinas: the very white whale, the somewhat less white whale, the still grayish whale.

At the appointed time a cheerful Shedd employee arrived to present her beluga talk. She told the assembled: The three whales in the tank were all about thirteen years old. One was a male, and the other two were pregnant females, halfway through their fifteen-month gestations and trained to submit to medical ultrasounds. I saw then that the females, identified by teats alongside their genital slits that, otherwise, resembled the male's, were indeed more rounded than their polygamous mate.

A focus of the Shedd's beluga program, the young woman told us, was reproduction. That is, they were trying to develop a breeding program. If belugas would successfully breed in captivity, the needs of aquariums could be filled without capturing wild animals. And, of course, the knowledge gained might be applied to protect and conserve animals in their natural environments. "The biggest problem for belugas today," the young woman said, "is pollution and habitat destruction. Caring about belugas is the first step in their conservation."

The beluga breeding program had not yet, eight years after the Shedd's whale addition opened, been a success. Another female—now with a mate in a separate tank—had given birth six months earlier, but the calf had been weak, unable—even with the help of human divers—to swim to the surface to breathe, and it had died.

At the end of the talk, I wandered down to the lower level where I discovered that it's one thing to watch whales from above, however clear the water might be, and something else entirely to see them below the surface, in their own, aqueous element. On the other side of the glass the three belugas circled, floated, and bounced up and down from vertical positions, with their heads out of the water, "spy-hopping." They cruised upside-down, bellies up and dorsal sides down, propelled by what seemed a mere flip of fluke and bend of body. They rubbed their backs on a fake-rock archway and brushed up against one another in what looked to be an affectionate manner. They swung past the glass, a nose-length (mine, not theirs) away. I could see every flaw in their skin, every muscle movement, the shine in their dark eyes.

And I could see another aspect of beluga physiology I had known to be true but had not imagined—the changing of their head shapes. Like something borrowed from science fiction or a distortion in a funhouse mirror, there they were—moving around the contents of their heads, shifting shape. Now, what I had read made sense. All that acoustical oil in the bulging front part of the head—the melon—can be moved at will, as we might tilt our heads, to best receive sound. When a beluga shapes its melon, as well as when it turns its head, it's focusing sound—in the same way that twisting certain flashlights will focus their light beams. This system applies to receiving both general sound in the beluga's environment and the returning "bounce" of its own echolocating clicks.

Bulge, shift, shrink, enlarge, flatten. I could see, with my own eyes, true shape-shifting, a real and uncanny no-special-effects morphing.

And then there were the sounds. I was finally hearing belugas. The chorus coming from overhead speakers was just as it's been described: a cacophony of clicks, squeaks, whistles, and trills. There were creaks like doors opening on rusty hinges and high-pitched electronic wheezes. I closed my eyes and imagined being in a tropical rainforest at dawn, surrounded by boisterous exotic birds. The voices were thick and various, echoing. They were, I found when I asked, recorded in the Canadian wild with a hydrophone.

While scientists hesitate to use the word *language* when they talk about the sounds that whales make, those sounds clearly make up communication systems. Killer whales have been found to have different dialects, depending on what pod and region they live within. Humpbacks famously sing, in patterns that repeat and seem to be copied and adapted among whales and across time and space. Belugas have a diverse repertoire—suggesting not only that they communicate within social groupings but that they may have a lot to communicate about. Belugas, researchers say, are very, very good at separating out specific, individual, and significant sounds from all the rest. Belugas are also imitative, and the ones at the Shedd, we were told, had learned to clank and wheeze along with the mechanical operations of their tanks.

At least a piece of what belugas and other cetaceans "say" is somewhat understood. The basic clicking appears to be, simply and complicatedly enough, the production of sound for echolocating, akin to what bats and sonar do. A beluga's clicks bounce off whatever's out there in its field of negotiation and are recaptured and "read" to determine shape, depth, solidity, and distance—even, apparently, behind barriers and around corners. I thought again about all the extreme conditions in which belugas live—sunless waters choked in ice, silty estuaries and shallow channels, Cook Inlet—and how much there might be to learn from the owner of what may be the world's most sophisticated navigational system.

I watched the belugas and listened to the recording, and then I stood back and watched and listened to other people watching and listening. The most common response from passers-by was along the lines of "Oh, look, belugas," or "Belugas! Cool!" or, to small whining children, "Look at the beluga, honey. He's trying to kiss you." It was a rare visitor who paused long enough to plant his or her feet in front of the glass wall. No one seemed to notice the head shape changing; no one seemed to cock an ear to the chorus, which may as well have been mall Muzak.

No one, reasonably enough, shared my obsession. It was something, I thought, that my fellow visitors at least knew the name of a strange animal they were unlikely ever to encounter in a natural habitat. The mothers and children, the men and the boys, the couple holding hands—they all saw the belugas and moved on to the interactive displays. They lit up a map of the world's sixteen Arctic and sub-Arctic beluga populations. They pushed buttons to show, by comparison, the sizes of the bigger whales—killers, sperms, and blues.

And then they went off to the choreographed dolphin show, clearly a crowd-pleaser. "We need to protect their habitat, the fish they eat, and the water they swim in," the woman there chanted. The training wasn't really to entertain us, she explained. It was to stimulate the dolphins mentally and to protect their health. That is, they were trained to hold still for procedures like having their blood taken. The circus music, the strutting of human attendants, the whole staged routine of synchronized jumping, tail-walking, and blowhole squeaking—all that, if I wasn't to be too cynical, got people through the door and into the seats so that they could hear about what was really important.

A way to help dolphins, the woman said at the conclusion of her presentation, was "to not throw trash in the street." Well, yes, that would be a start. And people who learn to care about belugas might not pour their used motor oil down storm drains? I supposed we could do worse than help humans make these elemental connections to the way they, and wild animals, live.

Back at the beluga tank, I watched the three belugas circle, again and again, past the glass wall just inches from my inquiring face. I tried to look beyond the anatomically curved smiley-mouths to read something in their expressions, and I imagined we were locking eyes. Beluga eyesight isn't great, I knew—little required in dark and turbidity, otherwise compensated for. Still, one way or another—through rods and cones or by reflected sound, assuming that the wall of the tank didn't act as a barrier—I felt sure the whales "saw" me standing beside them. Probably, I thought, they saw me with considerable precision. In the wild, they would surely need to know if what they approached was friend, foe, or food.

The bigger question seemed to be, what could these whales possibly care about any of the human forms—short, tall, fat, thin, calm, agitated, fast-paced, or lingering for an inordinately long time—that passed their wall, all day, every day? In their confined lives, perhaps they grasped what meager stimulation they could in whatever occasionally varied within the tank or beyond the wall. Perhaps they thought people were marched past for their own entertainment? What did it mean for a whale to "think"?

The complexity of whale brains rivals our own, and many of our species would like to attribute to theirs a kind of human intelligence. But there we are, homocentric as ever, so limited in our understandings and imaginings that we can only conceive of others in terms of ourselves. It's much more likely that the complex brains of whales are geared to different functions than ours—all that acoustical, echolocating ability, for a start.

One of the female whales bumped its head under an arch. Ouch! I was surprised it would be so clumsy. Then it did it again. The game, I observed after a few more repetitions, involved releasing air to be caught as bubbles under the arch, then striking the arch to send the bubbles, like little air balloons, to the surface. How bored does a whale need to be to invent such head-splitting play?

The male beluga swam directly at me, turned belly-to at the last minute, and loosed its penis from its genital slit. The long pink organ flailed out like a waving sea anemone or the tentacle of an octopus. I was being flashed! By a whale! What was it thinking? It seemed, most definitely, to have intentionally displayed itself not to one of the other whales but to me. In my surprise, I jerked away. The next moment, I smiled. Did the beluga record my reaction? Was its act one of hostility, curiosity, boredom, flirtation, anything to provoke a reaction? Or nothing—did it mean nothing at all, just normal whale behavior, whether anyone was present or not?

Later, I would read that captive dolphins, the belugas' cousins, are famously indiscriminate in their sexual displays. The Shedd publicist would also assure me that such beluga behavior is common. The interesting question (for me) remains one of motivation, one I suspect might be a challenge even to a beluga. In removing belugas from their usual situations and placing them in artificial ones, we've surely set the stage for abnormal behavior. We know this from our own species; look what happens to people kept in closets or raised by wolves.

I might have stayed all day with the belugas, insatiable in my desires to see and to know. When at last I tore myself away, I remembered the proverbial blind man who had known an elephant only by feeling one of its legs; at last I, like he, had extended my "touch." I carried away with me a beluga picture that would alter forever how I saw those white arcs rising from my home seas. But I still remembered something Barry Lopez had written about sperm whales, after compiling a list of astounding size, weight, diet, ambergris, and ability-to-sort-through-noise facts. "What makes them awesome is not so much these things, which are discoverable, but the mysteries that shroud them."

At the end of the following summer—the 1999 season that hunters had stood down—I learned that the two pregnant belugas at the Shedd Aquarium had given birth. One calf weakened and eventually died, but the other survived its infancy and was still prospering at year's end. Media coverage of the births and first weeks of life, the death, and the public display of the surviving calf were all extensive, not only in the Chicago area, but around the country. Clearly, on a leviathan scale, people were interested in and informed about the new and now famous cute-as-can-be baby beluga.

Cute is cute, but the proportions of concern seemed to me to be all wrong. *Hey, people,* I wanted to shout, *we've got whales in trouble here!*

What is it about human beings that allows us to respond so completely and empathetically to an individual (especially a baby) while remaining disinterested—even uninterested—in the collective? Probably there's some evolutionary reason—some family-first survival mechanism—behind such behavior. In any case, we all know examples. A kitten rescued from a tree is fought over by people who want to keep it, while the animal shelter overflows with unwanted pets it must euthanize. An abandoned baby elicits tremendous concern, a plethora of adoption offers, truckloads of teddy bears—while general population children in need of care or attention go wanting. A sad-eyed war orphan is rescued and repaired, but the war goes on, and misery without an individual face is ignored.

One captive killer whale—named Keiko—became the star of a major movie (*Free Willy*), and millions of dollars in donations from children and their families went to its rescue. Keiko was eventually moved to a floating pen off the coast of Iceland—near where it was captured in the 1980s—and over a period of years reintroduced to its wild brethren and the unique concept (to Keiko) of capturing its own food. Similarly, in 1988, three gray whales trapped in ice off Alaska became the objects of a worldwide rescue attempt, even as other whales, beyond the reach of video cameras, are routinely caught (and die) in the ice without fanfare or acknowledgment.

Organizations like the Save the Children Federation have long taken advantage of our fondness for faces. Donors don't give money to save children from starvation; they select Lili, age six, from Bolivia, with her hair in braids, or grinning Patrick, age seven, from Malawi. A number of whale conservation groups now pursue the same strategy, offering "for adoption" specific blue, fin, humpback, right, orca (the name preferred to killer, for obvious reasons, in most adoption cases), and beluga whales. These programs are particularly successful when individual whales (orcas, for example) can be clearly identified by markings. An "adoptive" family receives, for its fee (generally applied to research programs), a photo of the whale, its family history, and updates on sightings. One Canadian whale research and education organization even sloganizes: "Whales have faces!"

The whole population of Cook Inlet belugas was less than the high school enrollment in my small town. I imagined a yearbook of beluga faces, if only we could see them.

∽∽

The Vancouver Aquarium, in the year 2000, was best known for its killer whale, known as Bjossa, which had most recently been in the news for suffering and then recovering from a respiratory infection. (Bjossa was later moved to Sea World and died, from what was identified as "a chronic lung infection.") But it also housed five belugas, and I wanted—as I had earlier in Chicago—to see how belugas behaved in captivity, and how people behaved with them. And this time I had an appointment with the marine mammal curator, John Ford.

It was "a brutal day," Ford—an intense, dark-haired man with a trim moustache and beard—told me when I found him that Monday. A dead killer whale from the well-known "J" pod had washed ashore over the weekend, and he was besieged with media inquiries. He apologized, but he would have no time to talk with me, and the person who did most of the work with the aquarium's belugas was, unfortunately, away. The best I could do would be to sit with him while he was on the phone, and maybe we could talk a little between calls. He jingled his hands in this pockets and pulled out a tooth one of the aquarium belugas had just lost. "Now I can get an age," he said, and dropped the tooth, as he might a loose coin, into his desk drawer. The aquarium's adult belugas had been captured, like the Shedd's, in the Canadian Arctic, and thus their ages were only roughly established.

In the cluttered, underground office, windowless except for the one—high on a wall—that looked into the beluga pool, Ford took or returned one hurried phone call after another, and I heard the killer whale story. The necropsy, in which he had participated the day before, had found a massive infection and abscess in the animal known as J18 or (more popularly) Everett. I quickly understood from the talk that—there being so few resident killer whales on the west coast, all of them numbered and named and many of them well-known to the public—the death of this one whale was big news. Ford's concern, as he was telling various newspaper and radio reporters, was that high levels of PCBs in killer whales might be depressing immune systems and making it impossible for them to fight off infections. J18 was also emaciated, likely a result of the illness, but with salmon runs down, food availability could also be a problem.

At the window, the youngest, grayest beluga, a three-year-old born at the aquarium and known as Qila, flattened its melon against the Plexiglas as though peering into the room. I supposed it was, in fact, peering into the room. I had recently read that when killer whales had lived in that tank, one of them had been fond of studying photographs of other killer whales and dolphins that Ford held up.

I spotted, on the corner of Ford's desk, a copy of *Killer Whales: The Natural History and Genealogy of Orcinus orca in British Columbia and Washington State,* a book of which he was the lead author. Between calls, when I asked if I could look at it, he went into a near-panic; the copy was marked with his corrections for a new edition, and he'd completely forgotten about sending it on to the co-author. More calls—to the coauthor, to a courier—but yes, I could take a look. I quickly looked up the "J" pod. There was the photo—the standard ID shot of the whale's left side, showing its distinctive dorsal fin and white "saddle patch"—of J18, a male born in 1978. As of 1993, when the catalog data had been assembled, J18 was one of just twenty J pod members; only four others were males, and three more juveniles had not yet been identified by sex. Losing this one whale—a male in what should have been its prime—was serious indeed.

I thought about the belugas in Canada's St. Lawrence River—whales that were badly contaminated by industrial wastes. The females passed some of their contaminant load to their young, while the males kept accumulating over their lifetimes.

Later I would read more about J18's necropsy results. Scientists would agree that the bacterial infection would have been nonlethal except for a compromised immune system. The whale's reproductive organs were also found to be underdeveloped, another hazard of PCB contamination. The level of PCBs in the dead whale could not be tested because the animal was too wasted and had metabolized its body fat.

Very soon, Puget Sound killer whales would make headlines for being the most PCB-laden marine mammals on earth. The southern resident population—those whales found in Puget Sound, around the San Juan Islands and the southern half of Vancouver Island—fell from ninety-eight individuals in 1993 to seventy-eight in 2001. Puget Sound is polluted with industrial PCBs that have settled there over the years—but the area is not considered to be any more polluted than other marine areas around urban centers. As one Canadian scientist put it, "It has nothing to do with how close you are to the pollution source, but how you are on the food chain." The southern resident whales eat fish—200 pounds a day, mostly salmon—and orcas are long-lived, with the matriarchs in that population going back to the 1930s. All that food over all that time has sent to their fat layers and organs tremendously high contaminant levels. Males are living only half as long as females.

The levels of PCB for J18's population averaged a very high 146 parts per million, but the levels for the lesser-known transient whales—which feed primarily on marine mammals—were even higher—up to and more than 250 parts per million. Soon, too, there would be news from Alaska, where transient killer whales in Prince William Sound were also dying—and were found to have even higher PCB levels.

I was in Vancouver to look at captive belugas, but it seemed I'd found an interspecies cautionary tale.

Ford's young son, on spring break with the thousands of other children thronging the aquarium that day, breezed in for some computer games under Qila's watchful eye. I noticed his green ball cap and then looked again; it read "Free Willy."

How ironic was that? Perhaps the most famous killer whale in North America—now that Keiko had gone off to Iceland—was circling a pool just on the other side of us. At night, before bed, did the younger Ford pester the older to "free Bjossa"? Or did he understand that the whale, captured twenty years before, was too old to adapt to life in the wild and that Bjossa also served a useful purpose in captivity? Such, in fact, was the policy of the Vancouver Aquarium: Orcas released to the wild could not be guaranteed to succeed, and it was important to show them to people unlikely to encounter wild whales. A companion policy, however, stated that the aquarium would not acquire any more killer whales, from any sources, or any cetaceans of any kind from the wild. It would keep its belugas and hope that they would replace themselves.

It was time for Ford's TV interview beside the killer whale pool. He strode off to the bright lights and cameras, and I headed for the scheduled beluga show. At the tiered seating area, I found myself looking at—peacocks? Yes, peacocks—certainly unrelated to anything in the belugas' natural habitat—spread their elaborate tails from the rock cliffs behind the outdoor pool. Now the trainers—in rain gear and boots, carrying poles and buckets—pranced out, and the whales sped excitedly around the pool, blowing and squeaking. This activity was, it seemed, not a beluga "talk" like I'd heard at the Shedd but rather a performance.

Using hand signals and tossing fish from buckets, the trainers directed the belugas to spin around, squirt water, shake their heads, roll over, swipe with their tails. The whales wiggled their melons all around. They rose up vertically, high out of the water, to touch their lips to poles, then "stood on their heads" to wag their flukes in the air. They made "dolphin leaps" out of the water. It was—almost all of it—very unlike normal beluga behavior. The trainers patted them on their heads and splashed water into their mouths; they reached into their mouths to rub among their treacherous teeth.

It was a circus show, pure and simple, and part of me was repulsed by its artifice and rank exploitation. Another part of me, perhaps in equal measure, appreciated the show's lack of pretense. Here, there was no treacly speech about training the animals to have their blood taken. This show was, without apology, meant to entertain the legged creatures on my side of the low glass wall.

Beyond that, looking at these belugas swim and squirt and nod their heads, I had to wonder at the contrast with the hulking creatures I'd seen at the Shedd. Was it just that they were being fed, or were these whales having more fun? Was fun even supposed to count in the life of a whale?

Below, where the whales could be viewed underwater, I watched the five of them swim upside-down, rightside-up, together, and apart, and I watched people watching. I noticed, as I had not before, the dark veins in the whales' flukes, white in the corners of their eyes, the amount of sloughed skin that drifted through the water. Whether it was because there were so many parents with so many children, or because Canadians are less entertainment-jaded than their U.S. counterparts, or for some other reason, the crowd at the glass walls—indeed, throughout the aquarium—was pitched to a peak of excitement. Everywhere, people were oohing and ahhing, pointing things out, taking another look. Here they were examining the undersides of belugas to tell females from males; there they were discussing how cold the water might be. Small children were not whimpering but shouting with joy.

I wandered among people who loved belugas, around displays about Canadian beluga populations and the sounds that belugas both make and listen for—among the latter, those of killer whales, boats, moving ice, and hunters walking on ice. I read that in Canada several populations were hunted by Inuit people, who take 600–700 belugas each year for subsistence purposes. Three populations, I read, were currently endangered—the St. Lawrence one by industrial pollution, and the small (1,000 animals each) southeast Baffin Island (Northwest Territories) and Ungava Bay (Quebec) stocks as a result of earlier commercial hunting. (Later, I would learn that continued subsistence hunting was contributing to the decline of the latter two.)

Near the exit, I came to a sign that declared, "You've just helped belugas. By visiting the Vancouver Aquarium you've helped support research which will enable wildlife planners to better understand the needs of wild belugas."

Fair enough. I could accept that some portion of my admission contributed not only to the care and feeding of the captive belugas but also to the knowledge gained from them, knowledge that might be extended to their protection in the wild. Until belugas were bred in captivity, no one was sure how long the gestation period was. Now, it was possible to use that information to safeguard breeding and calving areas and pregnant females.

There was that—the things that money could do—and there was, I hoped, that other thing: what visitors might take away with them. I thought back, as I often do, to something Rachel Carson wrote. "Once the emotions have been aroused—a sense of the beautiful, the excitement of the new and the unknown, a feeling of sympathy, pity, admiration or love—then we wish for knowledge about the object of our emotional response."

It worked for me. I couldn't live around wild belugas and not be "aroused." Now, it seemed, I couldn't learn enough.

Every year thirty-two million Americans come face-to-face with marine mammals in zoos, aquariums, and marine parks. Would some fraction of the whale enthusiasts who swarmed the Vancouver Aquarium during spring break go on to learn more about belugas, and then follow their knowledge with action? What about all those people who were so moved by the advent of the Shedd Aquarium's baby beluga? Would they extend their Raffiesque love to the baby's wild relatives and the natural systems essential for the species' continuance? With so much competing in such rapid bursts for our everyday attentions, who among us can commit to understanding the interdependencies of whales and fish, whales and water and a livable Earth, whales and humans and the deep-rooted cultural ties that surround even the killing and eating of whales?

⨯⨯

I came back, again and again, to thinking about transformation, about the capriciousness of public opinion and the evolution of thought and belief. For thousands of years whales were simply "big fish," a source, when they could be scavenged or hunted, of nutrition and otherwise useful parts. For about two hundred years—a blink of the eye in our history together—whales amounted to storehouses of great wealth. The period of high-seas commercial whaling, the *Moby-Dick* days, commodified whales in a big way. Whale oil lit lamps, and light was highly desirable. The filtering plates in the mouths of the baleen whales, likewise, built demand for a thousand products, corset stays among them. Even after the wondrous new flammable known as kerosene devalued whale oil, whalers still found cutting out baleen worth their effort. It took the invention of the polymerization process before plastics would outdo baleen for plasticity and send that portion of the whale products market tumbling.

As I'd learned, right into the 1960s in Cook Inlet, belugas were famous for three things: as a novel variety of barbecue food, a scourge to fishermen, and a sport-hunting challenge. And then things changed. With an abrupt turn of temperament, the public—especially the American public—decided that whales were different. Whales—whether blue, gray, killer, humpback, minke, beluga, or any other species—were special. What began with concern about overexploitation and risk of extinction grew into something else: the idea that whales were "superior" to other animals, perhaps even to people, with whom they might share (or exceed) a level of intelligence while improving on gentleness and cooperation. In this new world, whales were smart *and* kind. They were international treasures to be honored. A whole new set of ethical questions about our relationships to whales arose. Why would we kill something that was so rare, so beautiful, so smart, and so gentle?

Even some whale biologists, perhaps most notably Roger Payne, joined this chorus. In the preface to his book, *Among Whales,* Payne wrote that he had turned to writing for a general audience "as I try to explain some of the reasons that many of us are so deeply fascinated by whales, and why it is that we object to people killing them." He also wrote, "I believe that the principal gift that whales offer humanity is that they are the only animals that can impress us enough to persuade us to change our minds about the importance of the wild world."

There are, of course, critics of this new order. They find what they call the "totemization" of whales annoying, short on scientific justification, and not particularly useful for dealing with issues that arise around whales. They fault the construct of a "super-whale," a creature that doesn't exist in reality but that combines characteristics of various species (as well as humans) into a mythic animal. The super-whale is the largest animal on Earth, the smartest, and the most endangered, and it exhibits various appealing behaviors, such as singing, approaching boats, and allowing admirers to pat it on its head. The super-whale image, like that of any superstar, makes it easy to pump people's emotions and to open their wallets for any number of purposes: as benign as supporting conservation programs and as nefarious as selling consumer goods. That image, percolating through human cultures, has finally turned world whale politics upside-down. The International Whaling Commission, initially designed as an organization of whaling nations to deal with conservation issues, is now heavily influenced if not dominated by antiwhaling nations.

In 1992, when respondents in six countries were questioned about the sale of various animal meats for human food, Americans were OK with chicken, lobster, and lamb, split on deer and wildfowl, and opposed to horse, seal, and whale. Eighty-eight percent were moderately or strongly opposed to whale meat being eaten as a commercial food. (The survey did not ask about non-commercial, subsistence use of whales.) That attitude contrasted with those in the whale-eating nations of Japan and Norway, where more people approved than disapproved of eating whale meat. When the question was phrased a little differently, asking people to respond to the statement, "Can't imagine why anyone would kill intelligent whales," fifty-seven percent of Americans agreed, twenty-five percent disagreed, and the remainder had no position. Forty-eight percent of Americans agreed that they were opposed to the hunting of any kind of whale under any circumstance.

The same study also tested people's knowledge about whales and found it lacking. Americans tended to think there were far fewer whales in the world than there really were and that most were facing extinction. Only one in one hundred Americans correctly placed the worldwide sperm whale population at more than a million. Likewise, a majority of Americans thought there were fewer than 10,000 minke whales in the world, in contrast to the actual population estimate of—similar to sperm whales—about a million. I had to wonder, how many Americans in 1992 had even heard of minke whales? Japanese knew about minkes because they badly wanted to resume commercial whaling of that species, but Americans had no such touchstone.

Later, I found another survey, conducted in 1997 by the World Conservation Trust—a nonprofit organization "promoting the sustainable use of wild resources" and in favor of allowing a limited harvest of some whale species. In that survey, ninety-two percent of Americans self-described themselves as knowing nothing about minke whales; ninety percent would not venture a guess about their status. More than half the respondents said that whale populations worldwide were threatened or endangered, eighteen percent did not know what status they had, and three percent said it would depend on the species.

In the popular press, I followed the controversy over the Makah gray whale hunt—the Washington state Indians eventually killed one whale for subsistence and ceremonial use—and additional debate about whaling of all kinds. One letter-writer, opposed to any form or degree of whaling, wrote, "Most importantly is the high probability that whales are sentient beings" and that "knowing this makes it hard to deny that killing them is immoral." Another, responding to my own argument that conservation and respectful use (including the eating of whales by people with those traditions) can be compatible and that the animals we wish to protect may best be served by working cooperatively to that end, insisted on moral absolutes. Some practices, he wrote, did *not* deserve respect: "subjugation of women, hatred of people different, glorification of insensitivity, as well as destructive exploitation of nature"— such as killing whales for any reason.

Like so many other things that divide us, we bring closely held beliefs to the whaling table—or to what might be considered a modern try-works.

There were good points to be made all around, and there was also something so *American* about feeling so sure that there was one right way, that if you weren't with us, you were against us. We hear this sentiment all the time from our political leaders. In other parts of the world—and in much of the world that resides within our own boundaries—that black-and-white moral certainty is recognized (and resented) as cultural imperialism.

Do we—modern Americans—make too much of whales and their "specialness?" Yes, probably, particularly when we pedestal them above all other creatures and reject on principle any human use, under any circumstances. Whale-love is not necessarily an attractive condition when it ignores scientific fact and cultural histories. Nor is it helpful to "save the whales and screw the shrimp," as the writer Joy Williams once titled a provocative essay.

On the other hand, there remain plenty of hazards to whales in our, and their, world. And perhaps a few million whales are not so many, certainly as opposed to six billion people and the damage we wreak on the oceans.

∽

Most whale species, of course, are too large to be housed in aquariums, and the only reasonable way for people to see them is in their natural environment. Whale-watching has become a gargantuan business in this country and, increasingly, in other parts of the world, including even in such whaling countries as Japan. From its beginnings in 1955 in California, whale-watching now takes place in at least eighty-seven countries and territories and involves nine million people per year. Can it be that more people are looking at whales each year than there are whales?

The growth of whale-watching and its economic contributions have led to American recommendations that the economic values of nonconsumptive use of whales (whale watching, essentially) be considered by the International Whaling Commission in any discussions about lifting the moratorium on commercial whaling. The argument is that nonconsumptive uses have become more valuable than consumable whale products.

Some whales are particularly suited to whale-watching. Gray whales, once the "devil fish" of whalers, who found them aggressively defensive of their young, are now considered "friendly," known for approaching boats and presenting their heads to be rubbed. Humpbacks throw themselves dramatically from the water. Killer whales, with their six-foot fins slicing the water and their predatory reputations as "wolves of the sea," keep the cameras clicking.

When I visited Washington state's San Juan Islands, the boat basin in Friday Harbor was deep in whale-watching boats, even as killer whales were declining and hard questions were being asked about the effects of too many boats chasing after too few whales. At the nearby Whale Museum—reportedly the biggest tourist draw in the islands—there were skeletons to study, pickled brains of a human and a fin whale to compare, orca genealogy charts, and a telephone booth where a person could "call up" various species to hear their vocalizations. (The call to the Atlantic gray whale received only silence—the sound of extinction.) Around town, the killer whale motif dominated, with everything from killer-whale-shaped mailboxes to fence tops cut like dorsal fins. It might have been a challenge to find a souvenir that didn't feature whales.

Alaska, late to trends, has been slow to tap the whale-watching potential—or perhaps simply has more natural wonders in competition for tourist dollars. The fishing community of Kodiak is one place that's trying, with a weeklong Whale Fest that celebrates the spring migration of gray whales by the island. Between a poetry reading devoted to whales and a slideshow/lecture about cleaning and assembling a gray whale skeleton, a Kodiak friend and I drove out past the new missile launching site and sat on a windy, high bluff to count and time the blows, like geysers roiling from the sea, of passing whales. The news was that the whales didn't always migrate by anymore—that some of them were staying year-round there by the island, in the generous waters of Whale Pass.

Another time, in Seward, I took a wildlife tour boat into Kenai Fjords, where we just happened to hit "Superpod" day, the one time a year when several killer whale pods come together for social purposes, thought to be their way of breeding outside of their own pods and family groups. More than forty of the "big fins" cut in and around one another, rubbed against one another, rose together sometimes three or four exactly side by side. They breached; they rolled sideways; once I saw, on a turning male, its penis probing after an adjacent female. On the same trip, we saw as well numerous humpback cows with calves—some of the very large whales launching themselves repeatedly into full, gravity-defying, water-spraying view. In their natural environment, going about their business, the whales were awe-inspiring in a way that aquarium performers could never be. The inherent conservation message—the need to protect the waters that were their homes—could not be lost on any of the passengers.

Who didn't love watching whales? The Kodiak fishermen and the schoolteachers from Iowa all thrilled to them. Whales are special, in a way that sea otters and sharks and puffins—fascinating animals in their own right—are not. They're big, they're mysterious, they're few enough. We humans respond in a visceral way; we like whales. We look at whales, and what we see—in our estrangement from our hunter-gatherer past—has nothing to do with food or use or even fear. Whales impress us on some other scale, one that, perhaps, measures who we want to be. The psychology of it is beyond me, but it's clear enough that whales operate today as powerful emotional triggers.

I remembered that early beluga meeting, when an environmentalist had asked Cook Inlet beluga hunters point-blank if they couldn't switch over from hunting belugas to taking people out whale-watching. The negative response—the not wanting food "looked at"—had been a cultural rather than a practical one. The issue of whether Cook Inlet's belugas could support some level of a whale-watching industry still hung out there in the world of possibility. Elsewhere, belugas draw tourists. Churchill, Manitoba, is known for polar bears in winter and belugas in summer, and in the St. Lawrence River belugas are one of several species typically spotted from whale-watching boats.

Belugas are neither large, as whales go, nor particularly dramatic in their behavior, but they do have other attractive attributes, including their rarity in natural environments outside of the hard-to-reach Arctic. Every spring, traffic along Turnagain Arm south of Anchorage nearly comes to a halt as drivers pull over to watch the belugas feeding on hooligan (the early and oily smelt-like fish known more formally as eulachon); I knew one person who, reaching from the rocky shoreline at high tide, touched a passing beluga.

Would passengers pay to go out on Cook Inlet for beluga-watching? Barbara Mahoney, at the Anchorage NMFS office, had told me that people with whale-watching proposals occasionally inquired about beluga viewing locations and regulations. In 1988 one operation, using a converted World War II tug, ran summer cruises into Knik Arm. The advertised highlights included beluga-watching as well as dinner, dancing, and seeing the sun set against Anchorage's glass skyscrapers. That business operated one season, and then the tug sank in a gale as it was being taken across the Gulf of Alaska to winter storage. In 2001, another proposal bloomed; this one involved a multimillion-dollar extension to the public boat ramp at Ship Creek to accommodate a floating dock accessible at all tides. Two-hour sightseeing tours would circle Knik Arm and the upper inlet to the west and would feature beluga-watching from a catamaran. Plans for the private venture were reviewed by government agencies, and the Port of Anchorage gave its blessing, but investors may have been less plentiful than tour-happy belugas.

∾∾

Many people get excited about belugas, but only one person has ever been described to me as a beluga fanatic. I first met Jim Diehl at a beluga meeting, where he'd made an emphatic and logical argument for establishing a response plan for beluga strandings. He seemed a reasonable although intense person, and he told me that he was associated with a organization called the Girdwood Cetacean Group. (Girdwood is a ski resort community along Turnagain Arm, about thirty-five miles south of Anchorage.) I sensed he wasn't a person with much stomach for sitting around at meetings or dealing with bureaucracy, and I didn't see him again. I only heard about him—that he kayaked the bore tides on Turnagain Arm, that he was a photographer and had photos of belugas, that he was a beluga fanatic. He was a guy who was out there with the whales and had come to admire and respect them.

When I arrived one June morning at his Girdwood cabin—a tiny, low log building at the end of a dirt road just downhill from the ski lifts—Jim was seated at his computer, looking at his photos of stranded killer whales. I ducked under log beams hung with pairs of skis, stepped around water jugs and a wiggly yellow Labrador. The clutter of outdoor equipment, myriad photographs, and just plain stuff suggested an active, much-involved life—and a man who lived alone, or alone with a dog.

"This is the one that died in '93," Jim said, barely looking up. "It was the same one that stranded in '91. See here where it vomited some beluga."

Indeed, in the photo, there are two chunks of white flesh lying on the mud before a completely out-of-the-water killer whale. One chunk looked like a base from a baseball game, the other less rectangular.

Jim skipped through some other photos, ones of himself splashing buckets of water onto killer whales. He handed me something he'd written after the 1991 stranding; the end he directed me to involved a dream that a bore tide was carrying him to his death against jagged rocks that transformed into killer whales with broken skin and oozing blubber, and a waking commitment to speak of what he'd seen. While I read, he disappeared into the smaller adjoining room and returned with clippings of Turnagain Arm whale strandings going back to 1988. He had thorough files, he said, of everything to do with strandings and responses. He'd talked to people all over the world about whale strandings and collected every sort of protocol and plan and theory about how best to respond to stranded whales.

Beluga strandings are a little different from most other whale strandings, we both knew. Most whales strand for unexplained reasons—and strandings have been with us since at least Aristotle's time, negating the notion that humans are necessarily responsible. In modern times there are famous examples of sperm and pilot whales that have run ashore in large groups—because they were confused, or sick, or perhaps following a leader that made a critically wrong turn. Those whales usually die, under the crushing weight of their bodies or from overheating in the sun. Beluga whales, on the other hand, seem to be built for stranding, and typically survive it. They have sturdy rib cages that support them on land, and their white skin reflects rather than absorbs the sun. In Cook Inlet, they've been known to strand while chasing fish or escaping killer whales, or by being caught in channels emptied by tide.

Jim and I headed off to Girdwood's Bake Shop for a late breakfast. It was a cool, overcast day, but Jim was wearing shorts and running shoes, with a fleece pullover covered in dog hair. The toughness in his voice was New York, where he'd grown up, the son of a cop. For twenty-five years he'd built a Girdwood life around seasonal jobs and community activism, and he now commuted to Anchorage to teach high-school English.

How, I asked, had he come by his interest in belugas and killer whales and, especially, responding to strandings?

He was, he said, one of a very small group of expert kayakers who, outfitted in dry suits and helmets, surfed the arm's famous bore tides—waves that ran up shallow Turnagain Arm as incoming tides folded over outgoing water. Riding waves that were often four or more feet high, Jim explored the arm in all its weather and conditions, often in the company of belugas.

His defining moment with belugas came in October 1988 when he and a friend paddled out to "visit" twenty-seven belugas stranded on the mud just south of Girdwood. It was, at that time, the largest beluga stranding ever recorded for Cook Inlet. "That was like a dream," he said. "That was something else. The adults had all the young corralled in the center. You could see they were protective of the young." At first, the belugas clicked and whistled, but then they quieted. "As we walked around them, they followed us with their eyes."

The two men used five-gallon buckets to wet the whales, to keep their skin moist in the cool breeze. Jim had the distinct impression that the belugas, watching from what he called a "restive and patient state," knew that he was there to help.

Fish and Wildlife officials eventually showed up in an inflatable boat and trudged through the mud to tell Jim and his friend that they were stressing the whales and in danger themselves; they needed to leave. Three weeks later, from the roadside, Jim spotted a pod of belugas and recognized two of them from the stranding—one with a curlicue scar and a very young gray one. They seemed, he told me, "like old friends." He thought that was the end of it, that such a stranding was a once-in-a-lifetime event.

Only it wasn't. When killer whales stranded on a sunny May day in 1991, Jim again helped by wetting animals down. The officials didn't approve and threatened him with a $25,000 fine for harassing marine mammals. Although the six whales appeared to swim off when the tide rose, Jim complained to the press, "Their skin was splayed open and smelled like cooked fish. These whales are candidates for parasitic infections." He was backed up by a California stranding expert—who agreed infection could be a problem and who said, "If an animal is being baked and its skin is splitting, I think somebody trying to offer aid would be more beneficial than worrying about stressing out the animal by approaching it"—and by a state Fish and Game marine mammal biologist who said, "I'm not going to criticize the National Marine Fisheries Service, but my feeling is that those guys don't do a very good job sometimes. They don't have a marine mammal expert on hand."

Jim organized for future strandings. He called stranding experts from all over the world and collected response plans and protocols. He assembled his kayaking friends, with their class-five whitewater expertise and safety training, into a volunteer force. He knew all about the Marine Mammal Stranding Network that operated on every coast except Alaska's and how that network was organized and operated under the authorization of the National Marine Fisheries Service. He had the book that detailed the use of kayakers as a response resource.

"'Fine,'" he quoted a NMFS official to me. "'You train your men, Mr. Diehl. If we need you, we'll call you.'"

Perhaps prompted by Jim's efforts, NMFS did work up a Turnagain Arm Marine Mammal Response Plan, as an agreement between NMFS and the U.S. Forest Service, which controls land adjacent to the arm. Published in early 1993, it laid out three objectives: limit actions so as not to endanger any response personnel, prevent mortality of any stranded marine mammal, and minimize stress to any stranded marine mammal. On its organizational chart, the position of volunteer coordinator or any additional information under "volunteer support" was never filled in, apparently because federal officials considered any response to be too dangerous. Jim received a letter from the Forest Service district ranger that read, in part, "I do not envision Forest Service personnel or any volunteers associated with us to be out on the mud to rescue marine mammals. I would not jeopardize human safety for extraordinary efforts to alleviate a particular whale stranding. I am concerned that your group envisions a role bordering on extraordinary to rescue stranded whales."

In June 1993, ten belugas stranded in Turnagain and later swam off. Two months later killer whales caused at least three small groups of belugas to strand—while they killed and wounded an unknown number. That same day, most dramatically, the killer whales themselves stranded in the arm, just north of Bird Point along the highway. Jim and three friends, uninvited, responded to that stranding and kept the five animals wet. One whale regurgitated beluga parts and subsequently died. Jim later spoke to stranding experts, who suggested that pressure on the animal's organs could have been relieved by using a small pump to displace the ground beneath it and dropping it into a pit of fluid mud.

Jim hoped that lessons from the stranding, including the need to control crowds that appeared at the roadside and tried to cross dangerous mudflats, would be incorporated into future responses and that increased cooperation among agencies and volunteers could lead, finally, to an efficient and adequate response to whale strandings. He and his friends continued to paddle Turnagain and to practice against its tides. "Besides having fun," he told a reporter, "we're establishing a record of our being able to handle Turnagain Arm. If NMFS is putting together a whale rescue team in Turnagain Arm, I want it to be the best damn rescue team in the United States." He also shared a bit of his motivation. "When I see whales, it makes me happy. When whales strand, I'm not so happy about that. Helping them might be a little bit of a way of repaying them for all that happiness."

Jim started teaching full-time that same year, and although his commitment to the whales of Turnagain Arm never lagged, he was less available to respond to strandings or to keep after NMFS to refine their response plan. Nine years later, the plan document was unchanged, with blank spaces for the volunteer effort and no updating of any other sections. No killer whale strandings have been reported since 1993, but groups of belugas continued to go aground.

In 1994, 190 belugas—at that time, perhaps *one-third* of the total inlet's population—stranded in several bunched clusters on flats just off the Susitna River. It was a sunny June day, and although most of the whales appeared to be alive and swimming after the tide returned, biologists thought it likely that at least a few died. In 1996, on a big minus tide, one hundred belugas were stranded in two different Turnagain locations, and at least four died. And then again, in 1999, more than fifty belugas went dry in the middle of Turnagain, and at least five died.

What was common to all the beluga strandings since the one that Jim Diehl responded to in 1988 was their inaccessibility; none could be easily reached from roadways or even by motorized boat. Only in the 1996 event did anyone attempt to get to any of the animals—in that case by helicopter, which landed for an hour on a sandbar while two biologists wetted the animals with a bucket and applied vitamin E to sun-baked backs. They found that some belugas were bloody from seagulls pecking at their skin and that four were dead. In 1999, although there was no response to the stranding, when some of the dead belugas later washed up on shore, biologists collected samples, and Native people salvaged muktuk.

In the Girdwood Bake Shop, Jim said his role now was to make sure that NMFS responded when it should. "They don't need to respond to everything out there, but on a hot day they need to," he said. He kept up his own beluga study. He'd watched fifty belugas at a time gather behind Bird Point to wait for the tide to bring them salmon, and he'd watched another group bounce along the bottom right behind a bore tide. He'd heard belugas sing. He was concerned about their numbers. There used to be pods of up to 200, maybe more. Then he would commonly see about fifty. Then there were fewer. Recently he'd seen groups of twenty. When he used to fret about strandings, NMFS officials had been unconcerned, he said, because they considered strandings a minor source of mortality compared to Native hunting. Now, he saw a lot of gray animals. He hoped they were "reproducing like crazy, trying to get their numbers up."

The hooligan run the belugas fed on in spring was pretty much over, and Jim hadn't seen any whales in about ten days. Still, we could take a look. My Subaru trailed Jim's Subaru—with a kayak strapped to its roof—to the scenic pull-out at Bird Point, just a few miles away. A newly installed public sculpture twisted along one side of the parking area: a line of white humps and two shiny beluga heads—one in a lift position, the other in a roll—protruding from a sea of gray concrete slabs.

We got out into a cool breeze and the beginnings of rain. Jim pointed to the gray water rising over mud. "This is where a lot of it happens." There on the north side of the point was where the killer whales had stranded in 1993; there on the south side was where he and his friends had put in their kayaks to make the approach; there on the north was where, other times, he'd seen killer whales waiting to "ambush" belugas as they came around the point.

Jim was wearing binoculars around his neck, but there was no need for them. There was nothing out there: just muddy water, the bottoms of mountains cut off by clouds, and a single low-flying gull. "I just got into kayaking, and the whales were a part of it," he said. "This is a really cool piece of water, and no one goes out there except a very few people.... You might see a canoe once in a while, but then you read about them drowning." He stared off up the inlet, into the distance, into the wind.

5

THE GREEN MACHINE

Pollution and noise from the inlet's oil and gas industry, contamination from wastewater and runoff, vessel traffic and noise, conflicts with fisheries, food shortage, disease, predation by killer whales, habitat loss due to human population growth and community development, climate change, strandings: All these are cited by environmentalists as dangers to the Cook Inlet belugas. "There's been an awful lot of attention on the hunting of the whales," Kris Balliet, from the Center for Marine Conservation, told a newspaper reporter in 1999. "Overhunting did contribute to this animal's precipitous decline. But we have moved beyond the place of looking at what brought us here, and to look not only to their recovery but their ability to survive extinction."

In May of 2000, when the National Marine Fisheries Service declared the Cook Inlet belugas depleted under the Marine Mammal Protection Act, a process to regulate Native hunting began. From the start, though, conservation and environmental groups had had concerns that went beyond hunting. A coalition of them first had petitioned to have the whales listed as endangered under the federal Endangered Species Act. When NMFS didn't respond to the petition within one year, as required by law, the coalition sued. When NMFS eventually ruled that the belugas were not endangered, the coalition sued again. Parallel to their actions with the federal agency, the groups also petitioned the state of Alaska to use a little-known state law to declare the whales an endangered species, to add another layer of protection. When the state rejected that petition, they filed a suit there too.

In the eyes of the coalition members, the only way that the belugas could be fully protected—with a recovery plan, attention to critical habitat, and oversight of activities that might pose threats—was through the Endangered Species Act. To an extent, the coalition sang a unified tune. But within the coalition—and outside it—the notes of concern ranged more widely.

Kris Balliet was an unlikely leader of the beluga-saving forces. Or maybe not. Other Alaskan environmentalists, more accustomed perhaps to working within the system and more aware of the dangers of missteps with the particular situation, held back. Kris was new. She was an outsider. When the beluga issue went public, it was Kris who took the leap. And it was Kris who stuck, like a suction cup on a beluga's back, with the twists and turns of what followed.

Over lunch one day—back in early 2000, when the belugas were still at the stage of only, belatedly, being proposed for "depleted" status—Kris told me how the issue had claimed her. The Center for Marine Conservation, a national group (now renamed the Ocean Conservancy), hired her to open an Anchorage office in December 1998, just after the Cook Inlet whales hit newspaper headlines. "I made my first priority to listen, to be like a sponge," she said. "I kept hearing about this beluga whale. In a three-week period I met all the players. A lot of information landed in my lap all at once."

Kris had not been entirely new to Alaska. She'd lived in Anchorage once before, briefly, when she did some contract work for a couple of environmental groups. More recently, she'd worked in the Northwest with a group called Save Our Salmon. She'd grown up on the East Coast—literally on the coast, on a barrier island in South Carolina—and was drawn west because, she said, she wanted more "wild." She has a law degree, and she talks like a lawyer—like, in fact, a prosecutor.

If Kris were a dog, she'd be a miniature Doberman. I don't mean that unkindly. What I mean is that, physically, she's a small, slight woman with a tenseness to her. In her presence, you feel like she could rip your throat out—if she wanted to. Behind her school-teacher glasses, her eyes are alert, calculating, intelligent. She speaks and moves quickly, and she knows her mind.

Kris had made other conservationists nervous. Partly there were issues of territoriality. Alaska has a wealth of home-grown environmental organizations, most of them working on shoestrings, most of them with memberships and constituencies to whom they answer, most of them with long histories in their areas of expertise and an "Alaska perspective" that puts such activities as hunting into historical and cultural contexts. Increasingly, national conservation organizations have moved in—perhaps not unlike tribes from another land. These—aside from generally being better funded—have not always found a fit with the locals. In some cases, they've been criticized for contributing little to problem-solving; they may exist to bring the allure (and fund-raising potential) of a few high-profile causes (like saving the Arctic National Wildlife Refuge) to their organizations. Often they're perceived to be drawing funding, volunteers, or media coverage away from the less-flashy Alaska-based groups and their nitty-gritty issues. Some of the nervousness comes from the real dangers of naïve newcomers entering complex situations and screwing up—damaging the long-term work that others have labored to achieve. The Center for Marine Conservation was a Washington, D.C.–based organization that was almost corporate in its structure and operations, with little Alaska membership. What might it, in the person of a dogged Kris Balliet, render unto Alaskans?

Kris made me nervous. Before I ever met her, I spoke with her on the phone and was taken aback by how much she assumed she knew. She was prone to using words like *parameters, facilitate,* and *stakeholders* in a jangle of jargon. "We are trying to dialogue with hunters," she said. She told me how well she worked with fishermen, but it didn't seem that she knew Cook Inlet fishermen or that their fisheries might be very different from those in the Northwest.

To her credit, Kris was aware that she made other people uncomfortable. Still, as she saw the situation, she was the one who started making noise on the issue, and the local and grassroots groups had rallied around—resulting in the loose coalition that moved forward to petition for the endangered listing. "That's what CMC was able to do," she said. "As a national organization, we acted as a catalyst."

Another helpful partner, she said, was the Center for Biological Diversity, a group without any local presence and known for pursuing endangered listings anywhere in the country, at every opportunity. Formerly the Southwest Center for Biological Diversity, CBD was described in a 1999 *New Yorker* article as "the most important radical environmental group in the country." Particularly in the Southwest, it had stopped one logging, grazing, and building operation after another—all through skillful and persistent use of the

Endangered Species Act. (Its education effort is perhaps not as skillful as its litigation, at least in terms of keeping facts straight; about belugas, its website states, "...this lovely and intelligent animal exists only in Cook Inlet in the United States.... The whale is now threatened by oil development, fishing and hunting, and discharge of urban and industrial wastes.")

In the end, the diverse collection of environmental groups that signed onto the petition also included the Alaska Center for the Environment, Alaska Community Action on Toxics, Alaska Wildlife Alliance, National Audubon Society, and the Anchorage environmental law firm Trustees for Alaska; former hunter Joel Blatchford, as an individual, was also one of the petitioners. All the groups supported Native subsistence hunting and were committed to providing beluga hunting opportunities to the extent that they were biologically defensible. The legal filing was done by Trustees for Alaska, where the attorney primarily in charge of marine mammal issues was Jack Sterne, Kris Balliet's husband. In the small world of Alaska environmentalism, "all in the family" took on literal meanings.

Kris remained the primary spokesperson for the coalition, and both CMC and CBD, with their considerable resources, continued to dominate the development of the legal case. Those two organizations had extensive staffs—not in Alaska—with legal and biological expertise, and both were able to fund the collection of additional data and expert testimony. Over our lunch in early 2000, Kris told me that in the previous twelve months, three-quarters of her time had been spent on belugas. She was still essentially a one-person office, with a clerical assistant.

Getting an endangered species listing was "the driving goal," Kris told me. She handed me a preaddressed, prestamped oversized postcard—part of a supply she was distributing to any and all takers, to be mailed to NMFS's Office of Protected Resources at their decision-making office in Maryland. The jammed-in text started with "Alaskans Want Recovery of Cook Inlet's Beluga Whales" and ended with "Only the Endangered Species Act has enough authority to do what needs to be done to ensure the Beluga Whale's recovery. Use the Endangered Species Act to PROTECT & RECOVER our belugas. LIST THEM ON AN EMERGENCY BASIS NOW."

"I don't think we can get to recovery until we have a listing," Kris said. "It's shuffling deck chairs." I pressed her on whether a halt to the hunting might not be enough to allow the stock to rebuild. She shook her head. "Had we done it a few hundred whales ago, it might have been enough. But not now. There are too many other threats."

She was not, she said, happy to be working on the issue; it was just that the work had to be done. "Frankly, if I had to do it over again," she said, "I wouldn't. Politically, it's the most challenging place I can think to be in." She mentioned the sensitivity of subsistence, the morass of inter-Native politics, the entrenchments of the oil and gas industry, how difficult any resource conflicts were and would be in Alaska's most populated area. "There's no way to work quietly on this issue. And no way to be subtle."

But now, it seemed, there was no turning back, no settling for the depletion designation and the halt to hunting. "Now what we have to do is force the agency to go beyond the obvious." She mentioned work NMFS had done to calculate recovery rates given yearly subsistence takes of zero, one, two, or more whales. "There's no factoring in all the other stuff. The whale's fate is being dealt with with an *appalling* lack of information."

There was also, Kris believed, another kind of calculating going on. A scientific review group, advisory to NMFS, had found the Cook Inlet belugas to be a high-risk stock and strongly advised the use of a conservative recovery factor when calculating the "potential biological removal"—the number of whales that could safely be hunted without further drawing down the population. But NMFS, Kris had been told, was going to ignore the recommendation and go with a higher number. "They're saying, 'We need to have a hunt,' and cooking the numbers to make it possible." Kris looked like she might choke on her cod taco. "This is *biology* we're talking about."

It was not that Kris was necessarily opposed to a limited hunt. She was extravagant in her praise of the hunters "standing down" the previous year and supportive of continuing the congressional rider that would allow a small take under a co-management agreement. She was concerned that too many hunters still thought that an endangered listing would automatically prevent any hunting. "We have great opportunities here," she said, suddenly adopting a rosier tone. "We need to turn the corner to collective thought—how to make this work in everyone's interests." Like the bowheads, she said. An endangered animal could still meet subsistence needs; protect the animal, and you were also protecting the culture, and respectful cultural practices played an important role in knowing the animal and assuring its continuance.

That reminded me of something else. Where were the animal rights groups? They were certainly sounding off about the Makah gray whale hunt—which involved a species that had recovered to what were thought to be historic numbers. Why was there not the smallest squeak from them about Cook Inlet's belugas? I'd heard that Kris and Trustees had taken pains to convince animal rights groups to keep a distance. For much of the public, including Native people, distinctions between environmental and animal rights groups were unclear or even irrelevant; one save-the-whales effort was as good, or as bad, as another. Any attack on Native hunting would have sent Natives behind the barricades and canceled any hope of getting past the hunting/overhunting question to the place where Kris and her colleagues wanted to be—where everyone might work together to protect beluga habitat, assure clean water and adequate prey, and provide for both whales and the people who eat them.

Kris confirmed that she had worked hard to hold animal rights groups back. One, the Animal Welfare Institute, had submitted its own petition for an endangered listing for the belugas, but that had been the extent of their involvement so far. "They're definitely coming," Kris said. "They're not staying away." And when they do "they're not going to be as thoughtful. Look at the situation in the 1980s with the Pribilof fur seals." Kris was referring to a national campaign by animal rights groups against the harvest of fur seals by Alaska's Pribilof Island Natives. The successful campaign played heavily on the emotions of animal lovers and demonstrated no understanding or sympathy for historical, biological, or cultural aspects; it created a great deal of resentment and did nothing to encourage people to work together for fur seal protection in the long run. There were plenty of elements of life in Alaska that people elsewhere, without having contexts for them, might find ugly or objectionable, and it would not, in Kris's opinion, be helpful to have the world looking at them. "I'd like to see us have the opportunity to work this out from the ground up. I'm hopeful we'll learn how to do it together."

For now, there was just one thing keeping the other groups on the sidelines, Kris said. "There's no place for them to be." As long as someone was doing something, they'd wait and see. "But if we stop, they'll come in and do it."

At the moment, we were all waiting. I asked Kris for her prediction. When all the hearings and analysis and consideration of petitions were done, what would NMFS do?

"They're going to stay with the depleted status, and we're going to sue them." She had absolutely no doubt that such would be the course and that a suit would eventually be successful. But meanwhile, she was fearful for the belugas. "I expect a catastrophe to happen. How could it not? The population is so low, and we're so busy in there," she said, referring to everything that was happening in the inlet. She mentioned again the possibilities of a mass stranding, food shortages, pollution. When she was growing up in South Carolina, she saw raw sewage being dumped directly into the ocean—a practice that was stopped only when the degradation became too terrible to ignore. She couldn't believe that Anchorage was allowed to get away with only primary treatment of its wastewater. Did we have to make the same mistakes everywhere?

The Endangered Species Act became law in the 1970s, a "green decade" when federal environmental laws were enacted. With its passage in 1973, Congress recognized that many native plants and animals in the United States were in danger of disappearing forever. Lawmakers recognized further that, although extinction was a natural process, the rate of extinction had greatly accelerated in recent times because of habitat destruction, environmental pollution, the introduction of nonnative organisms, and overexploitation—all primarily caused by human activities. Since the Pilgrims landed at Plymouth Rock, the country had lost more than 500 species, subspecies, and distinct population segments. (All three categories fall within the act's definition of "species.") Under the act, protections apply not just to the species identified as endangered or threatened but to their necessary habitats as well.

The act, which has since been reauthorized seven times (not since 1988) and variously amended, provides for listing species as either "endangered" (in danger of extinction throughout all or a significant portion of a range) or "threatened" (likely to become endangered within the foreseeable future). There is also a list of "candidate species"—species that may warrant listing as threatened or endangered but which have not yet been proposed for either. Many people—myself included—were surprised to discover that the Cook Inlet belugas had been added—very quietly—to the candidate species list in 1993. It was that listing that moved forward funding to cover the aerial surveys and other research.

What qualifies a species as threatened or endangered? The act was meant to be flexible. The secretary of commerce must conduct a status review of a proposed species and rely on the "best scientific and commercial data available to him." Five factors are considered, and any one of them, if deemed a threat, can justify a listing. In the case of Cook Inlet belugas, petitioners had argued that all five were operative. That is, the whales suffered from overutilization, inadequate regulatory mechanisms, threatened habitat, vulnerability to disease or predation, and the broad category of "other man-made factors" affecting their continued existence.

Today, the Endangered Species Act is under attack. Some who originally supported it have changed their minds and are actively trying to do away with it. Alaska's lone congressional representative, Don Young, has famously stated that when he originally voted for the act, he thought it was about saving "leopards and lions. We never in my wildest imagination were thinking about rats, cockroaches, blue lupine, snail darters, and spotted owls." One of his Republican colleagues, Rep. James Hansen of Utah, complained, "The rights of an endangered fly or a species of seaweed take precedence over national security, commerce, and many people's rights to the enjoyment of property and the pursuit of happiness." Hansen was promoting a bill to exempt from provisions of the act private property, military lands, and all plant life.

There are also critics on the other side—among scientists and others who want to save species from oblivion. They fault not the act but its implementation. A review by the National Academy of Sciences found the system far too slow, particularly for preserving "survival habitat" for newly listed species and for developing timely recovery plans.

By 2002 nearly a thousand animals and plants were classified as endangered—and about a quarter of those were still awaiting recovery plans. Only a handful of species—most notably the bald eagle, the gray whale, the California sea otter, the red wolf, and the peregrine falcon—had been upgraded since their original listings, and more than twenty had either gone extinct or had disappeared from sight and most probably joined the extinction crowd. Another eighty or more went extinct before even making the list. Despite these grim statistics, there is some progress: Some ten percent of listed species are improving, and more have stabilized.

It was no secret that Alaska's political leaders, and especially its congressional delegation, disliked the Endangered Species Act and the damper they felt it placed over the economic development they loved. The listing of Alaska's Steller sea lions (after the western population dropped by eighty percent) and subsequent restrictions on commercial fishing within critical habitat areas (forced by an environmental lawsuit) had infuriated Sen. Ted Stevens. Word on the street was that Sen. Stevens's amendment to restrict Cook Inlet beluga hunting was part of a deal; he took care of the immediate overhunting problem in exchange for an agency promise not to list the belugas as threatened or endangered.

If Kris Balliet was from the activist, litigious part of the environmental movement, John Schoen was from the more science-driven educational segment. Senior scientist with the National Audubon Society's Anchorage office, John was a biologist with a Ph.D. behind his name. For twenty years before signing on with Audubon, he'd worked for the Alaska Department of Fish and Game as a specialist in conservation biology.

Audubon's charge is not, as many people assume, only bird appreciation and protection; the organization is much more broadly dedicated to protecting wildlife and wild places, with an emphasis on habitat conservation. Science, in every case, rules. When we met in his Anchorage office in June 2001, while still awaiting a decision in the coalition's lawsuit filed more than a year earlier, John made clear where Audubon stood as a coalition member. "We base our positions on sound science. We need to have a position that a large portion of reasonable Alaskans can say, 'that makes sense.' If you can't look at the biological information and make a case, then we're not going to be there." Behind his trimmed moustache, John was as neat and well-organized as the rest of his realm—the small room with everything seemingly in its place, the file cabinets into which he easily reached to pluck the desired position paper and its scientific references.

Litigation, clearly, was not the first tool in the bag for which John Schoen reached. When it came to the Cook Inlet belugas, however, John didn't see any way around it. Those in charge had not followed the dictates of science; they had made political decisions initially to delay any actions that may have prevented a crisis situation and then to choose a depleted designation instead of an endangered listing. "It's a no-brainer," John said matter-of-factly. He didn't insist that anyone accept Audubon's opinion. He simply pointed out what various government and independent scientists had said, and continued to say, about the Cook Inlet whales.

In a newspaper column, John had quoted the formal recommendation of the federal Marine Mammal Commission: that NMFS "list the Cook Inlet beluga stock as either endangered or threatened." He further quoted the independent scientific review group's determination that "because of their low abundance, declining trend, limited range, and susceptibility to catastrophic events, [Cook Inlet belugas] may be facing a real threat of extinction" as well as the chair's statement that the belugas were "a textbook case for an ESA listing." He might have quoted as well from NMFS's own biologists, who in internal memos and e-mails obtained under the Freedom of Information Act made similar professional assessments. In his column, John railed in his own quiet, professional manner, "The decision not to list belugas... ignored overwhelming scientific evidence, including the agency's own experts."

The lawsuit, he told me, would be "a slam-dunk." He mentioned a number of agency people whose statements regarding the need for a listing were now part of the legal record. "I can't believe a judge would not agree, after all those people came out so strongly in support of listing. It's a very compelling case, with good science behind it."

Clearly, John respected his former colleagues, the scientists in the government trenches. "You can't expect a scientist to go to the press and say 'my agency is irresponsible,' but they'll answer questions honestly," he said. In writing up Audubon's beluga comments, he relied on the evidence the federal scientists themselves had assembled. "It's basic biology and common sense," he told me. Had the NMFS decision-makers only heeded the work and the sense of the agency's own experts, there would have been no need for a lawsuit. The problem, as John saw it, was "people at high levels bending to political pressure, swamping out biologists trying to do their jobs." Not that it hadn't been a challenging situation, with all the sensitivity to Native hunting rights. "People were afraid to suggest any restrictions, and the Marine Mammal Protection Act was itself vague about what was allowed or could be done. Still, NMFS was irresponsible to not take any actions earlier."

John was not uncritical of the environmental community. Without naming names, he made clear that he didn't necessarily agree with the positions or strategies of other groups, including some within the beluga coalition. Some groups, he suggested, tended to exaggerate and to play on emotions, or they took positions beyond what was supported by science. "That's one of my pet peeves. The conservation community needs to be more sophisticated. We bash 'oilies' all the time. There are people who work in industry who have a deep passion for the outdoors and can be allies on our issues." In the current case, he thought some of the "green" groups went too far to place blame for the belugas with the oil or other industries, when the cause of the decline clearly lay with hunting. Audubon had worked hard with the lawyers to make sure the lawsuit had differentiated between development activities as causative factors in the decline and as threats to recovery. To Audubon, the distinction was critically important. Inlet industries may well have had nothing at all to do with the decline, but with the beluga population now so small and vulnerable, every activity needed to be scrutinized for its effects on habitat and other beluga recovery needs.

The way John saw it, both sides in this and other issues could get more of what they wanted if they'd only be reasonable and try to work together with goodwill and in good faith—before crises developed. Conservationists could do a much better job by sticking with true science and by building relationships with agency people who knew that science. Developers could benefit from being less defensive and less adamantly opposed to regulation, no matter how small or justified. John had heard—as had I—some of the complaints, even hysteria, from people in the resource development ranks, who seemed to think an endangered listing would be the end of the world, or at least the end of their Cook Inlet activity. What he tried to explain at chamber of commerce meetings was that, in fact, a listing imposed a rather small, not unreasonable burden. The consultation requirement meant just that—usually an informal discussion with the agency and a limited evaluation. He knew the numbers by heart: Of past consultations in the United States, only 0.3 percent resulted in "jeopardy" findings, meaning that the proposed action would harm the endangered species, and only 0.05 percent resulted in withdrawn or terminated projects. The case he tried to make was that all Alaskans could benefit if they'd only agree that protecting Cook Inlet belugas was worthwhile and then work together to figure out the best way to do that.

This was not just idealistic rhetoric on John's part. A majority of his time was spent on brown bear protection and a process he hoped could be a new model for conservation generally. The issue with brown bears on the Kenai Peninsula (the land that runs alongside Cook Inlet, essentially between Anchorage and Homer) was, in some ways, similar to that of the Cook Inlet belugas. The bears form a small (perhaps 350 animals), isolated population that people value and want to maintain. Habitat loss and the cumulative impacts of human activities might be expected to take the bears down the road to extinction, following the rest of America's large predators. The Audubon project involved developing a conservation strategy now, instead of waiting until the bears were squeezed into the margins. The exact strategy was still in the works but was based on sound science and on collaboration among citizens, scientists, resource managers, and government officials; it would rely heavily on educational efforts and land-use planning as well as the development of a wildlife management plan.

All that was well and good as process for a species where habitat requirements were key and that habitat was disappearing with every felled tree, new house, and fisherman crowding a riverbank. I wasn't sure that the beluga situation was analogous. I put the question to John: Could it be that their depleted status and the cessation of hunting might give them all the protection they needed?

John shook his head. "We supported the depletion designation as one step, but we didn't think it went far enough. At a minimum, they should convene a recovery team and develop a clear strategy with milestones and objectives, and they should engage the best science and scientists to put that together. That would be required under the Endangered Species Act. The act would also require identifying critical habitat. Clearly, we know that Knik, Turnagain, the Susitna flats, parts of Chickaloon Bay—all those would be considered critical." The consultation process was necessary too, and John didn't see why it wouldn't be a rather simple one. A proposed action would be presented to NMFS, which would say whether it presented a problem, or not, for the belugas. John explained, "On some portion, NMFS might say, 'This could be a problem, but this is how you can make adjustments to avoid a problem.' We need that additional oversight so we don't do something harmful out of ignorance."

And the environmental community? What more could it do now, beyond the lawsuit?

"We haven't done enough," John said. It wasn't enough simply to respond to the various calls for comment, to participate in the steps along the way. And it certainly wasn't enough to file suit and leave it to the courts or, after winning in court, to those who would implement the law. "The goal is to restore the population. We need an aggressive outreach program. We need to work with NMFS to educate the public." Audubon had already joined with NMFS to increase the award offered for information about any illegal shooting or harassment. "It's in everyone's best interest to bring the population back. I hope we don't use the law to stop things that don't need to stop. Then we jeopardize the good will of the public, and the Endangered Species Act itself."

I asked John if outreach and education were key requirements, who would make sure they happened.

"That's a good question," he said. Audubon, in many ways well suited for the job, didn't have the resources. Despite John's "senior scientist" title, suggestive of a legion of Audubon workers, the Anchorage office had a total of three employees. "It's very difficult to get funding for a nonprofit conservation organization to do that kind of work. The traditional way is to make headlines and litigate. To work behind the scenes and not make headlines doesn't get the funding. You have to find a devil."

Bob Shavelson had a devil, although I doubted his devil helped bring much in the way of voluntary contributions to the Cook Inlet Keeper, the conservation organization he directed in Homer. When the Keeper began in 1995, its start-up funding came from a legal settlement between conservation interests and Cook Inlet oil companies who were accused of more than 4,200 violations of the Clean Water Act. Keeper's mission, to protect the Cook Inlet watershed and the life it sustains, means that it continues to monitor the inlet's oil industry.

There's certainly a case to be made for keeping an eye on the aging Cook Inlet fields and infrastructure, which tend to experience pipeline leaks and other problems. In addition, Cook Inlet is the only estuary in the United States where liberal offshore standards for oil discharges are allowed. In every other estuary in the country where oil drilling is allowed, wastes must be removed and disposed of elsewhere or be reinjected. In Cook Inlet, produced waters and drilling muds and cuttings—containing hazardous chemicals, hydrocarbons, and heavy metals—are legally discharged directly into inlet waters.

The inlet's belugas were a concern for Keeper, which had added its voice to the public record and had also initiated a program called Beluga Watch aimed at citizen awareness and participation in seeing that the whales weren't illegally harassed or hunted. Keeper had not, however, joined the lawsuit seeking an Endangered Species Act listing.

I visited Bob in his office one day to ask him about that. Bob was Homer-informal, wearing a beater blue sweater over a T-shirt and green cargo pants. As I made my way to a chair, he apologized for the state of his office. I'd been in and out of Keeper's offices—four different locations—since the beginning, and I was used to stepping around dogs, bicycles, and huge piles of paper, but a new move had brought disorder to a new high. Although Bob has six staff people (some part-time), most of Keeper's current funding was specified for water quality monitoring and educational projects, and the burden of advocacy work had fallen increasingly to Bob alone. (This situation seemed the opposite of the funding problem John Schoen at Audubon had lamented.) In any case, organizing his office and managing paper—never Bob's strengths— had not made the priority list.

Elsewhere in the country, members of a network of river and bay keepers largely raised their funds by winning clean-water lawsuits, but Bob—despite his training as a lawyer—had not hewn to that model. He told me, in a measured voice any politician would covet, "Cook Inlet Keeper looks at litigation as a last resort. In our six-year history, we've litigated only about a half-dozen cases."

One of those cases involved belugas. In 1999, when the state proceeded with a 4.2 million acre oil and gas leasing sale that included areas specifically identified by NMFS as key summer habitat for belugas, Keeper was the lead plaintiff among conservation groups that sued. "We argued that under the Alaska Constitution, leasing of oil and gas activities in sensitive beluga habitat was not in the best interest of the people of Alaska." They also used the NMFS habitat maps to argue that the federal agency's expertise in the matter should be respected. The judge agreed, and 600,000 acres of sensitive habitat—much of Knik and Turnagain Arms as well as the river mouths of major salmon streams—were removed from the sale. "That," Bob said, "is probably our proudest accomplishment in our litigation history."

Another habitat issue that might have gone to litigation involved dredging in Knik Arm, again in the heart of beluga habitat. The project was the deepening of a mile-long shipping channel, the most extensive work of its kind ever undertaken in Cook Inlet; it was designed to allow larger ships to come and go at low tide and save shippers up to $2 million a year. Trustees for Alaska, on behalf of Keeper and other groups, threatened to sue, then negotiated an administrative agreement with the Corps of Engineers in which the Corps agreed to consult with NMFS about protecting belugas from negative impacts (noise, displacement, disruption), to carry an on-board monitor to watch for belugas, and to halt dredging operations when belugas were in the area. Jack Sterne, Trustee's lawyer on the issue, had pointed out that the process set up by the settlement was very similar to what would be required under the consultation provision of the Endangered Species Act. If that was the case, it should have been reassuring to Cook Inlet development interests—and not totally satisfying to conservationists. When I asked about it, Bob wrinkled his nose and said, "I think it was successful in elevating the issue and by getting observers on the dredge and some additional information on whale behavior. That said, it was fairly clear that the whale was not going to be an impediment to this or similar projects that were cast as economically necessary."

What was the difference, I asked Bob, between these other legal actions and the endangered species suit? Why had Keeper gone in on the two instances of beluga habitat protection but not the overarching one? My impressions from past discussions with Bob and his staff were that there may have been a personality clash and, more important, that Keeper didn't like being—as some saw it—manipulated by NMFS, which knew what needed to be done but wasn't brave enough to do it without being forced by the nasty environmentalists. There'd been some discussion about being "used" in a way that would sap resources and win the organization no friends.

But this was not what Bob said. Instead, he told me, "We had a desire to show solidarity with Native subsistence hunting and, while we always wanted to see the strongest possible protections for the beluga, we felt that being a party to that lawsuit would have alienated our Native partners." I pointed out that it was precisely the same solidarity the groups that sued said they were after; their thinking was that an endangered listing would take the heat off hunting as the sole source and solution to the problem. Yes, he allowed, others saw it that way, but it was his (and his board of directors') call that the suit was more likely to damage than help relationships, without necessarily benefiting the belugas.

Keeper's interests in water quality, and its grievances with the oil industry and the government that regulated it, were pretty straight-forward. Bob summarized for me: "We start from the proposition that it's wrong to discharge toxics which we know harm people, fish, and whales, into an area frequented by all of them. Industry has so bastardized the interface between science and policy that the burden is on the public to show harm. When we're talking about such a complex and dynamic system as Cook Inlet, showing cause and effect relationships is like finding a needle in a haystack."

Indeed, there had been a number of studies, funded by government agencies or the oil industry itself, that had failed to tie oil industry discharges, legal or otherwise, to significant pollution levels. The general assessment was that the inlet was so large, the currents so swift at mixing and moving waters, and other sources of pollution so slight that contributions of oil, metals, and chemicals by the oil industry were sufficiently diluted and caused no harm. In most cases, industry contaminants were not even detectable. The solution to pollution is dilution, as we all used to know.

Bob calls this "the dumping toilet metaphor," the idea that it's OK to discharge toxics into Cook Inlet because the tides, with the freshwater input from rivers, "flush" them away. To Keeper, and to the lower inlet Native villages with which he worked—villages that depended upon subsistence seafoods—polluting the inlet was not defensible. "The results of the studies," Bob told me, "reveal not only shortcomings in our science but a true lack of desire to find the answers. We know that billions of gallons of toxics are discharged each year, and we know the chemicals are relatively persistent, so we have to assume that somewhere or somehow the effects of this pollution are playing out in the ecosystem."

The best thing we could do for Cook Inlet's belugas, Bob said, was to stop the toxic discharges. "We know from looking at the St. Lawrence belugas that toxics adversely affect whale reproduction and mortality. There also needs to be a hard look at seasonal restrictions on drilling and seismic activities." There were also noise issues. In Cook Inlet, they had had very little attention.

Outside, on the porch, Bob's dog—a big hairy one of indeterminate breed—was barking. Bob stood up to frown at it from the window. "The beluga," he summed up, "will continue to be a creature and a resource that we build many of our water and habitat protection arguments around. Like we've learned from the St. Lawrence, the beluga can act like the canary in the coal mine, as an indicator of ecosystem health."

In a state where average citizens eat moosemeat and dress in fur, the closest thing to an animal rights group is the Alaska Wildlife Alliance, another member group of the coalition that filed the endangered species lawsuit. I stopped one day in Anchorage to see Karen Deatherage, associate director, whom I knew from beluga meetings.

Karen, who speaks in a loud, firm voice, introduced me to her dog Ayla ("wolf" in Inuit, she told me), a malamute that accompanied her to work each day. Ayla was also featured on her computer screen and in a wall photo. The little reception area outside Karen's door was given over to wildlife pictures, most of them of wolves. Wolves were central in the Alliance's identity and work, and a passion of Karen's.

Some would (and do) say that the Alliance is one of those groups that is a little less scientifically inclined and appeals to people's emotions. Although it's based in Alaska, most of its membership comes from outside Alaska, and a review of its newsletter, "The Spirit," shows it's heavy on attractive wildlife photos and appeals to save various animals—wolves from hunting, caribou from Arctic drilling, sea lions from trawl fisheries. Its article featuring belugas likens one to "the famed childhood ghost Casper" and describes the Cook Inlet beluga as "perhaps the most threatened animal in Alaska." A sidebar, "Endangered in the Last Frontier," appeals to an image of Alaska as the last sanctuary for wildlife: "...Alaska is home to a growing list of threatened and endangered species. Habitat destruction, overhunting and pollution are taking a tremendous toll on her unique wildlife and fragile environment." None of that is *wrong*, exactly, but the strokes are broad and the rhetoric less precise than polemical.

Karen, whose background is in computer science and nonprofit management, fulfilled a childhood dream to live in Alaska when she moved from Virginia five years before and found her niche at the Alliance as one of its three employees. She was the first to admit that her organization had sometimes tread animal-rights ground, its swings dependent on its leadership from board and staff. Its mission is sufficiently vague: protection of Alaska's natural wildlife for its intrinsic values as well as for the benefit of present and future generations. The then-current executive director, who held a Ph.D. in zoology, was emphasizing wolf management. "It feels very solid and focused," Karen said, of the group's work. "We focus on predators and wildlife management and the management system. We play a role in connecting wildlife to habitat." One recent project was a study of moose pellets in Denali Park; the condition of fecal material, Karen said, showed the animals were stressed and helped the Park Service make the case that snowmobiles should be kept out of the park. "But we don't want to be the 'no' people, perceived as being against everything," Karen emphasized. She was also participating in the development of Anchorage's urban wildlife plan.

The Alaska Wildlife Alliance is "visionary," Karen told me. *Vision* and *visionary* are words she used often. The Alliance, she said, is the most visionary of any of the local environmental groups. It holds, among other things, a vision of a future Anchorage in which belugas are the pride of the city, where the residents are stewards of belugas and other urban wildlife, where locals and visitors watch whales from downtown cafés, where people work together to make sure the belugas prosper and, in turn, reap the economic profits that accrue to the attraction belugas present. "How many cities can you go to and see beluga whales while you're eating lunch?" Karen asked, referring to the fact that the whales sometimes feed near the mouth of Ship Creek, where they can be spotted from downtown.

The Alliance, Karen said, had played a unique role in the coalition involved with the beluga. First, it had almost misstepped. When it became aware of the overhunting problem in 1998, it drew up a resolution calling for all hunting to be stopped, with the idea of getting other groups to sign on. It backed off when it realized how complicated the Native element was and when other groups called for working more cooperatively with the hunters. The niche it made for itself within the coalition instead was one of bringing "viewing values" to the table and of working with national animal rights groups to convince them to let Alaskans work on a solution. It also initiated contacts with researchers who worked with belugas in the St. Lawrence River and brought references to their work on hydroacoustics and toxics to the development of the legal case.

"Clearly, hunting is the major cause of the decline," Karen conceded. "Our concern with toxins, sewage, shipping activity—all that—is the ability to recover. That's why it's so important to do the listing. It's been hard to get the agencies and media to understand this is our concern. If we can't prove that toxins caused the decline, they don't want to go there." She mentioned reports of Jet-ski activity among and around belugas in the upper inlet—a newly arrived sport and a disturbance no one would have anticipated a few years before. "Because they're such slow breeders, we have to look at what's coming up or they won't make it."

One of the Alliance's concerns, like Keeper's, was noise. The National Marine Fisheries Service had done no more than note that, in general, beluga responses to noise varied greatly and depended on such factors as what activities the whales were engaged in and how accustomed they were to the noise-making operations. Karen had located some work (unpublished in the scientific literature) that theorized that the noise levels in the St. Lawrence River were capable of causing permanent hearing loss in belugas. That study compared noise in the river with OSHA standards for humans in their work places and concluded that the St. Lawrence belugas were subjected to damaging decibel levels.

(Later, a study designed to quantify noise in Cook Inlet, noting that most industrial noise is at low frequencies whereas beluga hearing is keenest at high frequencies, would conclude that "the sound levels measured in Cook Inlet during this study would not be expected to have more than minor effect on the whales." The study did not measure noise associated with seismic surveying, used in the inlet and elsewhere to "read" underlying geology for the oil industry; such surveying typically involves series of explosions made by air guns and has been found, in other places with other whale species, to be harassment.)

The Alliance brought what it could to the beluga table—and left some aspects of the issue to others. It didn't, for example, try to work with Native hunters. "We were the least qualified group to do that," Karen said. "But the beluga issue showed us it's possible to work with Natives. Having the ecosystem intact benefits all of us. For us it's been a rare opportunity to go before the public and say we recognize the different values belugas have for people." I recalled one meeting when Karen had said as much. When other testimony had fallen back into debate about whether the belugas were or were not overhunted, Karen had taken her turn at the mike to say, "Let's stop talking about blame. Let's talk about what needs to be done now to assure there will be belugas for everyone."

It was not that the Alliance would ever be comfortable, itself, with whale killing. Its official position was neutrality in whether there should be a very small subsistence quota for the beluga hunters. "We have a hard time accepting any harvest now, given the low recruitment. I'd rather see it allowed, but not actually done." Karen frowned. "We do have a problem with killing any of these highly intelligent animals, but we accept it. We're working together for their long-term protection."

Karen was buoyant, though, about the vision of Anchorage's future that would include beluga viewing. Not long before, she'd driven the road along Turnagain Arm to look for belugas feeding on hooligan. At Twenty-mile River, people—mostly Natives and Asians—were dipnetting for the same oily fish, and a man was pointing at belugas and wondering what they were. "There's a wonderful opportunity there to educate people about the inlet and its residents"—especially, she emphasized, to reach a constituency often neglected by conservationists as well as agencies and the educational system. "Give them ownership for that part of the inlet," she said. There were no garbage cans where people were fishing, or signs, and Karen saw yet another opportunity to help people be good and aware citizens of the environment. Providing trash receptacles, signs, interpretive displays, and talks—it would be a perfect outreach campaign for the Alliance. "We need more education. We need to build from the ground up.

"I've got the vision," Karen said, "but never enough time."

One thing, however, she was confident about: the lawsuit. "I can't see how we can't prevail. This is a classic, *classic* candidate in all respects."

At the Trustees for Alaska office, nearly every doorway was blocked with a folding gate. The gates were dog gates, and behind them, in a warren of tiny offices, worked dog-owning attorneys. Jack Sterne, bookended by wagging black Labradors, handed me the two enormous volumes of administrative record used to support the endangered species case. I settled in at a conference table to examine for myself the paper trail I'd heard so much about.

As soon as I started reading, I felt a bit like I'd come across a cache of love letters. It was not that the content was personal in quite the same way but that my response was one of both wanting (voyeuristically) to read them and feeling (chastely) that I shouldn't—that really, these were private, not meant for me. It was true that the internal memos and e-mails were not meant for the public, but that's exactly the point of the Freedom of Information Act. The public has a right to know what the people it employs do and say; their work is our business.

This is some of what I read:

In the minutes of a January 1999 conference call among NMFS Alaska region people: "The consensus was to proceed with the dual MMPA and ESA listing process." The participants also agreed that time was short and the situation critical.

A month later, the head of the Alaska region recommended management actions to his superior: Proceed with a formal listing under the Endangered Species Act and, because such action would take time, also seek legislation action to impose a harvest moratorium or restrictions on hunting for 1999. "With your concurrence and approval, we will proceed immediately."

By April, there were references to the Stevens rider and increased vagueness about employing the Endangered Species Act. A new recommendation read, "Take immediate action to conserve the populations through legislation, status designation, and/or regulation under the MMPA/ESA."

In May, an option was considered to propose depleted status under the Marine Mammal Protection Act with language indicating that NMFS was reserving its decision on whether to proceed with an Endangered Species Act listing or not. The analysis is blunt. "PROS—is consistent with the request from the Alaska delegation, allows an ESA listing to move forward if there should be problems. CONS—will result in litigation by environmental interests; NMFS will lose the lawsuit."

A decision memo in June, recommending an MMPA depleted designation, stated: "Interest among Alaska congressional delegation is high, and resistant to ESA listing."

An e-mail from the chair of the Alaska Region Scientific Review Group said: "These factors make a textbook case for ESA listing, and I can see no way to make a credible argument otherwise."

E-mails from the director of the National Marine Mammal Lab included this analysis: "Scientifically, we can not make a strong case for depletion, while a very strong case can be made for threatened," and "I think most knowledgeable scientists would support a listing decision in the absence of politics because of the ESA charge to err on the side of the animal, although as to whether they would go with endangered versus threatened is harder to predict."

There was more, much more. What was clear enough was what the scientists and even lower-level policy people recommended "in the absence of politics" and what happened once absence turned to presence. No judge could fail to see that politics had trumped science and that a political decision had been substituted for the scientific one intended by our system of laws. The case was a slam-dunk, as John Schoen had so plainly put it. A slam-dunk and a no-brainer.

In July 2001, the endangered species case was finally heard by a district court judge in Washington, D.C. In oral arguments, Trustees for Alaska's Jack Sterne said, "The only reason not to list is political, and that simply is not allowed."

The heart of the case, as presented by Jack, was that, although the beluga decline might be attributed to NMFS's failure to prevent overharvesting by Native hunters, "numerous other human-caused and natural sources of mortality or harassment may cause further declines or prevent the recovery of the species." There was, he pointed out, no other marine mammal population as small as the Cook Inlet beluga stock not listed as endangered. Because of the population's small size, any number of stochastic events—random and uncontrollable events, which could include a mass stranding, an oil spill, an epidemic of disease—could threaten its existence. By failing to determine that a listing was warranted, NMFS had failed to do what was necessary to protect the Cook Inlet belugas and their habitat. The agency's determination that a listing was not warranted was therefore "arbitrary, capricious, and not in accordance with procedures required by law."

The NMFS attorney, in his argument, disputed that the belugas were threatened by anything more than hunting, which had now been halted. He told the judge, "There's no evidence in the record that these [other] factors contributed to the decline of the species or pose a future threat to the species." The government's position was that the agency's choice of the Marine Mammal Protection Act's depleted designation to control hunting was a legitimate policy choice, and adequate legislative and management actions had been taken to allow the beluga stock to recover.

A month later, Judge James Robertson delivered his ruling. The National Marine Fisheries Service, he declared, had acted within the law to designate the Cook Inlet belugas as depleted but not threatened or endangered under the Endangered Species Act. The environmentalists, he said, had not proved that NMFS officials, in rejecting the higher level of protection, had abused their discretion or otherwise departed from the law.

The judge, in his written opinion, went through the five factors listed in the Endangered Species Act—any one of which, he agreed, if "sufficiently implicated," would support a listing determination—and decided that the Cook Inlet beluga met the test of none. In answering plaintiffs' concern that the small population was particularly vulnerable, he ruled that NMFS was "not required by law to list any species with a historically small or a declining population" and, moreover, found that plaintiffs had not successfully rebutted an NMFS paper that used statistical modeling to determine that small populations would not, with "maximum environmental stochasticity," compute to extinction. The fact that the paper applied to hypothetical baleen whales and none of the unique specificity of the Cook Inlet belugas was not regarded as relevant, and an analysis by an opposing expert witness was stricken as extra-record material.

Regarding Sterne's argument that political considerations played an impermissible role in the decision-making, Judge Robertson found the allegation without support. "These bits of evidence show that the agency's decision was a difficult one and that political considerations may have been lurking in the corridors. They do not establish that, but for 'politics,' the whale would have been listed... or that political considerations became part of the decision making process."

In reading over the ruling, I kept coming back to a sentence in its introduction, in the judge's summation of "factual and procedural background": "...a listing under the MMPA does not have the regulatory, economic and environmental fallout of a listing as 'threatened' or 'endangered' under the ESA." *Fallout,* I thought, was an interesting choice of word, not exactly neutral. There was no companion sentence explaining the benefits of the Endangered Species Act to a listed animal.

The environmental coalition appealed the decision. Another year would pass before a three-judge panel would prepare to take up the case.

It was near the end of 2001 before I sat down with Kris Balliet again, nearly two years since we'd lunched in Homer. In all that time, she'd been hard to catch up with, even on the phone. She was always on the move—making frequent trips back and forth to what she called "headquarters" in Washington, D.C., sometimes around Alaska where her organization, now renamed the Ocean Conservancy, was expanding into fisheries and marine habitat conservation, including a controversial plan for marine reserves where no fishing would be allowed.

This time we met at her downtown Anchorage office, an expansive suite of open rooms with corporate-style furnishings and big windows looking out on the city, where ice fog was blooming in below-zero temperatures. A jungle of oversized potted plants—forty of them, Kris said—towered over the wood and chrome furnishings. Kris was quick to tell me she'd bought them "very cheap" from a nursery that leased them to corporations and took them back when they got too large. Kris had five staff people now (of one hundred Ocean Conservancy employees nationally); I glimpsed a couple of faces behind plants before Kris, buzzing with energy, led me into the conference room.

In the conference room, the handsome wooden table was arranged with a centerpiece of another (smaller) plant and a pair of whale rib bones. The bones, Kris said, were on loan from headquarters and may have come from a juvenile right whale. A painting on the wall, somewhat impressionistic, presented an aerial perspective of a white beluga with a gray calf among waters swirling with schools of fish, framed in by a rocky coastline and distant snowy mountains.

In Homer, Kris had told me that if she had the choice again, she wasn't sure she'd have taken on the beluga issue. I asked if she still felt that way.

Just for a second, her lips pressed together. Alaska's environmental community was very "conservative," she said. It wasn't that they didn't do good work. But it was like "good cops-bad cops," and she was always the bad cop, the one—as she saw it—willing to take the harder stance. "There were times I got really lonely out there by myself. I'm OK with it now," she said. "If I could do it over again, I'd try to figure out how to more graciously navigate between the Athabaskans and the people who have become Native to this region. I would have done cross-cultural work."

She was still keeping a hand in on the Native hunting issues. Of all the environmental groups, only the Ocean Conservancy had sought representation in the administrative hearing regarding proposed harvest regulations for the very small hunt that would be allowed. The judge was still working on a plan, and the Conservancy's concerns—about such things as whether a lactating female should be counted as one or two strikes (two, they argued) and whether hunts should take place after July 1 or July 15 to avoid pregnant females (July 15 was their choice)—were being represented by Trustees for Alaska.

And the endangered species lawsuit—its appeal—was still a focus. "We need a listing," Kris insisted. "The cynical me says, without one, there won't be a recovery. The less cynical me says, maybe there will be—but do we have the time and resources to address the myriad of issues? All we really want is consultation." Kris leaned back in the upholstered chair. "The burden should not be on us to prove harm."

Aside from those ongoing parts of the beluga issue, Kris was applying herself—and her office—to the Conservancy's tripartite program of advancing marine protected areas and ocean wilderness and preventing overfishing. The belugas, she said, fit under marine protected areas. She was working with "the local community"—mostly Native hunters to identify critical beluga habitat that should be protected, perhaps under the state's critical habitat program. Key areas had been identified, but, she stressed, the process was still in the formative stages and was going to take a "really long time." Unless, of course, there was some kind of catastrophe—an oil spill, a mass stranding—that would make the situation worse and get everyone's attention. The Conservancy had proposed very controversial marine wilderness areas elsewhere in Alaska but had not (yet) suggested anything for Cook Inlet. What Kris had in mind—in the absence of a listing—were possible "refugia." In such areas, there would be no hunting, no taking the belugas' food, and no activities (like dredging) that would interfere with the whales.

"We're working on a national message strategy," Kris said. "We haven't wanted to play the smiling little critter card, but we may. You have to tease out an icon, and belugas are a good icon. What we do in this office is to try to think of ways to engage a national audience in these issues—ways that are respectful of Native cultures."

Beyond the windows, weak winter light was seeping through the ice fog, and the outside world of roof lines looked soft and vague. Something that Barry Lopez had written came to me with a new, expanded, meaning. In *Arctic Dreams,* he'd quoted an anthropologist, who was referring at that moment to a group of Eskimos: "You ignore at your peril the variety in human culture." That variety, it was clear, existed not just in a split between Western and Native cultures but through all the nuances within and between. Native peoples—and Native people—may share some core values and history but were otherwise distinctly individual. Conservation groups were similarly dissimilar. And weren't we—every one of us, regardless of what culture we fit into—adding every day to what we knew?

6

THE OTHER REMNANT

In Alaska, I heard again and again about the beluga whales of eastern Canada's St. Lawrence River. Like Cook Inlet's, they were a southern remnant population. Like Cook Inlet's, they were few and troubled. Once, the St. Lawrence belugas had been hunted by Native Americans; later, European immigrants over-hunted them, and fishermen wanted them exterminated. As numbers dropped, the remaining animals kept to a smaller core area. They were observed to move seasonally, from upstream estuary areas in summer to a broader dispersal toward or into a more oceanic realm—the Gulf of St. Lawrence—in winter. With the end of hunting in the 1970s, numbers were expected to rebound. They didn't. For years the population was thought to be approximately 500; new survey techniques had recently raised the population estimate to between 1,000 and 1,400—but some researchers emphasized that the higher numbers only represented better counting methods and not an actual population increase.

The St. Lawrence belugas live in waters contaminated by industrial chemicals—substances well known for toxic effects on animal life and for interfering with reproduction and resistance to diseases. How many times had I heard that the St. Lawrence whales were "classified as hazardous waste," a half-truth linked to statements made by research scientist Pierre Béland? (What Béland had actually said was that some St. Lawrence belugas found dead "could qualify as hazardous waste," based on the levels of PCBs found in their fat.) How often had I heard fears and warnings that the Cook Inlet whales, could, if we weren't careful, go the way of the St. Lawrence's?

The St. Lawrence belugas were the most studied belugas in the world. Contaminants, noise, disturbance, social organization, habitat use, behaviors: These things had been studied in St. Lawrence belugas for twenty-five years. I was sure there were lessons to be learned for Cook Inlet; I just wasn't certain what they may be.

On a cool September day, I scanned for belugas from the cabin of a 26-foot research boat as it slid across the St. Lawrence River from the Quebec town of Tadoussac. Michel Moisan, head technician for the nonprofit GREMM (Groupe de Recherche et d'Éducation sur les Mammifères Marins, or the Marine Mammal Research and Education Group), steered the *Bleuvet* across the morning's barely rippled water while his assistant, Stephane Roy, kept an outlook from atop the boat's cabin.

"*Bleuvet,*" I said, giving the word my best French pronunciation. I had never been to Quebec before and was just learning how very French even the tourist towns were. At GREMM's educational center in Tadoussac, all the displays were in French, and English speakers were handed a translated script to consult. "Where does the boat's name come from?"

"It's a young beluga," Michel said, surveying the water before us. "Not a new calf, but one in its second or third year." Michel, whom I'd met for the first time just moments before, had already established himself as easy to be with. Before leaving the dock, he'd carefully emptied a plastic container of its nuts and washers, then used the container to trap a wasp against the window and carry it to freedom. Now, cheeks bristling with several days' beard, he pointed out some harbor porpoises. The day was unusually calm for so late in the season, and he was a happy man.

The boat was white fiberglass—whiter than a *bleuvet*—and rigged with a lot of gray aluminum railing. A blue flag featuring a beluga flew off the stern. We passed gulls feeding in a flock, seabirds diving, seals bobbing, and I thought how lovely—and more exact—the word *bleuvet* was, compared to our terms *calf* and *immature*. The land we faced, twelve miles across the river from Tadoussac, stretched tall and deeply green.

After an hour, as we approached an island close to the south shore, Stephane tapped on the roof. Belugas!

We had come to an area that had not recently been surveyed and where, Michel had warned me, it often took a long time to locate belugas. It was also an area known to be frequented by cows with calves, animals they found harder to approach than groups of males or curious juveniles.

Michel and Stephane changed places, so Stephane drove the boat with his fleece-bundled head through the open hatch, and Michel stepped to the bow strapped like a soldier with the tools of his trade: binoculars, camera, tape recorder, rifle. I took my assigned out-of-the-way spot on the cabin's roof, eager to see what would happen next. How was it possible to identify individual belugas, which all looked to me like the same smooth white backs? If you could do that, without attaching techno-gear, you could learn what habitats an individual used and when it traveled among them. You could learn with what other whales a given whale kept company and get some suggestion of family or social relationships. You could begin to judge the longevity of belugas you saw year after year. If you knew how often you saw the same whales, you may get a sense of how many whales there were altogether. And, if you were able to collect skin or fat samples from whales you identified, you may learn some of their more intimate information—sex, genetic heritage, health.

If you found a dead beluga, and you knew "who" it was, that whale would tell you a story—just as the killer whale that washed up near Vancouver had. But there was one big difference between killer whales and belugas: Killer whales have recognizable dorsal fins, individually shaped and nicked, as well as distinctive saddle patches. The researchers who studied them kept photo collections, and any sighting could be matched against the catalog.

The GREMM researchers were building a similar catalog of St. Lawrence beluga photographs, understandably more subtle in their differences. We motored and drifted among the scattered whales, taking their measure as they rose and fell around us, presumably feeding. Michel and Stephane moved easily around the boat, conversing in French, making notes about what they saw, switching to English for me. The art of photographing belugas, I saw, was not a simple one of driving up on the whales and taking their pictures. It was, instead, a more Zen-like way of being with the whales, involving long periods of waiting and watching, bursts of boat maneuvering, being ready for the exact moments when particular whales would present themselves beside the boat in proper lighting and silhouetted positions.

Michel squinted up at me. "So how do these compare to your whales?"

I took the question on its most basic behavioral level. "Ours are more skittish," I said. "Yours obviously haven't been hunted in a while." I'd been thinking about how, when I'd been with the researchers in Knik Arm, it had been impossible to stay with any group of belugas. I also thought about days at my fish camp, when groups of passing whales seemed much less shy and Ken and I had drifted among them.

Now, a number of belugas—young, gray animals especially—came right up to the *Bleuvet* as though looking us over; a couple lingered just off the stern, apparently enjoying the prop-wash as a person might enjoy the massage of water jets in a Jacuzzi pool. Once they'd checked us out, they went on about their business, circling the area, lifting through the water's surface to blow. They never seemed to speed up or slow down or to take long dives that left us staring at empty water, and they didn't try to move off or avoid us.

I guessed we were looking at approximately twenty whales, most of them white. Michel's practiced eye sorted through them and counted a dozen, eight whites and four grays. Moreover, he quickly saw that there was one group—three adults and two young—traveling together, sometimes close enough to be touching. We zeroed in on the group and tried to keep near it, with Stephane maneuvering the boat to position us alongside without crowding the whales or cutting off their lines of movement. Michel recognized two of the adults and worked at getting good, close-up photos of all of them, from both sides, to compare to what was already in the catalog and to record what was likely a family grouping. Between shooting, he spoke into his recorder, describing marks, behaviors, locations, and movements, every kind of field note that may eventually lead to a greater understanding of the whales and their social organization.

I tried to see what Michel was seeing and found my skills woefully undeveloped. Even when the whales rose right beside us and I could look directly at them from only a few feet away, I missed seeing what to Michel were distinguishing marks on their backs.

"Tell me," I asked Michel, "how you describe what you're seeing. What are the marks you're identifying?"

He pointed out one whale. That one, he said, had a small round depression near its tail, visible from one side. The other had a mark—a scrape or a scar—that crossed its back and could be seen from both sides as well as a pattern of nicks in its dorsal ridge.

Once I knew what to look for, I could see something like those marks. Then when we saw the whales at another angle, in different light, I missed the marks, or they looked different, or maybe I was looking at a different whale. I felt hopelessly incompetent.

Six years of staring at and comparing the backs of belugas had obviously developed in Michel a finely discriminating eye. I comforted myself by thinking of similar skills that Ken and I have in salmon fishing—the way we can detect the species in a salmon's jump or judge from the way a net hangs the number of salmon we'll find gilled in it. From May to October, Michel spent just about every weather-permitting day on the water with belugas—generally two or three days a week. He was the third researcher since the photo ID program was started in 1986 to so devote himself.

The day before, at GREMM's headquarters, I'd tested my identification skills on an interactive computer. I followed the directions to watch a video of surfacing belugas, then touch a beluga back on the screen as though I were taking its picture. The still photo I "took" was then displayed, and I was asked to compare it to five other photos that appeared on one side of the screen. All the whales were distinctively marked, and the photos were clear. Even so, the first time I tried to match my photo to the five choices, each of my picks only rang up a flat, disapproving, you-lose *blat!*, one after another, until I reached, by default, the very last choice. My second attempt, with another whale, was only slightly more successful.

The St. Lawrence beluga catalog held an impressive 800 whale identities. Some of them, however, were thought to be duplicates of the same whale—shot from different sides or just looking different after skin blemishes changed or were seen in different light—and some were of whales no longer thought to be alive. Nevertheless, 200 or more of the cataloged whales were well-known individuals with long sighting histories. Individual files tracked favored habitats, seasonal movements, reproductive success, family structures, and "friends"—the other whales with which they associated.

If the ID program was scientifically useful, it was also a financial boon. GREMM raised research money by "adopting" out individual belugas. For $5,000, the adoptive party receives a certificate, a photograph of the animal, a summary of what is known about it, a regular newsletter, and—if the beluga is unnamed—a chance to name it. I'd paged through the "family album" on display at the center, looking at photos and reading the detailed bios. Albert was adopted by a hotel chain, Blanchon by high-school students and hospital employees, Capone by another group of students and scouts, Doby Mick by a family. There were 105 adoptees, and "more are still waiting!"

A weak sun peered through a high, thin overcast sky. Along the shoreline, the yellows and oranges of birch and maple leaves glowed softly among the dominant evergreens. I was surprised to find the landscape so steep and rocky and so sparsely settled along the shore. Although the area has been inhabited by European comers for four hundred years and by Native people for who-knows-how-long before that, the toeholds for communities, still very rural, are few. And even though the St. Lawrence is considered a great shipping artery, I witnessed little traffic. I'd seen only one ship pass in the distance and, close in to Tadoussac, a few local tour boats out to show off some of the large whale species that inhabit the area seasonally. The waterway seemed to me wild and almost pristinely beautiful—and full of life.

It was hard to believe, just looking, that the St. Lawrence was one of the most contaminated waterways anywhere. For decades massive amounts of poisonous chemicals were discharged into its watershed—which includes the Great Lakes—by industries, agriculture, and urbanization. These contaminants include mercury, lead, hydrocarbons, tributyltin (an anti-fouling biocide used in boat paint and called by the World Wildlife Fund "the most toxic chemical ever deliberately released into the seas") and a wide range of organochlorines. The organochlorines include Mirex, produced on the shore of Lake Ontario as a stabilizer and pesticide; polychlorinated biphenyls (PCBs) used as flame retardants; and many pesticides, among them DDT. Pollution controls in the last fifteen years have greatly reduced both intentional and accidental discharges, but much contamination remains trapped in sediments, circulating through the food web.

In the briny water, so much clearer than muddy Cook Inlet, I got good at spotting belugas, like gray shadows, below the surface. When they rose, they sometimes lifted their heads first so that it was possible to get a quick glance at their front ends and bulbous melons. One whale, in the group of five we were watching, began to throw its flukes up into the air each time it went under. In whales generally, flukes are typically thrown when their owners angle themselves for long, vertical dives, but this beluga was not diving deeply. I asked Michel what was going on.

"Sometimes one whale will do it for a while, and then sometimes another will. What we've noticed is it's often females with calves, as though they're crowded or trying to brush the calves away." The fluking whale was, indeed, a cow followed very closely by a calf.

On the bow, Michel exchanged his camera for the biopsy rifle. The two adults he'd recognized—now well photographed—had not yet been sampled for genetic and chemical analysis. For a long time we continued boating among the whales, getting close, closer, not close enough, maneuvering again and again so that Michel could try to get a clear and sure shot at his target whale's back. And then he did. He fired; I saw the point with its bright red bit of plastic hit the whale and the whale flinch, splash, and dive, and then Michel was reeling in, with an ordinary fishing reel attached to the rifle, the line that brought back to him the hollow point now filled with a small plug of skin and fat. "Whale fishing," Michel said with a smile.

I wondered if the clearly unpleasant bite affected the whales' subsequent behavior. "Does darting them like that make them more wary the next time they see you?"

Michel stepped carefully around the deck as he replaced equipment. "They react just for a minute or two, and then they're back to normal." It was a few minutes before the pod circled by us again, and, indeed, they were as before, except that the one whale was lightly bleeding from the new small hole in the side of its back.

Michel took the biopsy plug into the cabin's forecastle and set up his "lab" on the table there. The plug, laid out on a sterilized surface, looked like a little white grub, less than an inch long and a small fraction wide. Michel cut it into pieces and popped them into vials to be sent off to labs—skin to be tested for sex and genetics, fat to be analyzed for chemical contaminants. "Number 148," he announced.

More waiting, more maneuvering, more watchfulness, and Michel shot and reeled in the milligrams of flesh from his other identified whale, Number 149. As he leaned over the new specimen at the table, I asked, "So, what are you learning from these? Are you finding high levels of contaminants?"

Michel, I thought, looked slightly uncomfortable with the question. He took a few seconds to answer. "Well," he said, "not as high as we expected. There appears to be stratification. You'll have to ask Robert about it." Robert Michaud, GREMM's founder and director, was in charge of the science. I made a note.

The wind had picked up and the water was ruffling, with a few crests breaking into whitecaps. We headed back across the St. Lawrence to its meeting with the more protected waters of the Saguenay River.

Right there, where the St. Lawrence and the Saguenay meet, lies one of the most remarkable marine habitat areas in the world. Fifty-four species of marine vertebrates, including eleven cetacean species, live at least seasonally at the confluence. Another 248 invertebrates swim, dig, and anchor themselves in the same area. What's so magic? The two rivers are really arms of the sea—an estuary and a fjord. The cold Labrador Current, entering from the Atlantic, carries a wealth of nutrients through the Gulf of St. Lawrence into the Laurentian Channel, which is a thousand feet deep. Where the St. Lawrence meets the Saguenay, the channel dead-ends at steep undersea cliffs, and upwellings force that rich nutrient soup to the surface. Meanwhile, the Saguenay also delivers its loads of nutrients from inland. Where the two water masses meet and their differing temperatures, salinities, and densities bump up against one another, "fronts" concentrate the nutrients and the organisms that feed upon them. Those organisms, prospering mightily at a generous table, serve, in their turn, as prey for larger species.

We were at, in fact, the center of summer beluga habitat, presumably the best place for the whales to eat. Nearly half the beluga population clusters in the St. Lawrence near the head of the channel, and most of the rest (especially females with young) frequent the warmer and more protected waters just upstream of the Saguenay. A small percent can usually be found within the Saguenay, most often near its mouth.

Slowly, with Stephane once again positioned on the roof as outlook, we proceeded up the Saguenay. Walls of Precambrian granite, polished smooth by four periods of glacial scouring and marked at their bases with several feet of tideline, rose abruptly from the water. Trees—deep greens broken by the straight white lines of birches and their golden leaves—clung to the hillsides above them. The wild land on both sides mostly fell within the protections of the provincial Saguenay Park, created in 1983, and for miles the only sign of humankind was a set of giant power pylons that spanned the fjord. At length we passed a small, quiet village where a road spur reached a nick of a bay.

We didn't, however, see any belugas. We drifted for a time in St. Marguerite Bay, fifteen miles upriver and as far as the belugas usually go. The bay is, in fact, a favored habitat for the whales, and the park maintains an onshore observation lookout and interpretative site at the end of another road spur. The stream that enters the bay hosts salmon and sea-run trout, but, Michel explained, there may well be other attributes that attract belugas to the location. He and others have observed that different belugas, in small groups, frequent the bay at different times and that while there, they behave differently than elsewhere. In St. Marguerite's, for example, they sometimes swim with their heads out of the water. "It's like a summer vacation place for them," Michel said, a place the whales take turns visiting to feed, to rest, or to enjoy a different temperature or salinity or a chance to rub away old skinwhatever it is they seek there. They stay for a few hours or a few days, and then they return downriver.

It was about four o'clock and the sun was nearly falling behind the trees when we motored back down the river. And then, not far above Tadoussac, we spotted more belugas. Six big white animals rose and fell together in a pack, and Michel—recognizing them—called out several of their numbers. When the animals passed beside us, even I could see how different they were from the ones we'd been among earlier. These were larger, heavier belugas, and each one was well marked with gouges or scars. They were a group of older males, friends who were most often seen together and who had lived long enough and dangerously enough to have become physically distinguished. Michel still lacked a biopsy from one of them, so he readied the rifle again.

We stayed with those whales for the next two hours. Although they weren't shy, neither were they easy to track. Stephane would maneuver the boat alongside their group, and then we wouldn't see them for several long minutes, and then we would see them again, across the river or farther up or down. The Saguenay is very deep, and the belugas, Michel said, likely were diving to its bottom to feed.

We drifted and waited and motored beside rocky cliffs, and we kept track of other belugas that were also in the vicinity, popping up mostly along the far shore. I began to understand what a challenge it must be to do population assessments in the St. Lawrence. Surveys had been conducted since the early 1970s, but their methodologies and geographic coverage differed widely and made them hard to compare. One scientist, Michael Kingsley, finally came up with factors to correct for the differences in order to get, if not necessarily more accurate numbers, at least index estimates that produced trend lines. His work suggested that trends have been upward—that the St. Lawrence beluga population has been slowly growing since hunting ceased in 1979.

Kingsley's work was a surprise to some because it was contrary to earlier analyses pointing to a population decline. Kingsley also argued that the correction factors generally applied to adjust counts for missed animals (such as those diving to feed) were too low. Later, work by one of his assistants, using a helicopter to track and count, justified a much larger correction factor and the population estimate now generally accepted, of between 1,000 and 1,400 animals.

The sun was falling below the trees, and we still hadn't gotten a shot at the elusive whale. A couple of younger belugas kept surfacing next to us, cutting to one side and another, swimming in tandem, lifting their heads. They were clearly playing with one another and with the boat, with us. They rolled forward and twisted sideways, like aquatic acrobats. One rose exactly beside Michel at the bow and blew water from its blowhole over him in a way that was obviously intentional. The three of us, laughing, leaned over the side, watching more of the dance. There was a thumping noise, and Michel called, "This one's under the hull, bumping us with his head!" Stephane dropped a rubber hose into the water and slapped his hand against its open end, making popping noises that drew the whales, again, to shoot around us and splash.

After a long day of serious work, of much patient waiting and watching on our part and of taking care of whale business on the parts of the young belugas, here was time for play. I was struck by how fully all five of us entered into it, how equally inventive both species appeared to be. Whatever may be said about the relative "intelligence" of humans and whales, there seemed no doubt that both are smart enough to know how to have fun and to engage one another in the pleasures we could both get and give.

"Every day is different," Michel said as he turned the boat homeward. Six years, and he never got tired of being with belugas. Like fishing, I thought. To an outsider, it can look like a lot of waiting and tedious repetitive work, but the person who fits into the rhythms and subtleties of the experience finds the felicity and the passion there and, always, something new.

Before I left Tadoussac, I stopped at the headquarters of the new Saguenay–St. Lawrence Marine Park (theme: Crossroads of Life, Site of Exchanges, Well-spring of Riches) and talked to biologist Nadia Ménard. Nadia was in charge of developing the park's management plan that would strive, among other things, to protect belugas and their habitat, and she had also been very involved in implementing parts of the St. Lawrence Beluga Recovery Plan developed in 1995. A lively, athletic woman—the kind of person you'd want for a hiking companionNadia met me in her office after an all-day meeting and seemed happy to talk belugas until well after all the other staff had left and her baby's daycare facility was within minutes of shutting down.

Cook Inlet's belugas would need a recovery or conservation plan, and it seemed to me that the St. Lawrence offered a potential model, despite differences between the two countries, their laws, and the specifics of their belugas. What struck me about the St. Lawrence plan (with its five broad strategies and fifty-five objectives) was its practical nature and workability. It wasn't some theoretical wish list of actions but rather a clear plan that ranked priorities and explained what actions needed to be done, who would do them, when they would happen, and how much they would cost. Much of it had already been implemented, and an update evaluated what had been achieved, what was ongoing, what obstacles had been encountered, and what might need to be done differently.

Except for the first, the five broad goals may well have fit Cook Inlet:

- Achieve in the St. Lawrence ecosystem an overall reduction in toxic contaminants believed to be having an impact on belugas;
- Reduce disturbance caused by human activities in areas frequented by belugas;
- Prevent ecological catastrophes and ensure emergency preparedness;
- Monitor the state of the population;
- Investigate other potential obstacles to beluga recovery.

I had gone to see Nadia primarily about the second item—reducing human disturbance—the goal with which she, and the park, were most involved. One of this goal's fifteen objectives, in fact, had been the establishment of the marine park. Once the park—fifty miles long and varying from six to ten miles wide—was legislatively established in 1998, beluga habitat within it was addressed in the park's voluminous management and conservation plans.

Mostly Nadia and I talked about whale-watching. An irony of the park's creation was that it brought more attention to the area and its resources—especially whales. Today a fleet of close to sixty tour boats make about 10,000 excursions each year between June and October, carrying half a million visitors into the marine park to see blue, fin, minke, humpback, sperm, and beluga whales. Everywhere in Tadoussac I was surrounded by signs advertising competing tours and gift shops selling whale-themed T-shirts, coffee cups, and fine art.

There were issues about all this whale-watching and its possible effects on whales. One study showed that fin whales exposed to boat traffic altered their diving patterns; it went on to suggest that such alteration could affect feeding success.

Fin whales were in fact the target species for the whale-watching operations. Fin whales are huge—measuring up to eighty feet in length and weighing nearly fifty tons. The only larger whale, the blue whale—the largest animal ever to have lived on Earth—is also found often enough in the St. Lawrence to be a draw. Humpback and sperm whales are possibilities, and minkes are common.

Because of its special status and the requirements of the recovery plan, the beluga is the one whale that's actually excluded from deliberate whale-watching from boats. First, members of the whale-watching industry agreed to a code of conduct that includes beluga protections. Then, regulations—still only proposed but to be adopted by the next season, Nadia told me—were drawn up with the same provisions. The park had recently produced a colorful brochure that encouraged visitors to think beyond whales, to enjoy all the wildlife, land forms, water conditions, lighthouses, and human history they encounter from the water. The brochure also included a short version of the code of conduct for observing whales in general and belugas in particular. Boats must reduce their speed to that which is necessary for maneuvering once they're within 400 meters of a whale, may not approach closer than 200 meters of a whale, and may not cut off a whale's path. The beluga section reads:

CAREFUL: BELUGAS! The beluga is the only whale species that inhabits the St. Lawrence year round. This small population is endangered, and disturbance caused by human activities poses a threat. TO HELP THE RECOVERY OF THE POPULATION, BELUGAS ARE EXCLUDED FROM WHALE WATCHING AT SEA. If you come across any belugas, you must remain at a distance of at least 400 metres. In case of an unexpected encounter with a beluga, the captain shall reduce his speed to the minimum required to manoeuvre his vessel and leave the vicinity.

When I first arrived in Tadoussac I'd more or less randomly selected a tour, wanting to see what the usual tourist might see by way of whales and presentation of whales. The boats seemed standardized to three-hour tours and were set to a schedule of spaced departures. Our boat, a catamaran capable of holding 175 passengers but less than full on a Sunday morning, took us directly to the confluence area just off the Tadoussac harbor. There, in an area of reefs and choppy water cluttered with gulls, we'd spent an hour with five minke whales feeding at the surface on schools of small fish. Our passengers were enthralled as the black backs and comma-shaped dorsal fins circled around us. The onboard naturalist narrated some of their facts (seven to eight meters long, surface feeders, worldwide distribution from the Arctic to the Antarctic) and pointed out one individual known as Broken Fin, which was very obviously missing most of its dorsal.

We did not stay 200 meters away. Our naturalist told us the recommended distance was 100 meters, which indeed, per the code's fine print, is permitted "in certain cases" depending on the number of boats involved. Even then, as the whales themselves turned and cut past us, we were often much closer. Other boats joined us, and at one point seven boats, varying from inflatables to a huge, three-story ship, surrounded the whales on three sides, very nearly boxing them in. I could see how tempting it must be to want to please eager passengers by getting as close as possible and also how difficult to keep a particular distance when the whales themselves were moving in unpredictable paths among the boats.

The naturalist teased us with a "surprise," which, after its build-up, ended up being a fin whale that had been spotted by another boat but that we weren't going to go to because it would be too hard to observe, and we'd likely only spot its blow. "We'd rather see a good show," she said, "so we'll stay here." She emphasized how lucky we were to be among the minkes. "Usually you can't see this!"

So we stayed with the minkes, looked at a lighthouse, looked with the underwater camera (relayed to video monitors) at the rich and varied life (colorful sea stars, sea urchins, waving sea plants) on the reef where the lighthouse stood, watched a big group of gray seals swim past, and were shown a hunk of feathery baleen. Then we headed up the Saguenay River while our naturalist told us about the area's glacial history and geology.

I spotted belugas ahead of us well before the naturalist brought them to our attention. When she did, she continued her lilting enthusiasm.

"We don't see them every day!" The boat slowed as it was supposed to, and her voice dropped to an amplified whisper. A portion of the pod was coming our way, and six or eight big adults, their fat backs lifting high from the water, passed us within a hundred feet. The naturalist told us about belugas being able to turn their heads, but she did not tell us about their endangered status and the special rules for minimizing disturbance.

Now, with Nadia, I confirmed what I'd heard from Michel—that this had been a poor year for spotting fin whales, which were more dispersed than usual, and the pressure to show whale-watchers whales was making targets out of belugas. I didn't think that the tour boat I'd taken had intentionally sought out belugas; most likely it had simply been conforming to the general efforts to extend the tours beyond whales to other aspects of the area's natural history and that our geology lesson in the fjord had only accidentally, or incidentally, corresponded to meeting some belugas. Nevertheless, the park people as well as the beluga recovery team were having to deal with the fact that with more focus on the belugas as a special, endangered population, more visitors would want to see them, and more educational and regulatory measures would be needed to protect them.

Nadia went over with me some of the ongoing efforts. Aside from the code of conduct/regulations to be followed by the whale-watching businesses, pending legislation would cap and reduce the number of whale-watching boats;

would provide a separate, limiting permit system for cruise ships; and would restrict all park waters to a speed limit of 25 knots. The park was moving toward a zoning plan aimed at protecting the most critical beluga habitat areas. There were also preliminary discussions about the creation of a marine protected area that might enclose waters several times the size of the marine park, or essentially all the beluga range.

"This is the challenge of working in conservation," Nadia said to me. "We're supposed to be the voice of those who can't speak."

Back in Quebec City, I spent an afternoon with two men who were instrumental in calling attention to the endangerment of the St. Lawrence belugas and who continue to contribute to their study and advocacy. At his modest office in an old bank building, I found Robert Michaud, GREMM founder and director of its research programs, with his mentor and friend, research scientist Pierre Béland, who'd come from Montreal for the day. Béland, chair of the St. Lawrence National Institute of Ecotoxicology, is the author of the 1996 book *Beluga: A Farewell to Whales,* in which he detailed his work investigating the causes of death of belugas found washed up on St. Lawrence shores. In the book, he concluded that unless humans change their ways and stop polluting the Earth, belugas as well as all other whales, and the natural systems they and we depend on, will be doomed. *Doomed* is his draconian word.

I had long wanted to meet both men and to pick their brains in their particular areas of expertise—beluga social organization in Robert's case, toxics and pathology in Pierre's. They in turn had questions about the Cook Inlet whales. Once we sat down together, we talked without a break for four hours.

With a wry half-smile, Robert told me his early work had been with fin whales and that he'd taken his first serious look at belugas in 1985, under pressure from Pierre. "OK, I'll look at your white maggots," he remembered telling Pierre. He went on to do a master's thesis in beluga distribution and movements, and his Ph.D. dissertation concerning beluga social organization would be complete in another year. It was only two years ago that he quit working seven days a week in the field during the warm months.

Robert ran down, in quick summary, some of his findings and ongoing work. All those hours identifying and tracking individual whales and their family groups had demonstrated that the sexes generally separate in the summers—with females and their young forming distinct but somewhat loosely organized communities likely based on matrilineal groupings, and males forming social groups that tend to be long-term and tightly bound. Juveniles roam widely and appear only gradually to fit into a network. The different groupings favor particular habitat areas. The genetics work, from the biopsies, will provide more information about relationships within groups. Another project—"we're quite excited about it," Robert said—will build on earlier work done with vocalizations to test whether there are differences between beluga communities, perhaps akin to the "dialects" discovered in killer whales. Hydrophones placed in three habitat areas will relay data to a research station.

"It's incredible that we can now speculate on these things," Pierre said, "when a few years ago we knew *nothing.*" Pierre, who has received a lot of press in recent years because of his work on the (ill) health of the St. Lawrence belugas and his somewhat maverick (for a scientist) style of outspokenness, was trying to hold back, to let me question Robert, who was more pressed for time and may have to leave. Still, I could see that quiet wasn't his normal state of being. With his gray hair and studious black-framed glasses, he made an authoritative presence.

We got quickly to the issue of population numbers and trends, which the two men were careful to divide. "Some questions are not good questions," Pierre said. "Like how many animals are there." Both—Pierre with a little more hesitation—accepted the new population estimate of 1,000–1,400, but neither thought that the higher numbers reflected anything other than improved counting techniques. "What I disagree with," Pierre said, "is saying there were 350 before and 1,000 now. There were probably the same number then as now."

Trends—specifically whether the St. Lawrence beluga population is now growing, shrinking, or stable—are the real issue, and trends had not been agreed upon. Once there were thousands of St. Lawrence belugas—before commercial hunting, bounties, even bomb attacks designed to reduce fishing competition. Then there were many fewer, and concern that the population was in danger of extinction led to its 1983 classification as endangered. Studies since then have not been standardized enough—or reliable enough—to determine exactly what the population is doing.

I brought up Michael Kingsley—the researcher who had tried to adjust the surveys so that they might be compared and who had concluded in 1998 that the population was slowly increasing. At that time he'd suggested that the St. Lawrence beluga status be upgraded from endangered to threatened. He had further suggested that those who insisted that the belugas were still endangered were doing so for unscientific reasons—because the funding of their research, even their organizations, depended on the whales being endangered.

Robert and Pierre bristled at Kingsley's name and at what they perceived as attacks on their professionalism as well as their organizations. They didn't find evidence, in the field or in Kingsley's work, to support his claim of an increasing population. They in fact had responded to Kingsley in the scientific literature, with an alternative analysis. If only the more recent and more reliable survey information (since 1988) was analyzed and updated to include results from 2000, they showed a flat line instead of an increase. This analysis, they emphasized to me, was reviewed and accepted by Canada's Department of Fisheries and Oceans.

"If there had been a big change," Robert said, "we'd have picked up some sign." With all the time he spent on the water, had he seen any changes? Yes, he said. "A few things have changed. We're now seeing larger groups of juveniles. And we used to see large groups of mostly adults together in the fall, but now we don't." He didn't know what either meant. There didn't seem to be more juveniles or fewer adults, just different organizations of them. "It could be simply changing habits." And although the range didn't seem to be expanding, there were reports of a few animals—usually single juveniles—showing up outside it. "Believe me," Robert said. "I'll be most happy if this population recovers."

Around the table, though, both he and Pierre were fond of using the word *precautionary.* When you don't have good data, they emphasized, the responsible track to take is to be conservative, prudent. Both thought it would be a major mistake, on the basis of preliminary and shaky data, to draw any conclusions other than that the St. Lawrence belugas were still in need of protection and more study.

We talked about ways, other than surveys, that might help get a handle on populations and trends. One way involved looking at the proportion of juveniles in the population; an increasing population will have proportionately more young animals. In earlier work, Pierre had developed an age-structured population model that placed the line between an increasing and decreasing population at the point when the population contained twenty-eight to thirty percent gray animals. A 1988 survey had found the percentage of gray animals in the St. Lawrence population to be in the range of twenty-one to twenty-six percent of the total population, suggesting a decreasing population. At present, the percentage of gray animals in the St. Lawrence population was thought to lie in the twenty-nine to thirty-two percent range, indicating (at least to Kingsley) that the population was growing, although not quickly. More recent population modeling had led Pierre to conclude that although the formula he'd come up with was valid in the long term, it was disrupted by "pulses" of calves. That is, rather than an even number of calves being born each year, he'd found that the number of calves born varies widely from year to year. "Females may find some advantage in synchronizing their reproductive activity," he told me.

Another way of getting at population numbers and trends, Robert said, was the capture-recapture method. I remembered it from a college ecology class; to estimate the number of carp in a pond, we'd netted one hundred and clipped their fins, threw them back to let them intermingle with the general population, netted another one hundred, and counted the marked fish. I wasn't too clear about the math anymore, but I got the concept. With the St. Lawrence belugas, Robert was trying to use the photo ID data. Instead of capturing or marking animals, they would track how often they saw the same ones. There were a number of challenges to this strategy, Robert admitted. "It only works if all the animals are equally likely to be 'captured.' But some animals are more shy, some are always together and some never are, and not all age and sex classes are equally 'marked', that is, identifiable." There were a lot of steps yet to be worked out to account for differences in spotting and recognizing individual animals, and Robert didn't try to oversell the system. "My faith in the final figure is not very high," he said. "I'll have to make a lot of assumptions. My guess is the conclusion will still be the same—we won't know for sure what they're doing, so we better be cautious. The information will be useful but not definitive."

We switched gears to talk about Pierre's work. For years, he'd run a stranding network that collected beluga carcasses from the St. Lawrence shores and performed necropsies. His findings, kept in what he called his "Book of the Dead," lay at the heart of his cautionary book, *Beluga*; they made a grim account of cancers and other diseases associated with compromises to the immune system. For this, the St. Lawrence beluga had become a symbol of the harm done to wildlife and the planet generally by industrial excess and irresponsibility. If in Cook Inlet both waters and belugas were relatively "clean," it may be important to know how to keep them that way—or what to watch for on the course of pollution control.

Pierre wasn't running the stranding network any longer, but, he said, "They're still finding the same stuff." Forty percent of examined adults were found to have tumors, and half of those were malignant. An unusual number of cancers were intestinal. Multiple lesions of the digestive system (fifty-three percent of animals) and mammary glands (forty-five percent of females) and numerous opportunistic viruses and infections were also found—conditions that exceeded by far anything else found in wild animal populations (except some fish from heavily polluted waters).

The dead belugas were also found to have very high levels of PCBs and other organochlorine contaminants. Levels of PCBs and DDT in the St. Lawrence belugas were twenty-five-fold higher than in belugas from Arctic Canada. Mirex—the pesticide once manufactured in a plant on Lake Ontario—was one hundred-fold higher. Heavy metals, such as lead and mercury, were also very high. Some of the most heavily contaminated animals, Pierre had found, were less than two years old—indicative of the transfer of "load" from females to their calves during pregnancy and nursing.

I knew already about the links between contaminants and animal health. In studies with laboratory and captive animals, organochlorines collectively have been shown to alter endocrine, reproductive, immune, metabolic, and neurological functions. High levels of PCBs in particular are associated with reproductive failure and depressed immune systems. Weakened immune systems make animals more vulnerable to cancers and opportunistic diseases. These are known facts; what is more difficult to discern is exactly how particular contaminants—in various concentrations and mixtures—act upon the systems of different animals at different stages of life development and in different habitats.

It certainly appeared that the levels of organochlorines and other chemicals in the St. Lawrence belugas were harming both their reproductive abilities and their physical well-being. Absolute proof between the chemical pollutants, reproductive problems, and causes of disease and death, I knew, had been harder to come by. Again, it was Michael Kingsley who had made the challenge. He had found the proportion of young belugas in the St. Lawrence to be similar to those in the Arcticsuggesting normal reproduction rates—and argued that examining only dead belugas, as Pierre had, was not going to determine much about live ones. Kingsley had also pointed out that the most harmful of the organochlorines, PCBs and Mirex, were now much better controlled, and contaminant levels had dropped in various tested species.

I pursued the Kingsley position with Pierre, partly playing devil's advocate, partly trying to understand the arguments myself. "If you only look at dead animals, well, of course they died of something."

If Pierre had been a wolf, or a dog, the fur on his back would have been standing. He was obviously defensive about having to explain, again, something that was to him as self-evidently true as the poor health of the whales he'd been working with for so many years. He collected himself before answering. "The question is whether the dead animals are representative of the population. We think they are. Of course I'm talking about belugas with diseases. I'm telling you that when they die, this is what they die of. It's crazy to say that what I'm describing is only diseases of dead animals. The live animals will eventually die, and they will die of these same things."

What else, Pierre asked, other than toxic chemicals could be causing so much cancer? In a small population, there could be a genetic variable, but no one had found any evidence of that, and such a thing was not terribly likely. It was also unlikely that anyone would ever find a given chemical that was the single cause of all the documented diseases. "There's not an easy explanation, or we would have found it a long time ago."

Another problem, of course, was that it was hard to do any kind of controlled experiment involving wild belugas. One study had taken lymphocytes (blood cells that play an important role in the immune system) from captive belugas and had exposed them to chemicals found in the St. Lawrence environment. Several of the chemicals, at concentration levels similar to those in the St. Lawrence, did indeed damage the cells and led researchers to conclude that, in a living whale, immune function would be suppressed. Additional testing found that cells were even more damaged by mixtures of chemicals.

Perhaps more telling than testing cells from captive belugas would be to evaluate the immune systems of living St. Lawrence belugas and to compare them to those of captive or Arctic animals. Such a study would require taking blood samples, which could be analyzed for immune response (how efficiently the cells function), other physiological parameters, and organochlorine levels. To get blood samples, animals would have to be captured. They would not have to be held long—just long enough to give blood—but they'd need to be immobilized. In 1996 an attempt was made to capture St. Lawrence belugas for this purpose, but the effort was unsuccessful and has not been reattempted. The St. Lawrence's characteristically deep water makes capture a challenging proposition, and the stress on an already stressed population isn't easily justified.

And what of the biopsies, now numbering 149? These only collect skin and fat, not useful for examining the immune system. They do, however, address the question of contaminants.

"Explain to me," I asked Pierre and Robert, "this issue of stratification."

Stratification was an issue, the two of them agreed, and one they didn't yet clearly understand. The beluga biopsies were showing lower levels of contaminants than the dead whales that had been previously sampled. There were, as well, differences in which chemicals were most abundant. "We're puzzled," Pierre said.

What was known, Robert said, was that stratification did occur in animal fat. That is, contaminants can vary in types and in concentrations between layers. The variation differs among species, and no one yet was very clear about how it worked in belugas. Tissues may differ in their metabolic processes at different levels; the superficial fat layers may process the chemicals or shunt them to deeper layers. "We need to obtain deeper biopsies," Robert said. There was also a problem in not generally knowing the ages of the animals they were darting as compared to the dead animals, whose ages were determined from their teeth. It would be useful to look at different layers in the old samples, but every chemical test was costly.

The stratification work that had been done by government researchers had been contradictory. One study of two dead St. Lawrence belugas found that PCB concentrations increased in the fat with depth. Meanwhile, another study of belugas hunted in Hudson Bay found organochlorine levels similar throughout the fat layers.

It's entirely possible, of course, that today's living belugas are generally less contaminated than the stranded animals (older and dead) analyzed earlier, animals that would have been living during the 1960s and 1970s when the St. Lawrence was at its toxic peak. Seals, seabirds, and eels in the St. Lawrence are "cleaner" today than in the past. In eels, a significant prey of the belugas, PCB levels have dropped sixty-eight percent since the 1980s. One study that compared organochlorines in dead St. Lawrence belugas from the 1980s and 1990s found that, in males, concentrations were lower in the 1990s. The trend was less clear for females, in which levels are affected by reproductive history. In any case, belugas, with their long lives and multiple food sources, will not "clean up" in any short order. One bioaccumulation model suggests that two generations, or more than twenty years, will be required to observe major changes in PCB levels in belugas.

After our afternoon together, I dropped Pierre back at the Quebec City train station. I went home to Alaska and reread his book. In it, he wrote about finding an old barrel of beluga oil, from an animal hunted in the 1950s, and of analyzing it for contaminants. He'd been shocked when the lab results showed eight parts per million for PCBs and twenty-nine parts per million for DDT. Serious pollution and its incorporation into the bodies of living creatures have been with us for more than fifty years—a long time in one sense, but a short one in terms of opportunity to learn how that pollution may play out in our natural systems, bodies, and future generations.

Today, the production and use of most of the most hazardous organo-chlorines have ended in North America, and the dumping of contaminants into waterways has been reduced. The Great Lakes, for example—from which came forty percent of the St. Lawrence's contaminants—have undergone a substantial cleanup. Elsewhere in the world greater controls over chemical use and disposal are now being exerted. Still, contaminants stored in marine sediments, washing out of agricultural lands, and going up in smoke continue to feed into the system. When cleanup efforts have gotten expensive, they have slowed. In the case of the Great Lakes, they've slowed to a standstill. Recent rollbacks in environmental protections, driven by conservative, industry-influenced politics, are a concern.

I gathered a few more dates and statistics. In 1976 a fourth of human breast milk tested in the United States contained PCB concentrations higher than what was legally allowed (2.5 parts per million) in formula. Between 1950 and 1991, the incidence of cancer in the United States rose forty-nine percent; forty percent of the U.S. population will contract cancer sometime within their lifetimes. In 1994 in Lake Superior between seventy-six and eighty-nine percent of PCBs came from the air; that is, air deposition in the Great Lakes is now one of the major sources of chemical contamination there. Seventy-five thousand chemicals are in use in the United States, and less than three percent have been tested for carcinogenicity.

Cook Inlet is not the St. Lawrence. Cook Inlet and its belugas have not suffered the huge chemical assaults that have been the fate of that other waterway and its inhabitants.

Still, there are lessons. What goes up in smoke in Chicago can come down near Anchorage, and what's flushed by Cook Inlet tides goes here, there, and everywhere. There's plenty yet to learn about cause and effect, about ecological roots and relationships. That learning is going on in many quarters and minds, in small pieces that eventually—sometimes only after decades—add up.

From the St. Lawrence there was also a lesson about recovery. Perhaps that beluga remnant wasn't doomed. Perhaps it would recover; perhaps it was already moving in that direction. The effort was aided not just by the banning of certain chemicals but by a plan of many parts, many in dividual objectives and acts. Habitat protection was central. It was not a perfect plan, Robert and Pierre told me. It was useful, certainly, to have goals and coordination, but there had never been enough money. They stressed again and again to me: With such a fragile population, it was important in all decisions to be precautionary.

7

ADAPTATION

Joel Blatchford's directions to his home in Kasilof were hard to follow, but after a few clarifying calls from my cell phone to his, I finally ended up down a dirt road toward a campground, and there was Joel, in the yard beside a small off-white house, waving at me. Joel's the kind of man who looks big, and it's only when I got out of my car and stood next to him that I realized he's barely taller than I am. He has dark, lively eyes beneath straight dark hair and a thin moustache with a goatee. Now he grinned and said, like a kid, "I know you."

Joel and his wife Dj had only recently moved from Anchorage to the Kenai Peninsula and now, in October 2000, lived in a rural setting practically on the bank of a major salmon river. Under a leaden sky, with fallen leaves skittering over the tourist-deserted road and a smell like coming snow in the air, it was a lovely, peaceful kind of place.

I had known Joel peripherally for a few years; he tended to be a dominant, or at least outspoken, presence at various beluga meetings. He was now forty-five years old, a retired heavy equipment operator who had taken on the beluga cause in a big way: the sole individual to have aligned with the six environmental organizations in pursuit of an endangered species listing. As a former hunter of the Cook Inlet belugas and an Inupiat Eskimo, he had strong feelings about the beluga situation, which he was happy to share, with anyone, anytime. Once inside the house, past his chrome-covered Big Dog motorcycle (parked in the living room and gleamingly well cared for), he immediately showed me the recently released environmental impact statement—required before the federal government could regulate Native hunting—and began critiquing its deficiencies.

I had never met Dj; I had only heard that she rode a motorcycle and was Joel's "new" wife, as opposed to the "old," divorced one. She greeted me warmly and said she'd just be working on the computer in a corner of the room while Joel and I talked, but very soon she joined us at the table to elaborate upon Joel's points. I could see that Joel had made a match with someone who believed passionately in both him and his cause. Dj let me know that she was also Inupiat (along with Athabaskan and French) and that she'd spent her early years learning the traditional ways with grandparents. Her grandfather and great-grandfather had both been beluga hunters.

Joel was, by strength of personality and public performance, the spokesperson for Anchorage beluga hunters, even as he aligned himself with environmentalists. He'd grown up in Anchorage and, starting at age three, had hunted belugas with his father, Percy. He no longer hunted for, apparently, various reasons. I'd heard him say he had stopped because he knew the belugas were overhunted and it was necessary to protect what remained; I'd heard him say he was afraid to eat them anymore because of all the pollutants in the inlet; and I'd also heard that he had to give up hunting (and equipment operating) because of a bad back. In addition, Percy's health had recently begun to fail, and the two could no longer hunt together. I'd met Percy at a couple of beluga meetings too, although not recently. The elder Blatchford was a kind man, easily approachable, and we had spoken about sea lions in the upper inlet, where they are generally not thought to appear and where we had both seen them on occasion.

I'd first learned of Joel and Percy in 1994 when they were the subjects of a lengthy Sunday feature in the *Anchorage Daily News,* "Whalers of the City: Little-known Cook Inlet Hunt Targets Belugas." I'd been surprised that Native beluga hunters had gone so public with their activities. There, splashed across the front page of the state's urban newspaper and continued inside, were full-color photos of a whale being shot and butchered. I was fascinated with the story and pleased with the window it opened into Native life, but I also wondered if other readers would be shocked to see one of their favorite animals turned into food. If Alaskans were generally supportive of Native subsistence as a concept, they also tended to think that subsistence occurred in villages and the vast country around them, away from urban centers. And whales—whales were not the same as, say, moose, which everyone expected to be eaten.

Anchorage beluga hunting had been, until then, low-profile—if not exactly a well-kept secret, then at least something that, like much of Native life, had operated in a realm beyond the sight of most Alaskans. I understood, later, that other Anchorage hunters were not pleased with the attention the article brought. They may also have thought that the Blatchfords were, in a very un-Native way, drawing too much attention to themselves.

That attention had come before most people knew there was a beluga conservation issue. Joel and his dad, back then, had been part of the invisible problem. As members of the Eskimo diaspora, living in Anchorage outside traditional tribal structures, they were maintaining subsistence patterns without knowing who else was doing the same and what cooperation might be called for. They fed a lot of people in those days, Joel told me. Now, Joel was trying to be part of the solution. I was interested in whether some of that solution was coming from—could come from—traditional Native sources, or whether Alaska's urban Natives were like the rest of us now, detached from our places and their care. So many of us were trying to share the commons, but we were not of one tribe.

In the cinnamon-smelling house, I asked Joel whether the move to Kasilof had anything to do with the beluga issue. It did, he said. "We moved here to get away from all the guff I'm getting." The "guff," from other Natives, had intensified with the endangered species lawsuit. According to Joel, it wasn't the Anchorage hunters—"the Eskimos"who were upset with him but rather "the Indians" from the villages around the inlet.

I could think of only one very public dispute in which Natives had been on opposing sides. In the debate over opening the Arctic National Wildlife Range to oil drilling, the Kaktovik Inupiat Eskimos (coastal people whose lives look to the ocean and the bowhead whale and who have economically benefited from North Slope oil development) had taken the pro-opening position, while the Gwich'in Athabaskan Indians (inland people whose lives look to caribou, the calving grounds of which would be invaded) had taken the keep-it-wild position. Now, what was being called "the Indian-Eskimo War" over Cook Inlet belugas was making Native leaders uncomfortable. If, in comparison to the refuge conflict, the beluga issue was less grand and more esoteric, leaving most observers unaware of the racial element, that created its own set of problems. The *Voice of the Times,* the editorial half-page that appeared in the *Anchorage Daily News* as a relic of an earlier newspaper war, was so clueless regarding the beluga depletion that it blamed the poor village of Tyonek, which took no more than two belugas in a year, for the entire 1998 estimated kill of seventy-eight Cook Inlet belugas.

In any case, the situation was awkward. The eight Cook Inlet tribes, excepting Tyonek, didn't even hunt belugas—at least not in recent times. Eskimos from elsewhere had come into their territory and not only hunted "their" animals without permission but had taken so many that the whales had been depleted, the very thing that Natives say that, in their hunting practices, they don't do. The tribal "Indians" were embarrassed at what had happened—that they had been made to look like poor stewards of their resources—and they also didn't want to lose their own rights to hunt belugas. The people of Tyonek were trying to maintain that tradition, and others may want to return to it sometime. For Joel to act as a spokesperson for beluga hunters didn't sit well with the tribes. When, by participating in the lawsuit, he raised the profile of the entire situation and the enmity of corporate and municipal interests that included those of the Cook Inlet villages and their business partners, he antagonized them even more.

Joel's role, mixed as it was with both inter-Native and environmental politics, was sometimes confusing. As the three of us talked, I began to glimpse the global scale of his concerns. He and Dj were advocates, all at once, for belugas, beluga hunters, Native (especially Eskimo) rights, a healthy environment, and respect for traditional ways. Joel had accepted that overhunting was the main cause of the belugas' population plunge, but he was also concerned about other threats to them—primarily from pollution. And although Joel and Dj both wanted hunting rights to be preserved in the long run, they didn't think there should be any hunting until the population began to recover. When hunting rights were restored, they wanted Eskimo hunters to have equal opportunity with Indians. "If you cut us off, you're taking away something we've had forever," Joel said. If you went back far enough, Eskimos had lived in Cook Inlet before the Indians came down out of the interior, he said. Eskimos taught the Indians how to hunt belugas. And just recently, they'd taught them again, after years in which few Cook Inlet villagers had attempted to hunt belugas. "There was a gap there. They were trying to hunt, and we had to show them how. We got the belugas for them."

For the summer just past, the National Marine Fisheries Service had signed an agreement with the Cook Inlet Marine Mammal Council—the group that represented the region's villages in marine mammal hunting matters—that allowed for one beluga to be taken by the people of Tyonek. Joel had been upset that the Anchorage Eskimo hunters had been excluded from the negotiations, and he had been displeased too that any hunt was going forward. In a letter to the *Anchorage Daily News,* he'd written, "We, the whale hunters of this city, have stood down and backed away from hunting belugas and taken our stand to protect these whales. Now we shall be punished because we are not considered a tribe." In the end, for a variety of reasons (a requirement to give NMFS seventy-two hours notice before a scheduled hunt, working around hunters' day jobs and fishing schedules, bad weather), Tyonek had not hunted.

Joel and his father had once been active with the marine mammal council, in the days before it had reorganized around the tribes. Now, Joel kept his distance. "They don't talk to me. They don't want me to be involved," he said. A year before, frustrated that the Anchorage hunters were cut out of the talks with NMFS, Joel had led about fifteen hunters to organize as the Alaska Native Marine Mammal Hunter Committee. As a competing group, it asked for recognition to negotiate its own agreement with NMFS. The agency, which didn't want to have to choose between organizations, for a while contemplated signing multiple agreements. Joel and the hunters, "for the sake of the whales," had since backed off, but the animosity had not diminished.

"All of us honored the stand-down," Dj said, meaning that the Anchorage hunters had first voluntarily agreed not to hunt in 1999 and then had complied with the hunting moratorium the following season. "All the Eskimos made the commitment." But if and when there was going to be hunting again, they wanted the same chance as the Indians. Later, over the phone, she clarified the issue for me. "Whether we hunt or not isn't the question. It's protecting our rights to hunt." Joel, she said, "is the leader of the hunters, and they all acknowledge that. We're just going to keep fighting for what's right."

I thought the "guff" resulting from the beluga controversy—and not just from Indians—must have been discouraging. Joel had separated himself from the Native community at large, and from all sorts of business interests, by joining with conservationists in the endangered species suit. Why, I asked him, had he decided to go in on that? Did he feel comfortable being so closely aligned with people who were, after all, somewhat suspect in the Native community for caring so much about animals and wilderness? I knew that Joel, with other Native hunters and tribal leaders, had been courted by the conservation groups, whose case was strengthened by his participation.

"I'm doing it for the people," he said, apparently quite clear about his mission. "I like being part of the suit because we're helping the whales. Now they're [the National Marine Fisheries Service] doing the studies. They have to start doing it the right way. They don't have enough research, and they were going to allow a hunt. You can see there aren't very many." Joel, as one of the hunters invited by NMFS to go along on survey flights of the inlet, had gone several times and kept his own count of belugas. "I've never seen more than 150."

Dj added, "Joel's family comes from a lot of healing people. We want to work this so we can move in a healing direction, to help the belugas. Why would we want to kill off our meat when they could build up and be enough for anyone?"

Was that naïve, I wondered to myself, to imagine there could ever be enough Cook Inlet belugas "for anyone"? Wasn't that precisely the problem—that the anyones and everyones were too many? I was doubtful that, realistically, the three of us would ever again see more than a token amount of beluga hunting allowed in the inlet—certainly nothing on the scale of what had occurred in the 1990s or that would begin to meet the needs of all local Natives. I thought again of the meetings where officials had pled with the Natives to "find a mechanism" to control hunting. I'd heard from the same people, again and again, about the need to keep Natives on board. It wasn't clear to me if hunters were, in fact, finding a way to agree on collective action.

We talked about the lawsuit. Joel was convinced the Endangered Species Act was the way to go, the only way that could broadly help the belugas. The belugas needed habitat protection, assured food supplies, evaluation of other threats. The sooner the beluga population recovered, the sooner some level of hunting could be restored.

If subsistence use and a healthy environment were the only Native interests to be considered, Joel's backing of the endangered species suit may have gone unchallenged. The Cook Inlet villages, which have the most long-term interest in their environment, would have had good reason to join him. But subsistence and good health, I'd learned, weren't the only interests being considered. The villages around the inlet, and their corporate shareholders, had multiple and overarching economic interests that had nothing in common with, and were sometimes in direct conflict with, subsistence use. Tyonek's village corporation, as one example, either owned or held investments in a port, an oil field construction and supply company, a hunting and fishing lodge, a logging business, and numerous commercial fishing operations.

Joel, individual plaintiff, was about as popular as a snail darter in the way of a dam or a spotted owl nested in a big old tree.

Our talk drifted back to Joel's history of beluga hunting. On the wall at one end of the room, I couldn't help noticing, hung a fancy wooden plaque laminated with the masthead from the Anchorage paper and the 1994 photo of Joel with the dead whale. A company that made plaques, Joel said, had made it for him, free, because they liked the picture so much. Indeed, it's an impressive photo, with Joel standing proudly on the bank, the white whale drawn up in the foreground, a rope around its flukes. As in a standard hunting or fishing photo, the animal is emphasized, magnified by the lens, made to seem larger than life.

The newspaper story, which I'd reviewed prior to our meeting, covered a hunt from the time the reporter and photographer met Percy at his Anchorage home to the time, the next day, when they all returned to town. After launching Percy's 18-foot boat from the ramp in Anchorage's industrial heart, they'd motored thirty miles west to the mouth of the Susitna River. There, they met dozens of beluga whales. Percy, driving the boat, cut a large white one from the pod and herded it into shallow water, and Joel shot and harpooned it. (Their harpoon attached by line to a float made from the most modern of materials—a cluster of plastic orange juice jugs.) The father and son then dragged the whale up to the bank and, standing in hip boots in the shallow water, stripped it of its muktuk, blubber, meat, flippers, and flukes, to pack into coolers. The carcass was returned to the inlet.

The reporter wrote, "Among Anchorage's 240,000 residents there are perhaps two or three dozen subsistence whale hunters.... Few non-Natives know that the hunters exist. Yet in Anchorage's growing Native communities, beluga whale hunts have become a source of food and an urban adaptation of village subsistence culture. The hunts are an important cog in an underground barter and cash economy reaching between the city and dozens of villages." Beluga muktuk and meat, he wrote, fed people in Anchorage and were also sent to friends and relatives in distant villages, in exchange for other Native foods—seal oil, caribou meat, fish—that Anchorage Natives desired.

By 1994, Percy had been hunting belugas in Cook Inlet for fifty years. Originally from Elim (the same Norton Sound village Charles Saccheus, who had helped with the Cook Inlet tagging operation, was from), Percy had come to the Anchorage area as a World War II draftee. He stayed with the military, serving in the Air Force for thirty years as an at-sea rescue paramedic. His mis-

sions took him from the polar icecap to Central American jungles; he made 326
parachute jumps; and although he had finished only three grades of school, he
helped write the Air Force Arctic survival manual. After his retirement as a master sergeant, he worked for ten years for the state, driving heavy equipment.

Despite what may have looked from the outside like a life integrated into
the American mainstream, Percy stuck with many traditional ways. From the
beginning, he kept a skiff to take him onto Cook Inlet for hunting and fishing, he established camps along the Susitna, and he generally maintained the
subsistence ways he'd grown up with. Even in his 70s, after his wife's death
and after three of his four children had moved away, he still hunted one or two
belugas each year with Joel. He also went after seals and land mammals like
moose and caribou, fished for salmon and halibut, and picked berries. All his
life, his efforts fed himself, his family, relatives, and friends.

Joel, the article said, had "gone down the wrong path in his younger days"
and "had had little interest in hunting or his Inupiat roots. Both finally helped
save him." I asked him about this. All he wanted to say about it was that he'd
been an angry teenager and kept getting into trouble, especially in school, but
that hunting finally "brought me back into survival mode." It was the elemental act of going out and getting food and in the process learning, by watching
and doing, tenets of Inupiat right behavior—patience, respect, cooperation,
sharing—that helped Joel define a positive role for himself. Joel has never been
to his father's village—never especially wanted to—but he was thinking that
he'd like to go, soon, with his father. Percy had made a regular habit of visiting
his home ground, staying in touch with his people there.

In one photo with the article Percy is cutting a slab of muktuk into small
pieces. The partially filled pot next to him was later set on a Coleman stove
and boiled, and the two hunters took a break from butchering to eat. "High
protein," Percy told the reporter. "Keeps you warm." From where they butchered and ate, they could see sunlight reflecting off picture windows in the
swanky hillside part of Anchorage.

Meanwhile, another Inupiat family from Anchorage had taken another
beluga nearby and had put up tents at a camp along the shore. Percy and Joel's
camp was farther up, on a slough reachable only on a high tide. That night
they stayed in a duck-hunting shack, where they ate whale steaks with boiled
potatoes and pilot bread.

Absent from the butchering and bounty, the article noted, were any internal organs. Both Percy and Joel told the reporter that they worried about
toxins that can bioaccumulate at the top of a food chain.

Today, Joel continues to worry about pollutants and the health effects of eating beluga and other Native foods. Overhunting, he emphasized again to me, wasn't the only problem for belugas. He believes Cook Inlet suffers from oil pollution and other insults from people and industries—what the scientists call anthropogenic factors—and that an endangered listing for the belugas would force NMFS at long last to document those effects. "Everything in the inlet is going down," he said. "There used to be 800 seals along the Susitna. Salmon have dropped so much. We got to do this research *right now*. We told the researchers for years [that there were problems, that fish and marine mammal populations were falling, that they were unhealthy], but they kept saying, 'We can't do anything, they're not threatened or endangered.'"

Dj nodded her agreement. "To blame it totally on the hunters isn't right. The oil people I've talked to totally blame the hunters. They say they're not doing any harm. Yet the numbers keep going down."

Joel jumped up and brought me two reports—*Alaska Native Cancer Update 1984–96* and *Alaska Pollution Issues*. There were too many toxics in the environment, he said, and they were poisoning people. "If you keep eating and eating and you know your fatty tissues are loading up, how long before you explode? All our food now is sick. All subsistence is going to end up in the museum." He opened one of the reports and pointed to a chart. "Look, 360 parts per billion. That's terrible."

Dj mentioned that one of her nephews had a rare cancer.

I knew it was true that Alaska Natives had elevated and increasing cancer rates compared to other Alaskans and Americans, but I also knew that many of those cancers were attributed to behaviors—especially tobacco use. Forty-five percent of Alaska Natives smoke, and smokeless tobacco use by Natives is four times the national rate. Joel smoked.

There had been various studies regarding the health of subsistence foods, particularly following the 1989 *Exxon Valdez* oil spill, but to my knowledge, none had suggested that traditional foods should be avoided. Except for the obvious, of course—such as mussel beds coated with oil.

I was not a toxicologist; I certainly could not make an independent judgment about what level of what contaminant was healthy or unhealthy. I had to believe the experts. Joel wasn't a toxicologist either, but he had drawn his own conclusions. I was also seeing that his approach to the subject of beluga health was different than mine—that there was, in fact, a duality to consider. There was the concern about what might harm belugas—parasites, disease, contaminant levels—and there was another concern about what was in belugas that might harm humans who ate them. An emphasis on the whales didn't necessarily address human concerns. I was thinking of management goals that would discourage the take of female belugas and direct hunting to older males, less essential to building a population. From an eating point of view, mature males, with the likelihood of higher contaminant levels, would be less desirable.

Dj said, "I'm not eating our Native foods anymore because it's too contaminated."

I looked up from my note-taking. "Really?"

Joel said, "Since 1995, I haven't eaten any subsistence foods."

Dj said, "Instead of seal oil, now I substitute olive oil and soy sauce. But I miss the taste. I love herring eggs on needles, but I gave it up."

"But you must eat salmon," I said. Alaska's wild salmon were famous for being healthful. Salmon marketers always make a big point of the health benefits of eating fish from Alaska's clean, cold waters—and back the claims up with tests showing very low levels of contaminants like mercury that are so pervasive elsewhere.

Joel shook his head. "Salmon's part of the food chain."

I didn't know what to say. I felt fortunate, myself, to be able to eat an Alaskan diet of salmon and halibut, caribou, local potatoes, berries I pick in the woods and fields. Those foods were without a doubt healthier than farmed fish, feedlot cattle, chickens raised in cages, fruits imported from countries that don't regulate pesticide use, packaged foods that had all the life and nutrition processed out of them, sugars. That Joel and Dj lived along a major salmon stream and didn't eat salmon seemed wrong. There was something unjust—not about the condition of our front-yard foods but with the way information got to people to guide their choices.

Joel's father, I knew, suffered from diabetes, an all-too-common (and increasing) disease in Native Americans and Alaska Natives. Diabetes has two risk factors—genetics and lifestyle. Natives who have substituted modernity—that is, physical inactivity, obesity, and diets high in junk food sugars and fats—for traditional foods and ways are highly vulnerable to diabetes and its dreaded body break-downs.

I didn't say any of this—not about most cancers resulting from smoking, not about knowing for a fact that Cook Inlet's salmon were among the healthiest foods on the planet, not about the pollution and food safety reports I'd read and been assured by, not about the data specific to beluga contaminant loads that both Joel and I had seen presented at meetings. I also didn't mention the salvaging of dead belugas the year before—the only Cook Inlet beluga muktuk that had been available for two years now. I'd been reviewing that newspaper clipping too—about how a dozen people, Indians and Eskimos both, had worked together to strip a whale that washed up along Turnagain Arm after the big 1999 stranding. One of the women who helped with the butchering and then drove around town with plastic bags of muktuk and fat had said she felt like Santa Claus. She said a lot of the elderly people she delivered to cried because they were so happy, and one old man was so afraid he might miss her that he waited outside his house for two hours.

Later, I'd seek out more information regarding the health of subsistence foods. There was, it turned out, very little that was Alaska-specific. One government report concluded that Cook Inlet seafoods were "nutritionally sound" with "contamination concentrations generally . . . lower than or within the range of other seafoods and commercial foods." It did, however, find certain hydrocarbons and PCBs "higher than comparison data." And it did *not* test marine mammals or seabirds and their eggs, foods most likely to biomagnify contaminants.

A different kind of study, of maternal blood in women from Canada, Greenland, Iceland, and Norway, showed that Inuit women dependent on marine mammals, fish, and seabird eggs had much higher levels of PCBs and DDT than women who ate "European" diets. Breast-fed Inuit babies from northern Quebec, in yet another study, were found to have many times more infectious diseases—possibly associated with compromised immune systems—than babies elsewhere. It was a terrible irony that so many dangerous chemicals ended up in the "pristine" Arctic, far from their manufacture and use, to accumulate in marine mammals particularly poor at degrading them—and where, furthermore, lived people most in need of eating their local foods.

Alaska Native infants, like those evaluated in Quebec, also suffer from high rates of infections, something another report said "may be due to a complicated set of factors," potentially including exposure to PCBs. That report emphasized the nutritional value of traditional foods and said, "It is not always clear what public health measures should be taken to reduce the exposure of populations who rely on traditional foods. . . . The goal of public health actions should be to reduce exposure to contaminants without threatening the social, cultural, spiritual, and physical well-being that is connected to collecting, sharing, and consuming traditional foods."

Later, too, I would look up killer whale and beluga PCB levels to compare them. People don't eat killer whales—which is a good thing because whales dying in Puget and Prince William Sounds were found with PCB levels at 250, 370, and an astounding 661 parts per million. By comparison, the mean PCB level for males among the St. Lawrence belugas was seventy-six parts per million, in Alaska's Arctic belugas five parts per million, and in Cook Inlet belugas one and a half parts per million. The U.S. FDA standard for PCBs in fish for human consumption is two parts per million.

I didn't want to start a debate about food choices with Joel and Dj. Still, I would keep wondering. Why wasn't necessary information—not only about dangers but also about what was good and healthy and just—getting to people who needed it? Can't we reach some common understandings of what things are and mean? Or does everyone have his or her own reality, based on a belief system that's like faith? You don't argue with religious people about God. How could I convince someone that 360 parts per billion of some chemical was OK if he believed it was not? How did I know that it was OK? There are, in fact, no safe dosages of carcinogens. And dioxins, those ubiquitous organochlorines that come from the production of other chemicals and from the burning of plastics, are capable of altering biological processes at a few parts per trillion.

I remembered Joel, at a beluga meeting, saying that he'd thrown away entire belugas because they were sick, diseased, their fat "all runny." The biologists, without samples, hadn't known what to say. Animals do get sick from time to time. Fat could look runny at a certain time of year, or at a stage in development or the whale's reproductive cycle, or because it was bruised, or who knew why? I remembered as well his father insisting that he'd once caught a whale that was full of radioactivity, that he'd in fact had it tested for radioactivity. But where was the record of that? It had, according to Joel, burned up in a house fire.

I did not, not for a second, think that either Joel or his father had fabricated any of their claims, to deflect attention from hunting or for any other reason. Whatever they said, I knew they believed. And they were right to be wary of the many pollution sources feeding into Cook Inlet. Military lands adjacent to Cook Inlet are known to be contaminated with toxics; the Eagle River Flats, draining into Knik Arm right where so many belugas gathered, was the site of a major cleanup after thousands of waterfowl died from white phosphorus poisoning. Then, water quality sampling at Ship Creek, Anchorage's urban (and salmon fishing) creek, found DDT. It wasn't a lot, but it was still an active form of DDT, suggesting that either the chemical, which hadn't been used in thirty years, took a long time to break down in the cold, or that it was leaking afresh from somewhere along the creek where it had been spilled or stored.

Still, I remembered, uncomfortably, all the times at meetings that Native people had expressed their concerns about toxics in the Cook Inlet ecosystem, toxics affecting belugas and their own health, and no one, except the oil industry lobbyists with an agenda of their own, challenged them on their assertions. Most uncomfortably, I recalled my environmentalist friends—who didn't support the claims, not exactly, but who nevertheless didn't disagree with them. They told the Native people that they shared their concerns about toxics and that the way to address toxics was to pursue endangered species protection for the whales. They used health concerns to support their own goals. They wanted to stop oil pollution—some critics say oil *development*— in the inlet; they wanted more than primary treatment of Anchorage's sewage; they wanted human activities in general to be more closely scrutinized for their effects on the marine environment.

I, too, thought that Cook Inlet should be less a dumping ground, more a respected habitat for all of us. Of course it would be better for it to be cleaner, as it would be better in general, everywhere, if we would use less, dump less, waste less, keep our waterways and oceans as pure as possible. The inlet should not be degraded as human population and industrial use grow, in the familiar pattern we've seen in all the other places from which we've come. But right now, relative to the rest of the world, Cook Inlet was not a danger zone. It was wrong to encourage people, especially people who depended on—or had depended on—its foods, to think so.

Joel and Dj, although they may have stopped eating subsistence foods, remained deeply entwined throughout their lives and passions with whales and other sea animals. Before I left, they showed me their matching wedding rings—shaped from platinum to be kissing belugas, with green diamonds as blowholes. Dj insisted that Joel show me his belt buckle, which he had carved from walrus ivory: a large, fat, nicely detailed gray whale. Joel disappeared and returned with a fur jacket. I immediately recognized the luxuriously dense fur as sea otter.

Sea otters were the wealth that brought Russians to Alaska and for which Chinese royalty once paid fortunes. Sea otters were so coveted by invading hunters that Alaska's Native people were enslaved to secure all they could get, in every bay and passage along the state's long southern and western reach, until the species came perilously close to extinction, until no more could be found to take. They've since made a remarkable comeback—except that, only recently, the population in the Aleutians has taken a dive perhaps related to killer whale predation, itself related to the decline in sea lions, which is attributed to food stress due to ecosystem changes and fisheries development. Everything connects, as Native people have been pointing out for a very long time.

Not so long ago, in the 1980s, when Alaska Natives petitioned to be allowed to take sea otters for subsistence purposes—to make from their fur crafts and clothing—there were those who argued against it because there was little in the historic record to prove that Natives had ever made such use of sea otter fur or because, at the least, whatever traditional use there had been had been lost for generations, and therefore what right did today's Natives have to it? The historic record, of course, had not begun until Russian fur traders had transformed sea otter furs into commercial wealth. Who could think that, before that happened, such a fur would not have had great utility, not to mention value, among those who lived with otters? As for the argument about long-broken tradition—wasn't this precisely what the beluga hunters were afraid of? If they gave up hunting the whales, would they ever be allowed to hunt them again, even when the whales increased to numbers that could justify a take?

To be fair, those opposing Native take of sea otters had a perhaps not unreasonable fear that sea otter hunting might once again become an industry, with Natives taking them less for personal use and crafts than, for example, roughly sewing a couple of skins together and claiming they'd made a blanket, in order to simply sell skins, as might have been allowed under broad interpretations of the Marine Mammal Protection Act's Native exemption. Subsistence sea otter take is today monitored by a commission that assures Native participation in management decisions, and the take is relatively small.

I admired Joel's jacket, which was not only gorgeous, with blond streaks running symmetrically down the front, but which he had sewn himself, from pelts of sea otters he'd hunted twenty years earlier in Kachemak Bay. Against the sweep of my palm, the fur was unbelievably soft. Joel held the jacket open and insisted I try it on. The weight of it, and the still-cool silk lining against my wrists, reminded me how rich we truly were—in the wealth of a place where, still, people can make a living and a life from the land and the sea, can make beauty, can prosper without destroying the system that provides.

Dj had something for me too, pressed into my hand. It was a memory she'd written about being taken beluga hunting on Norton Sound by her grandfather and great-grandfather when she was a tiny child. In it she recalled the bouncing of the boat on waves, harpoons in the boat's bottom, a rope whirling out with a "ropy-wheezing sound," shouts, and a smell of blood. "None would go to waste," she wrote. "We believed the great Beluga gave itself up to feed us with empty tables. So it is a circle of life."

8

THE BEACH PEOPLE

I kept thinking, *Indian time.*

I wouldn't have voiced the words; they are too often used by white people in a derogatory sense, implying that Natives had no sense of time, no respect for being on time or doing things in a timely manner. The implication was *lazy,* or *irresponsible.* That wasn't what I thought about my wait in Tyonek. Instead, I appreciated that, as a generalization if not a stereotype, Native people are more relaxed about time than are white people. Village life has a different pace, a different timetable, another form of attendance, even when what's being attended to isn't the wait for an animal to present itself or the tide to bring fish, this day or another. Time moves as it will. That being in the world without being driven by clocks was something I valued about Natives I knew, about village life, even about the life I assumed at my fish camp.

I might have known when I checked in with Peter Merryman, the village council president, at nine that morning—when the council meeting was supposed to begin, and he was the only one who had yet arrivedand he told me to return at 10:30, that that didn't mean that I would appear before the council at that time. I waited in the big round room that was the center of the Tribal Center, outside the door to the council room, past noon, past one o'clock. Just around the corner, at the school, the three teachers expected me to work with their classes; twice I ran back to reschedule.

I was not in a hurry myself. I'd given myself time, three May days in Tyonek, so that I could get more than the briefest glimpse of life there. Now, as I waited, I watched a stream of village residents, the women trailed by small children, pass through the room. A representative of the Alaska Department of Fish and Game had come for the day with the paperwork people needed for the subsistence king salmon fishery scheduled to begin the following week. The fishery is a special one, allowed just along Tyonek beaches, that permitted each household to catch seventy fish for their own use and for sharing with others. This fishery is different from the later commercial fishery that some villagers also participate in, and it recognizes the community's long relationship with the big fish that are the first, and the fattiest, of the five salmon species that return each summer to Cook Inlet streams. I had to remind myself that, as much as the fishery was accepted as an integral part of Tyonek life in 2001, it hadn't always been so. Overharvesting of king salmon by the inlet's commercial fisheries had led to a closure of all king salmon fishing between 1964 and 1980, and it took a lawsuit to return the subsistence fishery to Tyonek after the runs recovered and sport fishing was reinstated. Those years of closure had been tough ones for Tyonek, not only for the loss of food but also for the generational break in the teaching of traditional skills and values.

The Fish and Game man, Ron Stanek, greeted by name many who stopped at his table; he clearly had a friendly and long-term relationship with them. For many years his job had included monitoring and documenting subsistence use. I knew Ron from beluga meetings and had read and reread various of his papers, including one I carried with me, "The Subsistence Use of Beluga Whale in Cook Inlet by Alaska Natives, 1993." I listened to him inquire after people's families and how their winters had been, and I heard one woman, passing parts of an orange to toddlers playing under the table, say, "I want to get Jet-skis. We tried them in Hawaii. They were so fun." I listened to another woman tell him she'd been down at her camp on the beach for the weekend, and someone had spotted a bear by the creek.

Waiting, I read notices on the bulletin board and walls: "Applying for a Federal Job," "Vocational Rehabilitation: Are You Eligible?," "A Summary of VA Benefits." I studied the banner over a doorway *Tebughna of Tyonek,* which I knew meant Beach People of Tyonek—and recalled that anthropologists had concluded that "beach people" was so basic a name that the Tebughna must have been the first Dena'ina Athabaskans to have settled on the inlet and taken up ways that looked to the sea as well as to the forests and lakes.

Against another wall, I looked at framed photos of people and awards and plaques, none of them recent. I visited with the tribe's accountant, down from Anchorage, also waiting, and with the tribe's attorney, also down from Anchorage and finally emerged from the meeting room; we compared the ways we brined, smoked, and canned salmon. When Ron Stanek was free for a moment, I spoke to him.

Although the state Department of Fish and Game lacks management authority over belugas, which, like all marine mammals, "belong" to federal jurisdiction, Ron had been the one, earlier, to monitor harvest levels and to suggest they may be too high. Now, Ron felt the halt in beluga hunting was, while necessary, unfortunate—especially for Tyonek. "They never killed many whales," he said. "And they have the longest standing tradition. I think it's *tragic.* For the Anchorage hunters too, the ones who were conscientious. It's also a tragedy that everyone couldn't get together to control the harvest and refine the techniques." He shook his head. "I guess it was unavoidable in that regard. We never even knew who all the hunters were."

The hunting moratorium held out the prospect for a limited take under a negotiated agreement, and Tyonek hoped to be able to hunt a beluga in the approaching summer. Peter Merryman had recently been elected by the Cook Inlet tribes to be the new chair of the Cook Inlet Marine Mammal Council, the organization torn up by fighting between tribes and the Anchorage hunters and still expected to work out with the National Marine Fisheries Service whether there should be a hunt and, if so, under what terms. Ron wished the village hunters well, but his face, drawn tight, and his emphasis of the word *tragic,* suggested he wasn't feeling very optimistic. He knew too much about Tyonek's past to imagine an easy adjustment.

Although my fish camp lay just down the coast, maybe fifty miles away—no great distance in Alaskan terms—I had never been to Tyonek before. As a west-side-of-the-inlet village accessible only by small plane and adventurous boaters, Tyonek is not on the way to anywhere else. Although a few of its residents had recently begun doing some hunting and sport fish guiding, the village did not have accommodations for travelers and did not expect tourists. Tyonek had, in fact, a reputation for being isolationist, for not being particularly welcoming to white people. Years before, in the early 1980s, the village had attempted to ban non-Natives from living there. The precise situation had

had to do with a particular school employee, a housing conflict, personalities, but it had looked ugly in the papers—a racial disturbance gone deep into mistrust.

Tyonek's history with non-Natives is long—very long compared to many other Native communities in Alaska—and not terribly cheerful. When I consider the forces that have worked over Tyonek for generations, I have to be impressed with the people's resilience. The fact that they endure, when so many other villages are now only names on maps—or less—is one kind of success story.

Captain James Cook, that intrepid traveler, was the first foreigner to come by, in 1778; in his limited contact, he noted that the people already had metal knives and beads they'd acquired from Russians through their trade connections with other Natives. The Russians themselves, in pursuit of fur and fish, soon built outposts around the inlet, but much of the early Russian/Dena'ina contact was said to have been violent, including a notable attack on a Russian fort in Tyonek in the 1790s, with much loss of life (mainly Indian) and later reprisals. The fort was destroyed and never rebuilt. Oral history has it that the upper inlet people, including those in Tyonek, were too fierce to interfere with; they simply didn't allow Russians to establish themselves and killed the ones who tried.

Disease, however, proved more of a challenge. Between 1836 and 1840, half the region's Indians died from smallpox, and the reduced population, in Tyonek and elsewhere, became much more vulnerable to socioeconomic change. By 1875, a few years after the United States' purchase of Alaska from Russia, the Alaska Commercial Company was operating a trading post in Tyonek. The commercial salmon fishing that began in the 1880s brought cash income to the beach people and other Native fishermen but also displaced fishermen from traditional sites and soon overfished local stocks. In the 1890s a gold rush to the upper inlet used Tyonek as a debarkation point for goods and people; in 1896, swollen with white prospectors and adventurers, Tyonek was said to be the largest town on Cook Inlet. (Anchorage wasn't founded, as a railroad construction camp, until 1913.)

Early in the twentieth century, a small number of Alaska Native reservations, on the model of those for Indians in the western states, was established by presidential order. One of these, in 1915, was the Tyonek Reservation. The person assigned to reconnoiter Cook Inlet for a reservation site reported: "The Natives are quite fond of Tyonek and its neighborhood. I am assured that there is no better fishing ground for nets anywhere on the shores of the inlet." He observed that white fishermen were crowding out Indian nets on the beach in front of the village and wrote, "No white man would stand for it. But Natives do not possess the knowledge or the pluck to defend themselves against being thus victimized. A reservation expressly including exclusive net, weir and trap fishing rights is necessary if these Natives are to be protected in their fishing industry."

Disease struck again. Whooping cough, measles, finally the influenza pandemic of 1918–1919, which killed so many poorly resistant indigenous people throughout Alaska and the world, very nearly wiped out the Tyonek people. Villages consolidated; survivors from Kustatan, to the south (near where I fish), and from Susitna, to the north, moved to Tyonek. Tyonek became the last functioning Native village on the western sweep of inlet shore.

Cornelius Osgood, an anthropologist who visited Cook Inlet in the 1930s, wrote that the Native culture had been disrupted in so many ways for so long, that there was little left. On the final page of his *Ethnology of the Tanaina* (Tanaina being the earlier spelling of what we now call Dena'ina), he wrote, "Of native arts little or nothing has survived. Many of the younger Tanaina have even lost much of the traditional forest lore, so commonly thought of as the essence of Indian heritage... Culturally speaking, the real Tanaina are dead or dying." That same decade Tyonek established its village council under the Indian Reorganization Act, giving it a level of political recognition, and commercial fishing became a major source of cash for residents, with boats coming from Anchorage to buy the catch. Osgood commented positively on those developments, calling Tyonek "a cooperative village" and "one of the most hopeful developments to be seen." He wrote, "Although the aboriginal material culture has disappeared as elsewhere, some attempt has been made to adapt the social culture to modern conditions."

Certainly much had been lost, but I also doubt that Osgood was aware of all that was going on around the corners of his sight, or of that which his informants chose not to disclose. Today we understand that much of Dena'ina culture didn't disappear; it went underground, was hidden and even repressed, carried on in homes and families in ways a visitor would not discover. After all, Russian Orthodox priests had forbidden talk of spirits, shamans, all the old beliefs. U.S. schools beat children who spoke the Dena'ina language. If you had been told by priests, teachers, game wardens, cannery bosses, government agents, and others that what you thought and/or did was wrong, would you not also have kept those thoughts and actions to yourself and your group? The culture changed, as cultures do. It adapted to new ways, not by losing the old ways but by being less obvious about them and by creatively reforming the culture to fit new circumstances.

Tyonek's population dropped again when Anchorage grew up as a regional center, and people moved there for jobs, services, schools, and medical care. Just forty-three miles across some of the world's most treacherous water, Anchorage beckoned with both opportunities and temptations of the worst kind.

Then came oil. Starting in the late 1950s, Alaska's first big strikes came in and around Cook Inlet. When the Bureau of Indian Affairs put reservation lands up for lease, Tyonek sued, claiming monies received should go to it—not the government. The village, under the leadership of a very young half-Hawaiian (Albert Kaloa Jr.: His father was a seaman who had married into the village in the 1920s and had been himself a prominent village leader), won in federal court. Tyonek subsequently collected all the money from the lease sale (and additional bids it accepted) to earn the village $12.9 million. As it happened, gas but no significant oil deposits were found—and that was the end of Tyonek's oil wealth. As it also happened, the promising young leader died in an Anchorage fire even before the drilling began.

Tyonek's oil money had one significant consequence that went far beyond Tyonek. After paying for sixty new homes and making individual payments to villagers, some of the money was spent on a first-ever meeting of Alaska's Natives and then to assist the fledgling Alaska Federation of Natives, the organization that led all Alaska's Natives to the settlement of their land claims. The Alaska Native Claims Settlement Act of 1971 revoked Tyonek's reservation status and established in its place today's system of village and regional corporations. Tyonek Native Corporation now controls more than 193,000 acres of wooded uplands, lakes, and coastline. Headquartered in Anchorage and concerned with making money, the corporation developed a logging industry that exported spruce logs from its lands to Asian markets. It has in recent years pursued—without success, yet—economic opportunities in the forms of coal exports, an iron carbide plant, and natural gas liquefaction. Tyonek residents also belong to a profitable regional corporation (Cook Inlet Region Incorporated) that pays them dividends on its investments. (The layered corporate structures are separate from and not to be confused with the tribal organization, Native Village of Tyonek, of which Peter Merryman is president. The tribe deals with community matters such as water and sewer, social programs, and subsistence traditions.)

Who could expect a history such as Tyonek's to provide easy passage? Like so many other Native villages, in recent decades Tyonek has suffered from unemployment and poverty, family fragmentations, alcohol and drug abuse, violence (usually as a result of alcohol), and the restlessness and sometimes despair of its youth. It has also gone through periods of relative stability and cultural revival in which its elders and its traditions have been honored and young people helped to know and to feel pride in their heritage. The beluga hunts have been part of that revival.

Today, Tyonek's population stands at 193, of whom 184 identify themselves as Alaska Native or Indian and nine as white. The 2000 census data showed a much improved economic situation over that of 1990: Median household income stood at $26,667 (compared to $11,261 ten years before), with fourteen percent of the population below the poverty line (compared to thirty-seven percent ten years before). Fifty-six percent of adults were either unemployed or not seeking work. The job category with the most people employed was "education, health, and social services," followed by "public administration" and "construction." Twenty residents owned commercial fishing permits. Of 134 housing units, sixty-eight were vacant—but of those vacant homes, fifty-six were used seasonally. That is, Tyonek people who lived in Anchorage or elsewhere still came home—in summer and/or for holidays, to be with family.

In a subsistence community, which Tyonek is said to be, income and employment numbers mean less than they might elsewhere. Subsistence as an economic system means that products come less from stores than from the land and the sea. People's work is, thus, not bringing home a paycheck, but providing for themselves. In theory, cash does not have the same significance in a subsistence village that it has in the rest of the United States; money is not the ultimate measure of well-being. But of course, even in the bush, everyone needs some money. There's gas for the boat and the snowmobile (not to mention the boat and the snowmobile themselves), warm winter clothes (synthetics are uncontestably more practical than fur), air travel to Anchorage ($90 round trip), and beyond.

Coming to Tyonek as an outsider, I knew I was intruding where I didn't belong and that I would have little basis from which to understand whatever I did experience. How could I gather more than impressions, impressions dulled by my own blind spots? I had no right to expect anyone to befriend me, to be my guide. But then, I really had no expectations for this trip, only to meet the village council, to explain to them, as I had earlier to Peter Merryman, my interest in belugas, and to ask if I might return another time. The school visit had been a secondary idea. I knew how tired villagers in general were of people—anthropologists, linguists, researchers of one kind or another—popping in on them to get what they wanted; outsiders always seemed to be taking from them. I thought it would be nice if I gave something back: some time in the school, talking about reading and writing, working on reading and writing. The principal had been enthusiastic. "Anything," he said. "These kids get so little. Just having another person come in, that will really be a good thing." The school could also be my base, a place to park my sleeping bag.

The invitation to meet with the council had come earlier. When I asked Peter about visiting Tyonek, he'd said, "Come to a council meeting. Second Wednesday every month." I planned my visit for May, told Peter over the phone what I wanted to do at the school, and asked if it would be all right if I stayed for three days. He was very agreeable, and not overly talkative. He said, "Don't forget the donuts."

I didn't bring donuts. I did bring homemade chocolate chip cookies. As it turned out, the cookies went well with the Subway sandwiches that arrived, just before two o'clock, on a plane from Anchorage. (That plane was one of five scheduled each weekday from Anchorage, in addition to two that came from Kenai, about the same distance south across the inlet. These were small planes—a handful of passengers at a time—but still, it was a lot of coming and going. On the Cessna 206 I'd taken from Kenai that morning, there'd been two other passengers—an itinerant special ed teacher and a silent man headed for the Tyonek timber camp.) The council took a lunch break and invited me to have a sandwich with them.

There were eight on the council—men and a couple of women, all of them chatting amiably around the table. When the sandwich wrappers and chip bags were swept away, I explained who I was and what I wanted. I said I hoped to talk to people about the importance of belugas to the village and to learn something about how traditional skills were being passed to younger people. I said I was interested in the ways that the beluga decline and hunting restrictions had affected the community—and how some degree of local control may be retained through the new tool of co-management. I said that, if they were agreeable, I would like to visit again after they'd hunted a whale—if they did—so I could see firsthand something of the value of the hunt and of beluga to Tyonek.

They had questions. How was I going to get people to talk to me—was I going to go around knocking on doors? (I said I hoped some of them might talk with me, or introduce me to others.) What would be the benefit for

Tyonek? (I said something about presenting the value of subsistence beluga hunting to a general audience, helping people understand another way of life, that they may then be more supportive of it.) A couple of them spoke about subsistence generally—how subsistence rights had been eroded, how it was a constant struggle to hold on to what they had. For years they'd been restricted to hunting moose during the "sport" season in September, and they'd had to fight to finally get a winter season more in line with traditional patterns. Someone mentioned the newspaper editorial that had blamed them for taking seventy-eight belugas and how unfair that was. They asked about where I fished and who had fished there before me, and who I knew along that beach, and about the new oil development at Kustatan. They were, I thought, trying to judge my character.

And then it seemed that we were through. They looked like they were OK with what I'd said and what I asked to do, but they didn't say so. I looked to Peter. "Should I come talk to you tomorrow, then?"

He nodded. "I'll be in after nine."

May is an unpretty time of year in that part of the north, and Tyonek as a landscape was not at its most attractive—not that the village would ever suggest a bucolic beauty. The snow had melted and uncovered everything that had been stored or lost or just left beneath it, and the leafing and greening that would soften, as well as re-cover, the views was still some weeks away. As in any rural area, where indoor space is at a premium (I think of my own fish camp), there was a lot of "stuff" that looked like trash but was merely awaiting its next use. Between the rough-logged Tribal Center and the peeling turquoise school building, past the Russian Orthodox church with its weedy yard, past rows of boxy HUD homes that had not withstood the climate particularly well, up the hill to the trailers that served as teacher housing and the water tower, and down to the beach, I took a look at Tyonek.

There were no commercial buildings to speak of—no store but a snack bar run by the tribe and an ice cream "shop" in someone's home. There were a total of three miles of roads (none paved) in the village, connecting to the airstrip and to a newer residential subdivision known as the Sub; rough roads also connected to the timber camp and settlements called Beluga (after the Beluga River and home of the Beluga Power Plant, a source of gas-fired electricity for Anchorage) and Shirleyville (after a local woman and home of a roadhouse). I was drawn away from the dusty roads where I felt conspicuous—no one else seemed to walk—to the beach. There, drift logs were piled near a raging creek, and fishing skiffs were pulled up behind berms for the winter. To the south, a graveyard, with its Russian crosses and plastic flowers, brightened a hillside.

· What I didn't see in Tyonek were what I might have expected as outward signs of a subsistence life—no racks hung with drying seal meat, no stretched furs curing, no moose bones left for dogs to chew, no one carrying home a brace of ducks or a bucket of hooligan or sitting in the sun mending net for the upcoming fishery.

I remembered the report I had from 1984, the only one that had ever documented Tyonek's dependence on local resources. Back then, edible resources harvested in a year averaged 272 pounds per capita. The most relied-upon foods were salmon (seventy-one percent) and moose (twenty-one percent), but clams (gathered on boat trips down the inlet), hooligan and other fish, seals and beluga (a single beluga was taken in the study year), small game, waterfowl, and plants (especially berries) were all a part of the Tyonek diet and seasonal subsistence round.

It was spring, a traditional time of renewed activity and resource plenty, but I saw nothing that would tell me that. What I did notice were new pickup trucks, bright and shiny. In the most recent of notable events, money had come to Tyonek. The previous December, all the shareholders in the village—those who had been living in 1971 when the Alaska Native Claims Settlement Act passed, or who had inherited shares since then—received special corporate dividends from Cook Inlet Region Incorporated, their regional corporation, that averaged $50,000 apiece. Another $15,000 was forthcoming. The payments came from the corporation's sale of a few million shares of VoiceStream Wireless Corp., a high-tech investment that had proven successful beyond anyone's wildest dreams.

As a rule, Native people do not aim to either amass personal wealth or to save for the future. Abundance, when it comes, is a matter of good fortune, meant to be used in the moment, enjoyed, and shared. The whole potlatch system, a part of traditional Dena'ina culture, was based on accumulating goods only in order to give them away. With their dividend checks, Tyonek people had purchased items like new trucks; had taken vacations to Hawaii, Las Vegas, Disneyland; had gone to Anchorage and not yet returned.

In the morning, I waited at the table where the Fish and Game man had been stationed the day before, while Peter Merryman took a call in the office and then returned, a couple pounds of keys jangling at his waist. Peter has a lined face and graying hair, and a quiet sense of humor. When I asked him his age, he said, "Right now, about 168." He was sixty-one years old, younger than I would have guessed.

The times I'd seen Peter before were in Anchorage—once at a meeting where he testified that taking away beluga hunting would hurt Tyonek's elders, and once, back in December, when he'd appeared in a courtroom before a black-robed judge from San Diego, who was supposed to decide if the government's proposed hunting regulations were justified. The proposed regulations called for, among other things, hunting to occur only under terms of a co-management agreement, a harvest of no more than two strikes, and no commercial sales of beluga parts. Tyonek wanted to make sure that, if there were two strikes, it got at least one of them. For most of the contentious three-day hearing (which replayed before a new audience—the naïve judge—all the "Indian-Eskimo war," confrontational debate between environmental and developmental interests, and agency indecision), the village was represented by a lawyer, but on the third day Peter was sworn in to give formal testimony. He answered questions put to him by the lawyer about Tyonek's historic use and the importance of beluga hunting to the culture. Under cross-examination, he was clearly uneasy when asked to suggest under what circumstances strikes should be limited to one, disallowed altogether, or increased. "You're asking me a tough question." He knew the belugas had declined, he said. "People are worried. Are we going to lose our way of living?"

Here in Tyonek, Peter was, in contrast, very much at ease. The teachers had told me—what I'd also heard elsewhere—that Peter was extremely well liked in the village and that he was the person most responsible for maintaining the beluga hunting tradition. "It wouldn't be happening without him," the one teacher who had lived in the village for longer than the current school year told me. Peter reportedly doted upon his sixth-grade grandson, who lived with him, and had taken the boy on past hunts.

Peter had grown up in the village but, beginning while he was still in his teens, had spent a lot of time living and working "away," all over the state. He had been a contractor, running his own finish carpentry business. Now, settled back in Tyonek, he was in his third term as tribal president.

"Which do you prefer to be called?" I asked. "President or chief? When I saw you in Anchorage, at that hearing with the judge, they called you 'chief.'"

"Either way." Peter shrugged. Then, after three beats, with the perfect timing of a stand-up comic, he said, "I used to be the fire chief." Another beat. "That's why they call me chief." The last traditional chief, he clarified, was

Simeon Chickalusion, who had been a revered leader until his death in 1958. After that, it had been more like elections.

Belugas, Peter confirmed, were at the heart of his leadership goals and a reason he'd been chosen as president. The villagers—the older people especially—wanted him as president because they wanted someone to promote traditional use. From the late 1940s to the late 1970s, there had been very little beluga hunting. He'd gone to the elders, gotten their advice, and started going on hunts and teaching the younger people. They never took more than a couple of animals, "so that everyone has a taste of it."

"If you hadn't done that?"

"It would have died off."

And why, I asked, was beluga hunting an important tradition to continue?

Peter looked at me with just a hint of a sideways glance, as though he wondered if I really were very smart. But then he explained, patiently. "It's our way of living. The way things are going, we're losing everything. Moose, fish, now beluga. I like to see the teenagers and young adults learn how to do it. That way they'll never have to go hungry. Seals, too. We get seals when we go for beluga. I don't want our people to lose their ability to hunt. At least they'll know how to do it. Then they can teach the next generation." His face lightened up again. "Hopefully everything won't die out when I croak."

We talked for a while about moose. I'd read that the reason villagers had stopped beluga hunting in the 1940s was largely because they switched to moose, which had moved into the area with vegetation change. Now there were not many moose again, Peter was telling me. There were more bears and wolves eating moose and fewer for hunters. Wolves flourished, in part, because not many people were trapping anymore. A few villagers, Peter said, still went out after beaver, when they were hungry for Native food.

I thought of the Subway sandwiches, and I thought of the figures—the 1984 statistics—I'd read about Tyonek subsistence and the reliance, especially, on salmon and moose. I didn't know how much resource harvest was taking place in twenty-first-century Tyonek or who was eating what. I knew I was seeing Tyonek at an unusual time, when people were able to participate rather fully in the cash economy, when money and what it could buy were no doubt obscuring tradition. Money could buy grocery-store food, and it could buy fishing nets, rifles, outboards, snowmobiles for winter hunting—any of the necessary or desirable tools to allow a person to participate effectively in subsistence activities. However it was spent, for many people that sudden wealth would be just as suddenly gone. A hard fact was that there were not many paying jobs in Tyonek, and subsistence was not a feel-good tradition like fly-fishing or baking scones but a necessary and very literal way of putting food on the table.

And how, I asked Peter, did the younger people like beluga hunting?

"Quite a few young adults are really interested. Basically they need to have a leader. They don't go out without me. I've got to try to teach them not to wait for me."

Maybe, I suggested, they didn't go without him out of respect because he was their leader.

That could be part of it, he agreed, but they were also not sure of themselves. "There are some good hunters among them. I take one guy out with me who I think will be a good leader, but he doesn't know that yet." Peter laughed.

I asked about his procedures for hunting.

Generally, he said, they took just one boat, a 19-foot Boston Whaler with two 90-horsepower engines. There would be four men. (And your grandson? I asked. Yes, but—Peter laughed again "he don't count.") They would follow one whale, get it into the shallows, tire it out, shoot it, and harpoon it. "Now we've got to change our techniques," he said, referring to the new requirement from NMFS that the whale be harpooned first. "It'll make more fun out of it. It makes sense. Other times you'd be shooting and it'd sink on you and you don't know." The harpoon-first requirement assured that multiple whales wouldn't be shot at in pursuit of one, and that a struck whale would be unlikely to be lost. It would also require the hunters to get close enough to whales to tell if they were accompanied by calves and to avoid those that were.

"The work," Peter emphasized, "begins after we get 'em. The whole village will come down [to the beach]. We never did have a problem running short of help when we get a beluga. We never have too muchone or two whales. Everybody gets some."

It was one thing, I supposed, to be in charge of the hunt, responsible for doing it the right way according to tradition and for teaching the younger people. Now Peter also had to comply with new federal harvest regulations and negotiate, as chair of the marine mammal council, the agreement that would lay out the minutiae of details by which the hunt would be conducted. The previous summer the requirements had been burdensome. Tyonek had had to notify the enforcement arm of NMFS seventy-two hours in advance of their planned hunt so that the agency could be prepared to monitor it. It was hard to plan that far ahead, and, inevitably, each time they did, the weather blew up and prevented them from going out. The agency also insisted that the hunt not occur before July 15 so that pregnant females wouldn't accidentally be taken; presumably, after that date the hunters would be able to identify females with calves and would avoid them, as required.

This year, the agreement was still in negotiation. Peter was hoping the notice requirement could be reduced to twenty-four hours and that the hunt could take place in June, which was, because it preceded the busy salmon fishing season, a more convenient time. It would be easier to hunt before fishing buoys were anchored in place, creating an obstacle course, and when belugas were known to be in the area. Whales had passed the village in April, Peter said. That would have been a good time to go; in the old days that's when they would have. If you wait until the peak of the salmon season is over in late July, you typically face stormy weather. If you're further limited to weekends because some of the crew have jobs during the week, the possible days disappear all too quickly. That's what happened the previous year, and Tyonek, for all its negotiating and planning, had gone without a whale.

If all that wasn't enough for him, Peter's new leadership role extended his responsibilities to represent all eight Cook Inlet tribes in marine mammal matters in general and to somehow accommodate the needs and concerns of the Anchorage Eskimo hunters as well. Many people were hoping that he might lead all of Cook Inlet's beluga hunters to cooperation and harmony and oversee the recovery of the belugas so that all might again hunt. Indeed, he'd been giving a lot of thought to his role. "I want to be fair," he told me. "Natives are known to share. Maybe I'm kind-hearted." He wanted the Anchorage hunters to participate in the marine mammal council. He hoped NMFS would come forward with more funding for the council so that it could fulfill its responsibilities. All the efforts to cooperate and negotiate and involve people cost money. Tyonek had paid thousands of dollars to an attorney just to try to hold onto the village's chance to go after one beluga.

When it came down to it, the agreement between NMFS and the Cook Inlet Marine Mammal Council was a far different animal than the concept that had been so hailed by so many since—and even before—its federal enactment in 1994. What was being billed as a "co-management agreement" was merely an agreement specifying the details of that year's hunt. The Marine Mammal Council, with Peter as chair, agreed to a single beluga strike for 2001, and that the strike would be allocated to Tyonek.

In earlier discussions of establishing a co-management framework, Natives from around the state had insisted that co-management—which was only broadly sketched in the federal law—result, as much as possible, in equal sharing of management decisions. In the past, they complained, federal and state agencies had taken an attitude of "we manage and you cooperate." Although there was still no singular definition of co-management, by now there seemed to be a general acceptance of the ideas that subsistence users were, themselves, managers of resources; that they should be involved in the design of research programs from the start; and that their experience and the traditional ecological knowledge of communities should be incorporated, along with Western science, into the knowledge base and management decisions.

There were successful examples of co-management to point to. The Fish and Wildlife Service had turned to co-management years earlier when facing dramatic declines in western Alaska goose species. A plan that involved local people in research, the development of hunting regulations, education, and enforcement headed off a crisis, and the waterfowl conservation committee that developed out of it continues to guide recovery. There was also the Alaska Eskimo Whaling Commission, which demonstrated its ability to identify and design necessary research, to allocate bowhead quotas, and to enforce whaling practices. More recently, an agreement for conserving harbor seals while protecting subsistence hunting rights provided for hunter involvement in population monitoring, harvest management, education, both cross-cultural and technical training, and the identification of research needs.

Now there was also a good model specific to belugas. The co-management agreement signed in 1999 between the Alaska Beluga Whale Committee and NMFS for the co-management of western Alaska's beluga whales (that is, all Alaska's belugas except those of Cook Inlet) lays out specific responsibilities for each party and provides for consultation and the development of regional management plans. Even before the agreement's signing, beluga hunters had contributed considerably to designing and carrying out research. Hunter observations of beluga behavior and migration patterns had led them to pose questions about stock separations, and their collection of tissue samples provided DNA for testing. The resulting scientific analysis helped everyone involved understand more about the ranges and seasonal overlaps of the western beluga stocks—and how to assure both conservation and sustainable hunting.

As an example of how hunter knowledge was earning new respect, Alaskans were well represented in the decade-old field of study known as traditional ecological knowledge, or TEK. The idea of TEK—sometimes also referred to as indigenous knowledge—is that close observation over long periods of time provides a valuable way of understanding not just the behaviors of observed species or natural phenomena (e.g., ice conditions) but of ecological relationships and that, furthermore, this kind of knowledge can complement and enhance what is understood by science.

A few years earlier, researchers had worked with hunters on a TEK study that brought together a wealth of beluga-related knowledge from both the Alaska and Russia sides of the Chukchi and northern Bering Seas. That had been followed, more recently, by a study for Cook Inlet. The ten participants included both Tyonek hunters (who asked to be anonymous) and Eskimo hunters from Anchorage and the Kenai Peninsula. At a beluga meeting where the printed reports were handed out, the researcher who conducted the interviews and compiled what was said reported that the Cook Inlet TEK was generally consistent with what was in the scientific literature. Regarding winter habitat, the report stated, "Where belugas go during winter is unknown, and is a topic of great interest. Whether they migrate to the lower Inlet, into the Gulf of Alaska, or beyond is a significant question." Hunters also agreed, "Summer feeding is very important to Cook Inlet belugas. When they arrive in the upper Inlet in spring, the belugas are thin and sink easily. Their skin is thin, and their blubber is only about two or three inches thick. By fall, belugas may have blubber up to a foot thick."

In the report, hunters said they'd noticed changes in the distribution and abundance of the Cook Inlet whales. They thought the change in distribution may be the result of changes in fish runs or hunting pressure or may be a long-term trend in response to greater levels of human activity in the inlet. Regarding abundance, a key section reads, "[S]ome hunters note that fewer belugas have appeared in the upper Inlet in recent years. Overhunting may be a factor, and some hunters note an increase in the number of struck-and-lost belugas washing up on shore in summer, particularly on the west side of the Inlet. The specific details of hunting, other causes of mortality, and changes in the timing and size of fish runs require more attention to come to a common understanding of the various factors affecting belugas in upper Cook Inlet."

Hunters also remarked that they encountered few white (fully mature) belugas. Most of the belugas were shades of gray, and hunters observed gray belugas with calves—a situation they said was unusual and that suggested to them that the whales were becoming sexually mature at earlier ages.

I wondered whether there was science to support that piece of TEK or if there existed other TEK along the same lines. If the whales were breeding at earlier ages, that could affect recovery rates. If people thought they were breeding at earlier ages, that could affect expectations about recovery.

I learned from the researcher that one hunter was responsible for the observation and that he (the researcher) didn't know what scientists made of it. He suspected that it was "one of those observations that is really hard to verify, and probably causes many scientists to shake their heads" at some aspects of TEK. When I checked with Rod Hobbs at the National Marine Mammal Lab, he wrote back, "We have no evidence that female Cook Inlet belugas are giving birth at younger ages or remaining gray to older ages than in the past. To my knowledge a decreased female maturation age resulting from a decrease in population density has not been demonstrated for any cetacean population." He suggested the observation could result from the fact that there were indeed more gray animals in the population (due to the removal by hunting of mature white animals) and that because female belugas generally mature before becoming completely white, hunters could be seeing more gray animals with calves. Young females with calves would be more obvious in the population without necessarily having calves at earlier ages. Of course, the fact that there was "no evidence" of early maturation didn't mean early maturation might not be the case. There were simply no data. According to Doug DeMaster, at the same lab, there are data suggesting that marine mammals—but not necessarily cetaceans—reproduce at a younger age when the environment is favorable. But there were no data for Cook Inlet belugas, and there were not likely to be any. To determine the age of a beluga, one needs to count rings in its teeth, and there were too few teeth available from either the past or the present to compare.

Another question I had for the TEK researcher was whether there isn't a difference between traditional knowledge (which I define as multigenerational, passed down, belonging to the culture) and experiential (which I define as arising from a person's own experience, what he has learned himself) and if Cook Inlet hunters, because of the broken tradition and the in-migration of Eskimos, didn't primarily possess the latter. He agreed that there were differences—"most of this is shades of gray that are probably similar in their grayness"—but that he had not noted differences in either depth or consistency of knowledge regarding Cook Inlet belugas compared to what he'd gathered in other parts of Alaska. He was mainly interested, he said, in determining how hunters see the natural world and the belugas in it "so we can come closer to a common understanding for management purposes. If we can agree on a problem, we can come to solutions."

I saw his point. If people are going to go along with management plans, they have to agree about what's being managed and why. For the responsible management of Cook Inlet belugas, it was necessary to include what hunters knew about beluga numbers, movements, and behaviors and to consider their concerns. What didn't entirely make sense to me was what I saw as a quasi-legitimization of belief, without that belief having to be supported by something other than someone, or even a group of people, saying that something was true.

In the case of the Cook Inlet belugas, the TEK report made various references to declines in fish runs. One section reads, "The number of fish in Cook Inlet has declined over the past few decades, with sharp declines the past few years. Changes in the abundance of fish and other aspects of the food chain is a major factor in changes of beluga distribution and abundance in the Inlet."

Numbers of salmon—the main Cook Inlet fish—are a matter of record, and it is not in fact true that they have declined. Salmon numbers were at their lowest in the 1960s, when belugas were by all accounts plentiful. They were at record numbers in the 1980s, and declines in the 1990s still resulted in runs above historical averages. Thus, it was hard to calculate a food shortage for the belugas.

Still, there are regional differences, with fewer salmon making their way through to some rivers at the head of the inlet—bringing lower catches to Tyonek's nets in recent years and certainly, combined with a dramatic fall in salmon prices, leading to the perception of a decline. Increases in sport fishing had also led to smaller bag limits and to conservation concerns. In the lower inlet, what appeared to be a regime shift related to climate change had, since the 1970s, resulted in the near-disappearance of shellfish and a ballooning of the populations of other species, like pollock. Throughout the inlet, herring had become spotty, and no one seemed to know much about the hooligan that beluga feed on in spring.

How shall any of us explain that the place (the northern end of the inlet) where salmon runs have been least robust is the exact place where the belugas have been concentrating in recent years? This is further confounded by its also being the place closest to Anchorage and all of its human activity *and* the place where most beluga hunting has occurred. There had to be a good reason for Cook Inlet's belugas to be spending their time where they did. As the hunters said and documented with their observations of feeding behavior, belugas follow fish.

Beluga questions can surely use all the knowledge and wisdom that can be brought to them. But I was still concerned with whether what was brought to the table as knowledge was, in fact, *fact*. The source of the Cook Inlet beluga decline was the very thing that had been argued for too long before hunting was curtailed. If hunters continued to insist that food rather than overhunting was the problem for belugas, how did that serve management goals? I supposed it could help direct more research to beluga diet and food availability, which would be a useful thing in itself.

Peter was one who thought that food availability was a problem. About the TEK report, he said, "We all told him [the researcher] the same thing"— that a lack of food had caused the decline.

I thought to challenge him on this, but then held back. I knew that Tyonek had an interest in keeping the peace—in not blaming the Anchorage hunters for overhunting. If pointing elsewhere could help hunters save face and get along, and if hunting was restricted—as it was and would be—did it really matter if overhunting was denied? Did it matter if the denial was self-delusional or if it was a pragmatic political move? Did it matter if the denial appeared in a formal report that was meant to be accepted as a form of truth?

Later I would read more about using TEK in scientific and management contexts. In discussing some of the resistance to wider incorporation of TEK into research projects and management strategies, the same researcher wrote that it was appropriate to be cautious about the "overselling of TEK. TEK, like other forms of knowledge (including science), is sometimes wrong.... Unquestioning acceptance of TEK is as foolish as its unquestioning rejection."

Fair enough. Science was sometimes wrong, too. It was also sometimes manipulated for political purposes. If in science there were systems in place for testing hypotheses and for peer review of methodologies and results, TEK—at least in theory—had some similar checks and balances. Observers were always testing what they learned from those who preceded them against what they saw for themselves, and then that collection of knowledge against what they continued to see and learn. There was also a kind of "peer review," one that had been incorporated into the Cook Inlet study; after compiling the information from the interviews, the researcher took it back to the hunters to see if they agreed with its representation, and anything that he'd misinterpreted or that they disagreed with as a group was corrected. In the end, too, much TEK could also be tested by science. If the hunters said, as they had, that Cook Inlet belugas were larger than belugas elsewhere, it was certainly possible to compare measurements. (And, in fact, scientists have noted that belugas tend to be larger at the southern ends of their range, something they attribute to marine productivity.) If the hunters said, as they also did, that there seemed to be four "types" of Cook Inlet belugas, distinguished by size and other characteristics, that too could be tested with genetic sampling to see whether there may be subpopulations. Concerning numbers of gray animals, the ratio between gray and white could be—and was being—compared with that in other populations and monitored for change.

The value of TEK, as many were learning, lay in the wealth of experience and understanding of ecological process and change held by people outside of the usual scientific disciplines—not just Natives but others with long tenure on the land and water. For too long, that base of knowledge had been ignored or discounted as nonscientific and anecdotal. Now, when it was beginning to get the respect it deserved, the challenge was in learning just how to apply it to management objectives. Managers were learning that TEK could bring with it a host of positive contributions—not just rich ecological insight, but ways for Native and local people to participate in the development of sounder and more equitable policies. In short, the benefits extended beyond the value of the information per se to ones of broader cultural and political significance.

"Was it a useful report?" I asked Peter, about the TEK study.

"Yeah." He hesitated. "I know some guys were complaining about it— some things weren't true. But mostly it was." One of the discrepancies may have been the timing for belugas to be around Tyonek. "We used to go out [hunting] in April," Peter said. The report mentioned late April and May.

Peter and I went on to talk a little about the old days and the old ways, including the spearing trees that the Tyonek people had used before they had rifles and power boats. He went to his office for a typescript copy of *Shem Pete's Alaska,* which, judging from his familiarity with its pages, he apparently referenced often to see how the earlier people did things. "Them days were harder, but simpler," he said. He turned to Shem Pete's account of beluga hunting, written in both English and Dena'ina. Pete, who was originally from Susitna and had lived in Tyonek in the 1930s and then again for ten years until his death in 1989, had never seen a spearing tree himself, but he'd heard about them from some of the last Tyonek people who had. His account closely details how the tree—the *yuyqul—*was planted upside-down in a mud-flat, how the hunters would wait in the hewed-out roots that formed a platform to spear a beluga, *quyushi,* when it swam below them, and how the "strong men who sat in bidarkas" chased it and sometimes got pulled along behind when they grabbed the inflated sealskin that acted as a drag. Finally, when the whale tired, they stabbed it. *Niqahyiltash.* They brought it ashore. *Nil'unihyilash.* They butchered it. *Nuughelkidi hyighush.* They cut the blubber into blocks.

Shem Pete's Alaska, largely about Cook Inlet place-names and the stories that go with them, is one of my own favorites. I was pleased that some of the treasury of knowledge held by Pete and the book's other contributors had been preserved on paper and that it was proving useful to those who shared that heritage. But the bookishness seemed a little sad too—the loss of the direct oral tradition, the substitution for the person-to-person passing-along of what was known. I still hoped to hear something of the old ways from people who remembered them or heard about them from their elders, although I certainly understood that they had little reason to talk to a stranger. I asked Peter, "Who are the elders who taught you?"

Peter mentioned one name, a man who had died the previous year. "He was our elder, a beluga hunter." He mentioned another, "but he's in town [Anchorage]. He's not well." He thought, then mentioned a woman. "She's in Anchorage. Most of the elders are all gone now."

Once, the beach people must have had entire sets of myths and rituals that explained the beluga and the relationships between people and belugas, as they had for all aspects and members of their environment. *Quyushi* must have been more than the object of a hunt, more than a food source. There must have been songs, dances, practices developed to encourage the animal to give itself, procedures for thanking it. There must have been the equivalent of a dictionary for describing its parts and behaviors, of an encyclopedia for understanding how it fit into the rest of the Dena'ina world.

In Prince William Sound, east of us and an area to which the Cook Inlet belugas sometimes range—perhaps more often in the past—an early ethnographic account that discussed whaling mentioned various rituals and taboos associated with the practice. It is, unfortunately, unclear about which rituals applied to which of the five species (including beluga) mentioned, and it may be that special procedures were limited to the larger whales. Nonetheless, the account talks of hunters making paintings in secret places for luck, dressing neatly for the hunt, and celebrating the successful hunt by smearing blood and fat on themselves; wives were required to stay at home while the men hunted and to keep everything in good order.

I've searched with scant success for accounts beyond Shem Pete's that speak of Cook Inlet Dena'ina beluga knowledge and practices. The

Dena'ina writer and scholar Peter Kalifornsky, who died in 1993, seldom mentioned belugas in either his traditional or his personal stories. In the old days, he wrote in *A Dena'ina Legacy*, the people at Kustatan kept clams in oil in beluga stomachs. Elsewhere he reported that he once shot a beluga in the Kenai River. But in another piece, he wrote, "Mrs. Austin was the last one to kill a beluga in the Kenai River in 1929. The old Dena'ina lifestyle is gone."

Of all Shem Pete's stories, one best captures for me the traditional importance of belugas to Tyonek. Pete wrote that he found Tyonek a hard place to live the subsistence life, at least as he preferred it. ("Pretty hard place to get by. No trout. No fur.") But Pete also reported that a "long time ago, before Russians or anybody came to this country," Tyonek had a reputation for a particular kind of food wealth. "They called Tyonek 'Mother of the Earth' because there are lots of things to eat all the time: clams, fish, beluga, seal, grease, and oil. But they call Susitna River 'Father of the Earth' because they always had lots of fur, lots of caribou meat, dry meat, dry fish, but not much oil." In Tyonek, "They never used to go hungry because there was lots of seals and belugas." In the spring, the villagers would hunt and put up oil and grease for their own use and for trade. People from inland villages and up the inlet came to Tyonek to trade furs and caribou and bear meat for seal meat, fish, and especially beluga oil.

The K–12 school in Tyonek, formerly called E. L. "Bob" Bartlett Elementary and High School (after one of Alaska's first two elected senators) and recently renamed Tebughna School, is the "home of the Chiefs." The school T-shirts, which students are encouraged to wear on Fridays—Spirit Days—feature a Plains Indian in full feathered headdress. I thought of the stereotypes and of a Native friend who had attended school in Anchorage and been called, not in a way that he appreciated, "Chief." I asked a teacher if there was an issue there, and she told me that everyone liked the name and symbol, that it was "Pan-Indian." I went to the school store, where students sold shirts, candy, and pop as a fundraiser, and bought one for myself. The Indian profile was uplifted and serious, with a straight nose and a pose I couldn't detach from the now-uncomfortable word "noble." But the image wasn't Chief Wahoo.

In the school, the fifty children were divided into three classrooms. The younger children were curious, eager, affectionate. They were fun to be around. I'd brought with me a learning kit from the museum at home, a file box of all sorts of things to do with birds, including specimens of beaks and feet meant to demonstrate the ways that birds are specialized. I thought that village kids would be comfortable with animal parts, and I was surprised when those in the early grades seemed a little fearful or repulsed by the beaks and feet. They asked, with considerable concern, what had happened to the birds. I was further surprised at how few birds the children knew by name or could identify as living around Tyonek. I quizzed them about the spruce grouse, spruce hen, spruce chicken, fool's hen—all names for a common bird that lived in their woods and provided a reliable meal for traditional people and homesteaders—but no one seemed to know it or to have eaten it.

I remembered a discussion at a meeting of the Alaska Beluga Whale Committee about village children losing touch with village ways and values. There had been a student vote on a proposition from the statewide ballot banning wolf snaring. Rural students, like their urban counterparts, had voted for the ban, despite the facts that wolves competed with villagers for moose and caribou, that fur trapping was an important part of the rural economy, and that snaring was an ancient Native practice. Analysts had concluded that village school children were more influenced by popular culture than by village culture. Children were spending far more time with television and videos and the influences of teachers and curricula geared to the U.S. mainstream than they were with the teachings and examples of parents and elders. The members of the beluga committee had voted to step up their own education efforts—to design and implement programs for teaching young people about the importance of belugas to their communities. There had been a lot of emphasis on collecting traditional ecological knowledge, but if that knowledge wasn't passed on to young people, how were the traditions to continue?

In grades three to six we talked about special places and how writers can make other people know those places if they use all the senses in their descriptions. I read to them about my fish camp and had them write about special places of their own: short compositions that were, I thought, remarkably evocative. A few included Disney characters from recent trips to California, but more involved village life, favorite beach boulders and a log that "felt rusty," the bushes that whipped past snowmobiles on the way to ice fishing lakes. Peter Merryman's grandson, a handsome, energetic boy, was one who wrote, beautifully, of a particular ice fishing trip with his grandfather.

I asked that group, the middle-grade students, who among them had seen belugas, and all the hands went up. I asked who had eaten beluga, and most hands went up. I asked who had hunted beluga, and Peter's grandson's hand went up, so high it pulled him out of his seat. I asked him to describe beluga hunting. He started at the beginning. "First we get a big boat on a trailer and hook it up to a pickup and back it into the water. Then we go out on the water and watch for them. The water has to be calm. You see them, their white backs. Then we shoot it and harpoon it. There's a buoy so you can follow it and when it dies you find it, so it won't sink. Then we tow it home and everyone pulls to get it up on the beach, and a winch pulls it up, and we cut it up and eat it. The tail too."

The boy had learned well, I thought. He was proof of the value of passing on traditions, of having pride in who you were and how you could contribute to the community.

The older students—the teenagers—were another story. Once they too must have been curious and eager, but now they seemed to hold only anger. Their teacher had abandoned any pretense of teaching, was counting the days of her contract. In their classroom, they listened to music on their headphones and shrieked insults at one another. Something was very wrong; life was not presenting itself in a way that made those young people look forward to who they might be, what they might do. I worried for them. They felt beyond my reach.

I talked to the school custodian, John Standifer, who also worried. He had grown up in Tyonek, went out to school, came back. He had been involved in the tribal government, was still active in fish and game issues, commercially fished in the summers, and had hunted belugas. I guessed he was in his mid-50s. For ten years he'd been working at the school; he knew the kids better than anyone, and he didn't like what he saw. The children, he complained, weren't being educated, weren't prepared for any kind of life. The teachers changed every year. A previous principal had said to him, "A good kid is a sleeping kid."

I shuddered. *The only good Indian is…* Could that principal have been unaware of what he was parodying? Why would he have said such a thing, even in jest?

John had, on his own, started coaching kids for the Native Youth Olympics, a program in which students compete in traditional games, like the high kick, the stick pull, the one-hand reach—games that, traditionally, had prepared young people with the toughening and the skills that would serve them in living on the land and sea. He'd taken kids who were headed for trouble and given them something they could prove themselves in. "Kids like something to work for," he told me. More than twenty Tyonek students had competed that year, training for months for the statewide meet.

John said, "The bottom line is that everything is dying. Everything about the Native way of life. It's so much easier to open a package than to get your hands bloody."

And then—this man who fished and hunted and valued Native traditions—surprised me. He said, "I've watched too many nature programs. My heart's getting bigger for all wildlife. I don't want a beluga popping up and asking me why I'm shooting at him."

Still and all, he thought that what Peter Merryman was doing was a very good thing, trying to keep the tradition alive—even if he himself didn't want to shoot any more belugas. And he was disturbed that the whales had been overhunted. "They never should have been selling them in the stores. They sure declined fast. I remember seeing hundreds and hundreds and hundreds of them, more than a thousand in one pod. You could see them as far as the eye can see." His look, under dense black eyebrows, went past the window of the staff room, into the space that was blue-sky memory.

It was hard to talk to people in Tyonek. Except for Peter, I didn't see any of the council members again. Elders didn't seem to be available. Many people were away, in Anchorage or elsewhere. I didn't want to be pushy or to seem foolish; I certainly didn't want to run around with my notepad asking, "And what do belugas mean to you?" I walked on the roads and only saw people behind the windshields of their pickups. I walked on the beach and saw no one. People tended to stay home, a teacher told me.

If the hunters took a whale that summer, Peter said, I could come back. If the timing worked out, I might even see it dragged up on the beach, see the community gather to cut it up and haul it home. There might be a celebration, a gathering, a potluck or potlatch—Peter was indefinite about this. I would try to talk to the hunters then, would see them being men who did something more than open a package. I would see women with sleeves rolled up, cutting and carrying, possibly cooking. I would see Peter's grandson again; he would be excited, and proud to have gone with the men.

⌇⌇⌇

As it worked out, NMFS insisted that the hunt take place no sooner than July 1. I was busy with other summer work. I was away; I came back. Tyonek hadn't hunted during either of the first two July weekends.

And then, in the news: a tragedy in Tyonek. One child had accidentally shot and killed another. I studied the three-inch story in the Anchorage paper.

A six-year-old from Anchorage, staying for the summer with his grandfather, was playing with a twelve-year-old cousin in a bedroom of the grandfather's home. "Troopers say the older boy was showing his .410 gauge shotgun to the six-year-old. When the older cousin opened the shotgun, it discharged and struck the younger boy in the head."

There are fifty children in Tyonek, and I knew only one twelve-yearold boy. I hoped it would be otherwise—not that the tragedy would be any less, not that the village wouldn't be shaken to its core by one more terrible accident, one more death. But it was true: The cousins were grandsons of Peter Merryman.

I stopped calling to check on Tyonek's plans. I couldn't bear to bother people who were grieving. I sent Peter a sympathy card. I thought about the statistics always brought out by the gun safety lobby—all those accidentally killed children. I thought about guns in Alaska, how everyone has them, how they're basic tools in so many families. I thought about a young boy, eager to hunt.

Then, I heard that Tyonek had hunted. On July 21, a Saturday, in compliance with the agreement, Peter Merryman and his hunters successfully struck and killed a beluga. I talked to Barbara Mahoney, the NMFS biologist who flew to Tyonek to collect samples from the dead whale. Overall, Barbara said, the hunt had gone well. NMFS enforcement personnel had observed it, had seen there'd been just the one strike. The villagers cooperated well with her, and she got good samples—skin, blubber, organs, jawbone with teeth—to send to labs. The labs would do a fatty acid analysis to provide information about the animal's diet, map its DNA, and check contaminant levels.

And there was one more thing. The whale had been female—a lactating female. Barbara had also taken the uterus and sent it off to find out about the animal's reproductive history and health.

Barbara wanted to emphasize the positive. She told me how impressed she was with the community participation and the "festive spirit" as everyone gathered around with plastic bags and containers. She said to me several times how "nice" it all was, and fun to see everyone together, and especially to be with the children who buzzed around and asked a million questions.

It took me longer to reach Peter Merryman, who'd left the village for a while after the hunt. But when I did get him on the phone at the end of the summer, he seemed happy to talk about the hunt.

"It was smooth," he said. "It was a lot of fun." He and his crew of four younger men, and his grandson, had motored north for about thirty miles, past the Beluga River, to the mouth of the Susitna River. They'd waited for the tide to flood, bringing in a group of belugas. They followed the one in the lead, isolated it, harpooned it, shot it. "Everything just fell in place." It was a small whale—eight or nine feet, Peter estimated.

I asked if they'd looked for a calf. They had, Peter said. "It didn't have a calf."

After the hunt, it took three hours to tow the beluga home. It was late—10:30 at night—when the whale was hauled from roughening seas onto the village beach. In the dim light, residents maneuvered a backhoe and trucks to shine their headlights on the white whale. "The whole village came down," Peter said. "We couldn't butcher it up fast enough. It was walking away before we could butcher it. They were hungry for it."

But first, in keeping with tradition, Peter cut off and presented a flipper to the harpooner. Then, people lined up, and "everybody got a chunk." In buckets and bags, the people of Tyonek hauled off muktuk and meat. Peter guessed that each family got as much as forty pounds. Over the next days, the meat was dried and frozen and canned, the fat was rendered into oil, the muktuk was boiled up and eaten with enthusiasm.

Peter had, he admitted, "kept it quiet." Except for the NMFS officials, he hadn't told anyone outside the village of the plan to hunt and hadn't announced it afterward. There'd never been anything in the papers. "I didn't want people bothering it," he said. He was feeling pretty good about NMFS, however. The enforcement people "did good. They worked with us real close." The co-management process, as awkward as it might be, seemed to Peter a useful way to go. "It takes a little time," he said. "We just got to learn how to work with each other."

After that, we talked a little about fishing. I'd been unable to sell any commercial catch that summer because, with prices down, no processors would send tenders to pick up salmon in my thinly populated part of the inlet. Peter said the village had had the same problem—no tender service. They'd flown some fish out, but it had been a poor and difficult season for the fishermen and their families.

Times were hard, as they nearly always seemed to be, in Tyonek. The beluga hunt had surely brought some purpose, some pride in being and doing, some cultural and nutritional value, to the people. One small beluga had not provided a great deal of food, but the hunt had been a good thing in a summer that had held both tremendous pain and grinding disappointment.

After I hung up the phone, the image that kept coming to me was nothing from the hunt as I imagined it or of Peter in his office, but from a beluga meeting two and a half years earlier. I kept seeing a stern John Burns, the biologist so well respected for his life's work with belugas, talking to hunters about the seriousness of taking females from the Cook Inlet population. After a while that started to fade, and then there was another picture in my mind—Peter's grandson, stretching out of his desk, arm waving to tell me about belugas. Then I could see him, a child no longer so childish, there in the boat, with the hunters, following the wake of a beluga and learning the ways of belugas and hunters, and holding his breath at the strike.

9

POINT LAY

From the beginning I knew that I needed to visit a village where beluga hunting was not only a significant subsistence activity but one significantly engaged in—that is, in more than an occasional or a symbolic way. I needed to see life tied into hunting and eating belugas so that I could better imagine the role belugas may once have held in Tyonek and other Native communities on Cook Inlet. Of equal importance, given the fact that most hunting of Cook Inlet's belugas in recent years had been done by Inupiat and Yupik hunters who had moved to Anchorage from northern and western villages, I needed to see, in a general sense, the kind of life from which those hunters had come. Without that, I didn't think I could begin to understand the values they lived by and had taken into a new geography.

There was more I wanted to see too. I knew, in theory, all about the Alaska Beluga Whale Committee and its oversight of all the beluga hunting in Alaska except Cook Inlet's. In twenty-four Native villages, the villagers themselves held the responsibility for hunting practices, non-wasteful take and use, and reporting. Villagers in many places were also trained and equipped to take biological samples, and they in various ways contributed their knowledge and skills to the ultimate goal—beluga conservation to benefit both whales and whale hunters. How did that actually work in practice?

One village drew my attention more than the others. Point Lay, an Inupiat village of 247 on the Chukchi Sea coast, lies about 150 miles southwest of Barrow and was the village where satellite tags were first used on belugas. In one report, Point Lay was described this way: "Point Lay depends on beluga whales to a greater extent than any other community in Alaska. Approximately two thirds of the annual subsistence production by weight is beluga, all of it taken in one cooperative hunt in early summer." In recent years, the hunts had generally taken thirty to forty belugas.

In Cook Inlet, with its depleted population, thirty to forty belugas would be a gluttony of whales. In Point Lay, they're cut from an Eastern Chukchi Sea population thought minimally to number 3,710 animals. There may, in fact, be several times that minimum number, based on the new satellite tagging data, that suggest aerial surveys may miss much even most—of the population. Biologists, in any case, agree that the number of belugas taken from the Eastern Chukchi population, about sixty a year total, is sustainable.

By luck, a woman in my town had lived in Point Lay for about fifteen years. Although she wasn't Native and had moved away a dozen years earlier, she'd been married to a Native man there and still maintained many close relationships. She loaned me her personal photo albums and scrapbooks and set about educating me. She talked to people in Point Lay about me and told them that I was a good person. At another meeting of the Alaska Beluga Whale Committee, I met Point Lay's new representative to the committee and spoke to the whole group about what I wanted to do. No one on the committee was thrilled to have someone writing about beluga hunting, and it was impressed upon me that too many villages had had unhappy experiences with writers, who accepted their hospitality and then wrote things that "made them look bad." In the end, after a series of phone calls and letters with village council representatives, I received formal council permission to visit during the hunt. I was also asked if, as part of my visit, I would help the village document some of its history of bowhead whaling; the villagers were hoping to join ten other Arctic villages allowed to take bowhead whales for subsistence.

At Barrow, I departed from the jetload of tourists who had flown from Fairbanks on a "Top of the World" day trip and hauled my duffle next door to Frontier Flying. The June 27 flight had been distinctly unscenic, and we had not punched through the clouds until our tundra-skimming approach to Barrow. The tourists had seemed surprised that there were no trees, and I kept hearing the word "barren." It was time for the *Nulukataq*—the blanket-toss festival that celebrates the success of the spring whaling season—and Barrow had had a particularly successful season, with twenty bowhead taken by its whaling crews. Another happy event was the recent bowhead census, which had found the population to be increasing at a good rate. I would have liked to have caught a little of the local celebration, but I didn't have time to wander. I checked in at Frontier, as one of four passengers on the day's flight to Point Lay.

For an hour and fifteen minutes we cruised down the coast in a small twin-engine plane, on a flight I wished would never end. Although I'd once visited the Arctic coast of Russia, I had never, in Alaska, been so far north. Below me lay the edge of the earth: straw-colored tundra pocked with thousands of ponds broken into portions of rotting ice and reflective water, and all that up against shore ice cut with open-water leads and, beyond, gray ocean running to gray sky. It was a huge canvas of patterned landscape—the kind of place, seen from the air or imagined as you might be placed within it, where you know you are very small and very inconsequential. Somehow, I hadn't expected the ice to be so varied—shades of blue and brown as well as white and gray, and anything but flat; even from the air I could see ridges and dips, cracks and jumbles, a matrix of Nature's design. We passed hooks of land, like lesser Cape Cods, reaching into the sea and still holding ice solidly in their grips. We flew inland over more brown tundra and potted ponds, to the coast again and past the village of Wainwright, tiny in our sight. We followed barrier islands down the coast, the sea ice piled up along them, passages here and there linking shiny water. Ahead there was blue sky, and the ocean below it, a blaze of brightest blue.

Lost in the landscape and the roar of the plane's engines, I thought about Point Lay and the writer who had preceded me there. Bill Hess, known mainly as a photographer, had worked for the North Slope Borough for many years on a publication that celebrated Inupiat culture. In an issue ten years previously, he'd featured the Point Lay beluga hunt. His new book, *Gift of the Whale*—mainly about bowhead whaling and packed with superb black and white photographs—included the Point Lay material as one chapter. In Point Lay, he'd been in a boat during the hunt and had shot from his camera as rifles fired around him and whales dove and splashed. Between photos and text, he'd given me a good picture of what the hunt entailed. It would be enough for me to watch from a distance and, like most of the women and children, only meet up with the hunters and whales when they reached the beach.

Whenever I looked at Hess's photos, I thought of how a Seattle woman I knew had described them to me; she said they were "gruesome." I'd been shocked, not by the photos, but by her word. The photos, I thought, were very beautiful, effective at conveying the life of a village engaged in serious and celebratory activity. Yes, there were pictures of people firing guns at belugas, of dead belugas with bullet holes and streaming blood, of piles of muktuk and meat. There were also pictures of old and young hunters with heads bent together, of children running and playing and helping to carry slabs of skin and fat, of a woman cutting muktuk to cook up on the spot.

It was a basic disconnect in our culture, I thought—that so many don't seem to recognize that grocery store foods in plastic packaging begin with something being killed. Do such people imagine that animals raised specifically for food are treated and killed more humanely than those that are hunted? Do urban people just not want to know where food comes from?

As we approached Point Lay, the long barrier islands separating the mainland from the sea became a dominant feature of the landscape, and I understood as I had not earlier the significance of Point Lay's geography. Kasegaluk Lagoon, fifty miles long, is the narrow, shallow waterway that fronts Point Lay, its waters protected by the barrier islands that separate it from the open ocean. During the annual beluga hunt, hunters in their skiffs literally herd a group of belugas through a pass in the islands and drive them right up alongside the village. This ideal physical layout means that villagers can hunt cooperatively—just once a year when the belugas migrate past—all the whales they need. Point Lay is thus uniquely dependent upon beluga whales because of its unique physical setting. Elsewhere, belugas are hunted less predictably and more opportunistically, and neighboring villages rely more on bowhead whales.

Point Lay is unique in another way as well. Although it had a long history as a community named Kali, located on the barrier island, in the 1950s nearly everyone left. A Distant Early Warning (DEW) Line radar station built nearby introduced alcohol and social problems that began to break up the community, and jobs elsewhere drew people away. Only one couple—Warren and Dorcas Neakok—stayed. After passage of the Alaska Native Claims Settlement Act in 1971, their children and others came back and reestablished the village. Those returnees, who had lived in many places around the country, grafted their broad experience in the larger world to a commitment to maintaining a traditional subsistence life. It's this unusual combination of worldliness and tradition in its middle-aged residents that makes Point Lay extraordinary.

The plane bounced lightly down the gravel field near the old, boarded-up DEW Line station with its giant golf ball, and I caught a ride the short distance to town with the village agent who was delivering freight to the store. As he pointed out the buildings that made up the village infrastructure, I was struck by the contrast to Tyonek, back in Cook Inlet. The North Slope Borough is enormously wealthy from taxes it collects on the oil industry, and villages within the borough share in that prosperity. Point Lay's shiny new school building includes a gym, swimming pool, and community library. There's a rumbling power plant, a brand-new water and sewer system (replacing water delivery by truck and the use of "honey buckets" for human waste), a fire station, a community center, a health clinic, a police station, a huge maintenance building for the village's vehicles, a store, and—surprise of surprises—a pizza restaurant. (One establishment noticeably absent from Point Lay, a dry community, is any kind of liquor store or bar.) There is one main, graveled road, and a beach at the end of town where aluminum skiffs were lined up across the sand. On a shore where tides rise and fall only a few inches, boats can be left on the beach, tethered only with anchors set farther ashore.

Snow was still heaped along the snow fence on the tundra side of the village and in the yards between houses, where water pooled into ponds as it melted. The houses themselves, most of them the modest kind of government-issue common to Alaska's villages generally, were set on pilings above the permafrost. Every yard seemed to contain at least one chained dog, sometimes amidst caribou leg bones, and a satellite dish. Many yards also included snow-mobiles and wooden sleds draped with caribou skins, and racks hung with drying meat—ugruk, or bearded seal, which hunters had only that week been able to reach on the ice beyond the islands. Hides—ugruk and one polar bear—were hung to cure, and a pair of dead ducks lay in a doorway. Women and girls, several piled onto one four-wheeler and clutching bags from the store, puttered past. Kids rode bicycles and played in the schoolyard. At the boat launch, hunters were shoving off into the lagoon still chunked with ice.

From the moment I arrived, all the talk was about belugas. The men moving boxes of groceries from the plane into a pickup, the woman and the passenger she was dropping off—all of them said the belugas were coming. The whales were in Kotzebue, Kivalina, Point Hope, coming next to Point Lay, they said.

At the school district house where I'd arranged to stay with the researchers, my housemates were sorting through gear and talking about belugas and migration patterns and the timing of hunts in previous years.

I headed to the village office to meet council secretary Joanne Neakok, who ran her tongue over her lips and said, longingly, how hungry she was for beluga. She'd just been to Point Hope and had some, fresh, and it was so, so good but just a tease for what she really wanted.

Down at the store, while looking at a computer-designed calendar of beluga butchering photos taped to the back of the door, I overheard women speaking together excitedly: "They're coming! They're at Point Hope!" There were rumors the belugas were even closer—but who had seen them and where? An airplane, someone said, had spotted a line twenty miles long.

While I waited with one of the researchers for pizza take-out, Point Layers stopped in for a soda, a snack, a box of Pop-Tarts. They were all checking with one another. Had anyone heard anything new? Had any hunters gone out? The owner, folding up a pizza box, told us her sister in Nome had asked her to save beluga back sinew for her sewing. Back at the other end of the street, the young man who lived across from the researchers' house worked steadily on his family's boat and motor.

There was concern, though, and it was about the ice. Spring had come late to the north, and the ice had not yet moved away from the outside of the barrier islands, opening a way for the belugas to approach the passes into Kasegaluk Lagoon. It was still early—the harvest sometimes took place in late June but more often about July 4th and occasionally as late as July 10—but still, people were worried. The year before, the ice hadn't moved out from shore when it normally did, and when it finally did, the wind had blown and the water was too rough. No belugas were even spotted. Everybody felt the loss, and the fact that other foods—including muktuk sent from other villages—kept anyone from actual hunger was no true substitute for what was missed.

In the constant daylight, we all waited. The community was focused on belugas—the coming belugas, the hunt, the food—in a way that was pervasive. I tried to think of an analogy and could only think of how a community of farmers might watch the sky, waiting for a rain they needed for their crops, a rain they knew would almost certainly come and which would feel so good, falling on them and their world, making everything else possible.

Commercial pilots kept watch along the coastline to our south and would notify the village as soon as they saw belugas on the way.

The hunters, we heard, were talking together. They were getting gas for their boats. They were having a meeting to go over how the hunt would take place.

Then the airplanes didn't see any whales. Maybe the belugas had turned back; maybe they had gone out wide.

I hung out with the six researchers, waiting. They'd assembled their inflatable boats, repacked their nets, wired the radio transmitters and programmed the computer, prepared their syringes and vials with egg yolk and the preservative DMSO. To get to know the area, and to practice in the boats, they took trips to the islands; they invited me to join them. We crossed to the old village site, Kali, to which the hunted belugas would be towed for butchering and where the beach was piled with old skulls and vertebrae and rib bones. On the top of the hill behind the beach, ice cellars, generations old and still used for storing beluga and other foods, were covered over with plywood. We boated into a cut in the island and walked to the outside coast, onto the ice. Hundredsmaybe thousands—of seals littered the ice in the distance like a fall of cinders onto a white sheet. We jumped cracks, threw snowballs at one another, examined tiny clam shells left on the ice by ducks, watched for polar bears. The sun was hot. The mosquitoes had not yet made their appearance.

Another day we boated to the pass called Five-Mile, where the hunters would drive the belugas from the ocean into the lagoon; to another island for beachcombing; to another where we surveyed snow goose nests and their eggs. Wildflowers—saxifrages and poppies and lousewortstrembled in the breeze, and birds rose and dove and soared past us on every side. I tried to keep a bird list in my head, repeating the whole of it each time I added a new species at the beginning, like a memory game: yellow-billed loon, Sabine's gull, parasitic jaeger, red-throated loon, Old Squaw duck, tundra swan, snow goose, Arctic loon, Arctic tern, common eider, snow bunting, Lapland longspur, ptarmigan, snowy owl, kittiwake.

Another trip, north: more beachcombing, walking on ice, seals, andthis time—walruses we could just see with binoculars, far out on the ice. We heard them before we saw them, and their cries were hollow and almost melodic, like wind blowing through rock canyons.

The Arctic edge, away from the village, opened out into an unparalleled world of strange and moving beauty. In its preservation of dry bone and washed-up wood and in its flat, sun-bright expansiveness, it reminded me of desert. In its vibrancy, its all-out explosion of life, it seemed an Edenic garden. I could see how, in the season we had just entered, it could be a generously providing place; a person could find in it sustenance for both body and spirit. I sat on a beach and picked through polished pebbles. I watched high clouds

curl into wisps. I breathed in the smell of the living Chukchi Sea. When
we motored back, Kali rose like a hill in the distance, reminding me of its
name—"mound" in Inupiaq—and its significance as a high point suitable for
settlement.

The beluga world—that is, the world of beluga research—is small. The
people who study belugas know one another, and one another's work, and
by the time I reached Point Lay I, too, had gotten to know who belonged
and what they did. Not surprisingly, beluga people share a passion not just
for belugas but for the marine environment and, beyond that, the natural
world and all its mysteries. I seldom find companions as devoted as I am to
beachcombing as I did in Point Lay, and so eager to pull apart greasy bird
skeletons and listen for the pipping of eggs. I was glad to have been allowed
among them.

Robert Suydam, a biologist with the North Slope Borough, was in charge
of the work at Point Lay. Now in his twelfth year of attending hunts, he'd established a cooperative relationship with the community for collecting samples
and, more recently, attaching radio transmitters to whales captured after the
hunts. I'd gotten to know Robert at beluga meetings, where his enthusiasm for
learning about beluga life history and population dynamics was contagious.

Then there was Greg O'Corry-Crowe, the geneticist with the Southwest
Fisheries Science Center, who was in his eighth summer of Point Lay beluga
research. Had it not been for Greg—who, so long ago, mentioned to me a
pending beluga conference—I might never have been drawn into the beluga
world and would not be awaiting belugas in Point Lay. Now, listening to him
fill the house with wild Irish stories, I had to laugh at my earlier stereotype.
Why did I ever assume that a geneticist would be a dull, stoop-shouldered
technician locked away in a lab, rotely working formulas like an actuary? How
was I to know that Greg would excel as a field biologist, and that he baked a
terrific Irish soda bread to boot?

A third researcher I already knew was Laura Litsky, who worked at the
National Marine Mammal Lab and was finishing a master's degree. One evening in Point Lay, we broke from watching *The Sopranos* on DVD to view
Laura's PowerPoint presentation about the model she'd developed to track the
ratio of old (white) to young (gray) Cook Inlet belugas. Her work addressed
the issue of getting accurate population counts and the reality that it may
take many years for surveys to confirm an increase in the Cook Inlet population—or to establish that the population was not growing as predicted. The
model, by looking at ratios in the videos and how they change with time,

might indicate much sooner than the counts themselves how the population was responding.

Of the other three, Lauren Hansen was Greg's assistant at the genetics lab and a high school science teacher, and two were veterinarians. The vets, normally associated with helping live animals, were sensitive about being even peripherally connected to a whale hunt and requested anonymity. Their project at Point Lay was a study of the sexual physiology of male belugas. Females—at least those studied in captivity—are known to come into estrus between February and May, but little was known about the sperm production or seasonality of males. The vets would be taking testes from dead whales to see whether the animals were in or out of breeding season, and they would be trying to save live sperm for future study. They hoped to find some clues about what may regulate seasonality; belugas don't seem to have melatonin—a hormone that responds to light—but perhaps there was something else—a different photo-sensitive hormone, some magnetic measurer of latitude? There were implications as well for the reproduction of belugas in captivity. I learned that when the vets talked about AI, they didn't mean "artificial intelligence." If viable sperm collected from dead belugas could be used to artificially inseminate captive females, it would be possible to both broaden the gene pool and to reduce the travel of captive animals. At present, beluga matchmaking required the physical transport of animals between facilities, an awkward and stressful process.

In between the waiting, the watching, the boat trips, I pursued the request of the village council that I help with their documentation of bowhead use. Point Lay needed to demonstrate to the Alaska Eskimo Whaling Commission a past history of whaling as well as a current subsistence and cultural need in order to be allowed to share in the bowhead whaling quota system. I met with Julius Rexford, the Alaska Beluga Whale Committee representative I'd met in Anchorage, and learned that, aside from being a beluga hunter, he was the captain of a bowhead whaling crew in Barrow. "I drive 200 miles to go whaling," he said to me, not as a way of complaining but of pointing up what seemed nonsensical. Julius, who I guessed was in his 30s, had whaled with his captain-father since the age of 14, had moved to Point Lay seven years ago, and had assumed the whaling captaincy at his father's death. He drove his snowmobiles to Barrow for the bowhead hunt and then drove back to Point Lay. Julius also had a regular job at the power plant.

What I'd read in a profile of Point Lay was this: "The deeply indented shoreline prevented effective bowhead whaling and the village never fully participated in the whaling culture. The villagers' traditional hunt of smaller, white beluga whales is similar to the bowhead whaling culture in other North Slope villages." But I'd also read that the people of Point Lay had historically taken at least a few bowhead near the village and had regularly traveled fifty miles north to a location known as Icy Cape for bowhead hunting. That history, known to a few elders, was rapidly being lost, and Julius and the others wanted to capture it before it was too late. I knew enough to think there was a good case to be made. Aside from a history of use, Point Lay was now large enough to use a bowhead (in the amount of food, roughly equal to fifty belugas), had the capacity in freezers and ice cellars to keep it, and had people with sufficient skills and the necessary equipment—not just Julius but at least two others who were actively whaling, in Barrow and Point Hope. The elders, Julius said, supported the idea of village whaling. "There's been an effort to do this since I moved here," he said. "I was approached by the elders. They want to revive it."

I went off to see a few of the Point Lay elders, pondering the issue of change—how much is allowed, how much is necessary. When it comes to Native cultures, we (those of us who make the rules) seem to want to allow them to continue as they were at a particular moment in time but not to change. (In the arguments over subsistence, there are always purists who say, "I'm all for subsistence, but let them do it the traditional way—no outboards, no rifles, no snowmobiles.") But cultures aren't like that. People aren't like that. Change is what we do: adapting to new conditions, trying new ideas, inventing. How dull we all would be if we didn't; how unhappy I would be if I had to live my life exactly as my grandmother lived hers.

We divide people by communities, but until very recently, northern peoples didn't live in permanent villages. They moved around, following food supplies, looking for something new or better, forming new alliances. Americans who visited the Chukchi coast as whalers, traders, missionaries, and coal miners in the late nineteenth and early twentieth centuries tell of people sometimes being in the Point Lay area, sometimes at Icy Cape, sometimes elsewhere along the coast. These same Americans, of course, also influenced the residents—by encouraging them to congregate in certain areas for trade and work at whaling stations, by whaling to excess and then starting on walrus. According to *To Keep the Past Alive: The Point Lay Cultural Resource Site Survey,* "For a while [early last century], Icy Cape and Point Lay vied as the region's major population center. However, changes in the topography of the coastline increased the difficulty of subsistence activities in the Icy Cape area, and by 1930 the trading post, the school, and most of the people had moved permanently to Point Lay." "Permanently" I'm not so sure of, given that the Point Lay population moved on again in the 1950s. But the point was, things changed. The land itself changed, just as it continues to change, with passes in the barrier islands opening and closing; the one nearest Point Lay closed just a few years ago, requiring hunters to boat either five miles south or eleven miles north to access the ocean.

And people keep moving. They come to Point Lay from Barrow, Point Hope, Noatak. They go from Point Lay to Barrow, Nome, Anchorage. No one lives at Icy Cape or at dozens of locations all along the coast where there were once settlements.

Over in Kali, the old village, we'd seen skeletal boats—wooden frames that once were covered with ugruk hides. Should we insist that the Point Lay people use those in their beluga hunts? In Barrow, the whalers still use umiaks, the traditional whaleboats, not out of some adherence to the past but because those lightweight, quiet, camouflaged vessels have not yet been improved upon for hunting bowheads in the spring leads. The Barrow whalers, however, also rely on aluminum boats with outboards to pursue struck whales or to tow dead ones and on snowmobiles to haul their boats to and from the ice edge.

In Tyonek, what if some system of management had decided years ago that beluga hunting was the subsistence tradition? When moose moved into the area, would the people have been prevented from shifting their hunting patterns? Because one community is said to have one sort of food source (beluga), shall it never be allowed to turn to another (moose, bowhead)? Perhaps, if Point Lay took a bowhead whale, they would take fewer beluga, just as in years of poor whaling success the bowhead communities may take more beluga to make up the difference, just as in poor beluga years in Point Lay people may eat more seal, caribou, or food from the store. That's what subsistence is all about—people being flexible and creative to get what they need.

There was of course a corollary here, and it could be dangerous. If change is accepted and traditions allowed to evolve, then some opponents of subsistence will make this argument: But you eat hamburgers (or Subway sandwiches, or pizza). Your culture has changed. You don't need subsistence foods anymore.

Warren and Dorcas Neakok, the couple who never abandoned Point Lay, are now in their eighties, living in a purple house across from the school.

Warren has lost his hearing and no longer speaks much, at least to strangers, but Dorcas, who has endured a lifetime of quizzing by researchers on every aspect of "the old days" and Inupiat life, submitted with great graciousness and good humor to my questioning. She apologized that her hearing aid was in Barrow but seemed to hear well enough if I spoke loudly, and she spun her wheelchair over sparkling white linoleum to clear me a place at her kitchen table. When I mentioned my friend who used to live in Point Lay, she said, "Oh, yes, you look like her," and made us both laugh.

Both Dorcas and Warren were, as "cultural resource specialists," primary contributors to the borough's 1985 cultural resource site survey, and I knew from reading the lengthy narratives in that document much of their personal history. Warren had been born near Icy Cape and had lived all up and down the coast with his parents and grandparents, engaged in subsistence pursuits that involved whale boats and dogsleds, ptarmigan and beluga and caribou, trapping and coal hauling. Dorcas was born near Point Hope; her father had been the chief reindeer herder, and she too traveled widely throughout the region as a child.

When I asked about bowhead whaling, Dorcas told me she remembered two occasions in the late 1930s when she and Warren were both teenagers and had used dog teams to haul muktuk and meat back to Point Lay, where it was put into ice cellars. "That was the last time," she said. She thought, though, that it would be a good idea to whale again. "Anytime they want to get a whale here, they can," she said. "They just need a quota." When the village was re-established in the 1970s, there was one effort made, one time, but the wind blew up. After that, everyone was too busy. "Everyone building new homes, no time to try. Now they settle down again, they have time to try."

Bowhead muktuk—what she called "black muktuk"—still found its way to Point Lay. She told me, "We get muktuk from Barrow, but it's too much work." That it took extra effort for friends and family to package it up and haul it to and from the airport. Freight shipments can be budget busters as well. (On my flight from Barrow, I'd had to pay $1.58 for each pound over the forty-pound luggage limit.) She gestured toward the freezer in the entryway. "This year my freezer is almost half full with it already. People are nice enough to send something. They never lie when they say they share with other towns. It's true."

Dorcas is proud of her children and her village. Her six children all went away to school; today some live in Point Lay, others in Barrow, Nome, and Anchorage. She seems to have always had a vision for Point Lay. When her children went away, "I tell them one of them have to be electrician, one engineer for the light plant. I must have been dreaming. Sounds like I was lying, but it come true." Her children and others of their generation came back to Point Lay with the skills to rebuild and operate it. "Now they've almost become elders." She also seemed to approve of the new people who had moved to Point Lay from Point Hope, Wainwright, "everywhere." "They like Point Lay. Nobody scold them."

We talked about belugas, and her round face softened even more when she spoke of the tender muktuk. She and Warren would not be going over to Kali for the butchering, but—she turned toward the window that looked out onto Kasegaluk and held her hands to her face, in circles suggesting binoculars—they would be watching. She laughed again. She told me how the hunters—"just like cowboys"—would herd the belugas into the lagoon "where they're easy to handle. They have to travel slowly and push. If you push them too fast, they go away. Then they make shares for everyone." She thought for a minute. "It take quite a while to teach them, too. After they go out to school, most of them come back and won't touch bloody meat."

Later, I spoke to elder Charlie Tuckfield Sr., who would be pleased to be confused with Charlie Tuckfield Jr., his son and a well-known Seattle artist. I think the second thing he told me was about his artist-son. The first thing, when I initially met him at the boat launch and we exchanged names, was that his grandfather was a New England whaler who married his auntie and adopted his father, and that he had Tuckfield relatives in Salt Lake City who were excited to have an Eskimo in the family. They'd invited him to visit, but they always asked in the summer, and he wasn't going to leave Point Lay in the summer.

He and his wife Esther had just come in from boating across the lagoon for a sunny-day picnic. Charlie was short, powerful, quick-moving, and about as gregarious as anyone I'd met; Esther was quiet and drove the four-wheeler.

The next day I visited with them in their home, where the walls were covered with family photos and artwork by Charlie Jr. and the CB radio erupted with announcements: The hunters were collecting gas drums to fill; a plane was arriving, and "anyone who wants to go to Wainwright, Barrow, Fairbanks, Anchorage, California, or Hawaii" should get down to the field; all the kids in town were invited to a birthday party.

Charlie's account of bowhead hunting was consistent with Dorcas's. He was "just a young kid," but he remembered two whales, two different years. There were two boats and two crews in Point Lay in those years. One belonged to Tony Joule, the Eskimo school teacher. The other was Alvie Sagoloak's. Charlie's father, who was a Point Hope whaler, went out with Joule. "That last one I remember pretty well," he said. "It was right straight out [from Kali]. We could see it from the top of the school building. Everyone went out—women, kids." The smaller bowhead they pulled up on the ice. The bigger one was too heavy, so they began butchering it in the water, then pulled up the head, butchered some more, pulled it up some more, until all of it was on the ice.

Charlie himself had whaled in Point Hope and had lived there most of his life, only moving back to Point Lay in 1982. "I used to stay out on the ice a week at a time," he said. "Now they have it made. They have snowmachines." Esther's father had been a whaler in Point Hope too, and she'd cooked at whaling camps since the age of twelve. It would be a good thing, they both thought, for Point Lay's young men to be able to whale. "There's quite a few guys who know a lot," Charlie said. "If they give them a quota, they'll get the equipment, no sweat. The community will help, they always do that."

Like Dorcas and her family, Charlie and Esther got bowhead muktuk from friends and family elsewhere. "They send it to us, and we send them beluga." The search and rescue plane, he explained, took muktuk back and forth on its practice flights. "We get sheefish from Kotzebue." Esther, who'd been half-watching a game show on the TV, got up and pulled a sheefish from the freezer to show me; it was long and narrow, with big scales I could see through the plastic wrap. Charlie continued, "We have all kinds of fish here. Salmon, Arctic char, herring, smelt." He told me that he used to fish through the ice. And go caribou hunting. "We had fun, you know. Life was good then."

"And now?" I asked.

"Life is good now too, but you got to pay for everything. And everyone was healthy then 'cause they worked all the time."

Two sons—the youngest a teenager—passed through the room and were introduced. I'd seen them playing basketball at the gym and knew they were among the best players. "The boys," Charlie said, making a face, "eat all that junk food from the store."

Charlie had been one of the participants in a study of traditional ecological knowledge about belugas a few years earlier. I was curious about one sentence in that report: *In the past, there have been years when belugas weren't seen at all, but now they appear every year.* Except for the previous year, Charlie couldn't remember the last time there had been no belugas at Point Lay. "They almost always come here," he said. "Usually the ice is all gone. They wait at

Omalik." Omalik was a rich lagoon area about fifty miles south where the belugas were known to gather for a couple of weeks before proceeding north when the ice opened. But in recent years the belugas had not always gathered or waited at Omalik. This year they had not been seen there yet, only farther south. In the report, hunters had worried that a fuel spill at Omalik had caused belugas to avoid the lagoon. There was now also talk of developing a coal mine and dock facilities in the area.

I asked Charlie if he would be going on this year's hunt. Probably, he said, but if it was at night just the boys would go. He and Esther would go across for the work once the belugas were brought ashore. "I usually sharpen the ulus," he said, referring to the curved blades used for cutting.

He was definitely looking forward to the year's first taste of beluga. "I like beluga and beluga muktuk," he said. "It's soft, real soft." His voice slithered away, and I was struck again with the intensity with which so many people spoke of the white muktuk, as though it were some sort of ambrosia, food for the gods, better than chocolate, better than anything. "You know," he said, "when I eat hamburger or spaghetti, I have to eat seal oil or muktuk for dessert, or I get a sour stomach." He also preferred dried beluga meat to that of ugruk and ate it by dipping it in beluga oil. He also liked, he added, steak.

"What kind of steak?"

"New York."

I must have looked confused.

"From the store," he said. "New York steak."

The store, indeed, seemed to do a fair business. I had been in several times, and there had always been shoppers. The range of available foods was impressive, even startling. The produce section had not been much, featuring hardy travelers like oranges, potatoes, and cabbages, but the frozen section mimicked, in miniature, that of an urban supermarket. You could buy a box of Banquet hot and spicy chicken wings for $4.75 or nine ounces of Lean Pockets Philly steak and cheese sandwiches for $4.85. Frozen beef short ribs went for $8.29 a pound. That staple of bush living, Spam, took up a good bit of shelf space—$4.05 for the twelve-ounce can. Cheerios were $6.09 for fifteen ounces (compared to the $3.99 I pay, spendy enough, at my local Safeway). Sodas were a dollar a can, whether you bought a single can, a six-pack, or a case. I watched people buying bologna and other packaged sandwich meats, Pop-Tarts, eggs, bread, cookies.

I wondered what, overall, the Point Lay diet looked like. How much of what was eaten consisted of traditional foods and how much came from the store or was otherwise shipped in? Such studies—like the 1984 one I had for Tyonek—are conducted from time to time, generally to establish subsistence needs related to hunting and fishing regulations, and I knew that there could be great variations between households and from year to year. One statewide analysis I'd seen for the 1990s put wild food harvests in the Arctic region at 516 pounds per person.

Of course, so much depended on how much cash economy there was. The 2000 census data for Point Lay indicated an astounding median household income of $68,750, nearly three times that of Tyonek. Most recently, though, construction work had trailed off, and local jobs were harder to come by. The oil wealth that drove the borough—and stateeconomy wouldn't last forever; indeed, it was declining steadily as the North Slope fields were pumped out.

There was a relationship between a cash economy and subsistence use, but what it was wasn't obvious or predictable. More money didn't necessarily mean more food from the store and less subsistence reliance, and more time at a paying job didn't always equate to less time on the ice or in the skiff. To the contrary, village households with sufficient income commonly spend some of it on "subsistence technologies"—boats, snowmobiles, gas—that allow them to harvest wild foods for themselves and to share with the less cash-rich. As I'd begun to see among my Point Lay acquaintances, the people most involved in the cash economy were often the same ones most involved in subsistence activities.

The wind that night, July 2, blew from the north, and began to move the ice away from shore. The hunters went out, late, down to Five-Mile Pass.

At the researchers' house, we woke in the morning to Greg's shouting. The belugas were in the lagoon! The researchers—minus Robert, who had left for London the day before to attend an International Whaling Commission meeting—went into a flurry of grabbing clothes and gear and running for the boat launch.

And there they were. The hunters and belugas were not only in the lagoon but in plain sight, barely south of the village. The boats—about twelve skiffs—were moving slowly across the flat water in a sort of box formation, herding belugas between and before them. With binoculars, I followed the backs of whales rising whitely. The village was strangely quiet. People were still asleep; some, perhaps, were watching from windows. I stood at the bluff with an elder, Don Neakok, and brushed away mosquitoes. A couple of pickups drove up slowly and parked nearby.

When it started, the shooting was a lot of *pop-pop-pop,* boats circling, splashes. I knew from the descriptions I'd both read and heard that to be in the middle of it would have been adrenalin-pumping, with rifles firing all around and wounded animals thrashing, but from shore it seemed eerily calm, a sort of slow-motion dance between glinty aluminum shells and curves of white. Very quickly the popping tailed off, and bright orange buoys began appearing, marking the dead whales. The boats spread out, chasing down the last wounded whales, checking that the dead didn't sink out of sight.

When the shooting was over and I could see boats beginning to tow belugas to the Kali shore, I went down to the boat launch and caught a ride across. The two vets were just pulling on their rubber gloves and seemed glad to have help. For the next few hours, they worked down the line of whales to cut out each pair of testicles. In whales, the testicles are tucked well within the body, and the vets had to first cut away slabs of skin and fat, like the squares the villagers would themselves soon strip away. I recorded overall length and fluke size measurements for each whale and bagged and labeled the warm, veiny, gray testicles tied off at their vas deferens ends. In size and shape the testicles, on average, resembled very plump, one-pound sausages. Boats towed in the last whales. There were thirty-five now, all lined up in a long row along the beach, tails to shore.

It was, surprisingly, lonely on the shore. The vets worked steadily and attentively, standing in the shallows in hip boots and bending achingly over the whales. A few kids who came by were given anatomy lessons. A couple of young men were hired to set the cutaway slabs on the grass and to help position the remaining whales. That was it. The hunters and their boats had disappeared. I had thought all the village would rush over and begin the butchering, but that's not how it went. The hunters had gone home to eat and sleep; the rest of the work would come later. There was no hurry. The dead belugas lay in the water at the edge of the beach and cooled. Mosquitoes swarmed us, bruise-colored clouds darkened the sky, and the water around the whales turned a deep red. One family, finally, came over and began stripping a whale. I was too busy to watch closely. Their kids carried fat slabs and then meat up the beach and piled it all in the grass. One whale and then another were quickly reduced to thin and bloody carcasses.

I was focused on taking measurements, holding knives and handing string, getting the right testicles into the correctly labeled Ziplocs, the job at hand. I was not reflecting on the death of whales, the fact that the bodies over which we worked had so recently been creatures moving through the sea; sensitive to the world as they knew it; alive to "thoughts" of the water around them, the social relationships among them, the impulses to avoid ice and danger and to take themselves northward. I held their rubbery tails as I measured them and as, sometimes, we wrestled the bodies in closer to shore, and I felt the skin that has often been described as feeling like hard-boiled egg. I saw the texture of skin (smooth, wrinkled, pocked, scratched) and the coloring (bright white, less white, gray-white, gray edging along tails and dorsal ridges, yellowing.) I watched the knives cut through skin and fat as through butter. I was aware of differences in body sizes and shapes, a tail that was large and broad and one that was narrow, the slits that held their sex, flippers that curled. Metric measurements formed columns in the back of my notebook, seventeen male belugas long. These Arctic whales were not as large as I'd expected; none of the lengths reached four meters. I thought about Cook Inlet whales being larger, and that they could be better fed; I thought about the uniqueness of species, of stocks, of individuals.

The beluga heads, facing out, hung down below the water's surface, out of sight. I only glimpsed them when one of the men, with taller boots, lifted them to hold the measuring tape to the end of what biologists sometimes call their "beaks." The faces seemed small and bird-like.

Later, I would wonder at my lack of emotional response. Death is a serious thing, and belugas are animals to which I have deep attachments. But death in service of life is something I understand. I've butchered moose, and I kill as many salmon as I'm able every summer. I love salmon and admire their design and beauty, but I have no issues about tearing their gills to bleed them to death. I handle them, I think, lovingly, as we did the belugas: by which I mean not sentimentally, but respectfully. Whether an animal is of a "higher" or "lower" order, in my mind the same applies: accept death without cheering it, and treat every animal seriously and with the intent of making good use of it. This ethic is close to that by which Native people have traditionally lived. No one in Point Lay had put this into words for me, but Bill Hess's book quotes an unnamed hunter saying about the beluga, "If we don't use them wisely and respect their gift, they will know, and they will go somewhere else."

Had I seen belugas slaughtered by trigger-happy yahoos, like the "sports" who annihilated buffalo from the prairies, or had I come upon bloated whales in a spill of toxic chemicals, my response would have been very different indeed. Had I seen thirty-five Cook Inlet belugas ten percent of that population—pulled up dead in one place, I would have been shocked to tears. But these deaths were not without purpose, and Kasegaluk Lagoon was not Cook Inlet.

Meanwhile, the other three researchers—Greg, Laura, and Lauren—had taken off as soon as the shooting stopped to try to corral some of the remaining whales in the lagoon for tagging. With two inflatable boats and hunter Jim Tazruk to guide them, they pushed a few whales into a shallow side lagoon and then set a net across the entrance. They succeeded in netting one whale, a good-sized female, and attaching a tag.

Females and juveniles were what they were after this time around. The question was, would females and juveniles, like the large males tagged in previous years, also travel far north under the pack ice—or would they favor other habitats and follow other patterns?

In mid-afternoon I was back at the house getting something to eat when Greg returned for more gas. "I don't suppose there's any chance you'd want more help out there?" I asked.

"Actually, yes," he said. "Another person would make it easier."

And so I got another boat trip down the lagoon where we all eventually caught up to Jim, who was slowly motoring along behind a beluga, following its wake. With the two boats we herded it into water only a few feet deep. The whale was tiring, moving more slowly and rising more often to blow noisy, exhausted-sounding breaths. Greg got into the boat with Jim, and they tried to motor alongside the whale so that Greg could set the hoop net over its head before jumping out next to it.

Between Jim's expert boat handling and Greg's earnest rodeoing, the two men nearly succeeded. Greg ended up, twice, in the water with hoop and whale and was once briefly towed in a new version of a Nantucket sleigh ride. Another time, the whale ran itself aground, and it seemed that Greg had it in the hoop—but then it thrashed free and was again creasing the water with its wake.

We went to Plan B. In waist-deep water, we stretched out a net, with Greg and Lauren holding its two ends, and we used the two inflatables to drive the whale toward it. The whale hit the net—and pushed under it. We turned it back again, and again it hit the net. This time it stuck. Greg, on the end very close to where the whale hit, quickly wrapped it in more net. The hoop went over the head, a tail rope went around the tail, the net was cut away, and the whale—not quite docile—was walked into shallower water until it was well grounded. Without a dry suit, I stayed with the boats and readied the tagging tools, the tag, and the DNA sample jar to hand over as needed. I wrote down the beluga's length when it was called to me.

And I watched the tagging operation, like someone in the gallery of an operating theater. The researchers, once the whale was secured, worked quickly, expertly, emotionlessly. They pushed the three nylon rods through the dorsal ridge and bolted the transmitter "package" to the rods with looped cables. The whale, meanwhile, blew furious, fast breaths and thrashed—within the limits of its restraints—its head and tail. It bled from its ("heavily vascular," Laura explained) tail where the rope chafed it and from the holes in its back. It made high-pitched squeals that sounded to me not like "vocalizations," which is what I wrote in the data book when requested, but terrified cries. It wasn't that the whale was in pain, particularly; the dorsal ridge, I'd heard often enough, has very few nerve endings. But it was certainly distressed. Compared to this whale, the hunted ones—so quickly dispatched—had had it easy.

I recalled the discussions I'd heard at Alaska Beluga Whale Committee meetings about tagging—the acknowledgment that tagging was not without its disruptions and dangers but was, for now, essential to learning things that could not be learned any other way. At the expense of temporarily tormenting individual animals, much could be learned that could help belugas in the long run. Anthropomorphizing is a dangerous thing, and I tried not to identify the beluga's brand of distress with the kind of fear I knew I'd feel if captured by strange beings and pierced with foreign objects. I hoped that belugas didn't have deep psyches or long memories and that this one, after this day, would return to a normal, non-traumatized life.

The tagging took about forty-five minutes, and then the tagging crew was pushing the whale back toward deeper water, slapping it on its haunch as though it were a cow being encouraged to head for the field. As soon as it got enough water under it, the whale was straightaway gone. The next day a satellite located both tagged whales at Icy Cape.

It was late evening by the time I got back to the beach at Kali. Despite weather that had turned cold and windy and was beginning to spit rain, at least a hundred people were carrying on the long day's effort and doing it in great good spirit. Some were carrying slabs of muktuk and meat between piles in the grass; some were resting and talking; some were ducking in or out of a wall tent, or eating boiled muktuk, or checking to be sure children had enough warm clothes. Children were everywhere, running after one another, flying up and down the hill, gathering around a chick one had found in a nest. Charlie Tuckfield appeared with a selection of old, bleached beluga bones; he held up a breastbone that resembled a fiddle and began to mime its playing.

Once the butchering had begun, it had gone quickly. What had been a line of white whales only hours before had been transformed into a line of stripped carcasses, much reduced and bearing very little resemblance to the originals. Were it not for the detached heads washing around in the water, the remains would have offered few clues to what species had been involved. (Later, I would learn that removing the heads of hunted animals is traditional Inupiat practice, meant to show respect to the animals and to allow their spirits to escape.) Now, all attention had moved beyond the shoreline to the next part of the process, the division of what would be eaten.

To my uninitiated eye, the carrying around of beluga pieces and chunks—held with hooks or from fingerholes cut into skin and fatlooked at first to be undirected and rather random. One pile got smaller, another larger; one flipper went in one direction, another came by going somewhere else. When I found Joanne Neakok, she explained.

"Everyone gets a share," she said. The big piles, where the muktuk and meat were first stacked in the grass, were redistributed into smaller piles, one for each household.

"How do you know whose is whose?"

"Everyone gets one, if they're here or not. Everyone gets the same."

I saw that Joanne had a piece of cardboard in her hand with, apparently, a list of Point Lay households, of which there were about fifty. The carrying around was to make each household's pile roughly the same in its overall size and portions. Households could then redistribute among themselves, giving away what was more than they would use, accepting what someone else didn't need. The essential point was that the common property—the belugas—was shared in common, regardless of who had gone on the hunt, who had shot or butchered what whale, who had helped in large or small ways or not at all. All the villagers, it was trusted, would eventually get what they wanted and needed.

A single beluga share was not all that large. I guessed if it were just taken as it was and packed away, it would not quite fill a large chest freezer. Of course, it wouldn't all be frozen. Much of the fat would be rendered into oil, and meat would be dried. I remembered reading Warren Neakok's account of his boyhood living with his grandparents. He said one beluga was enough for the year, meaning, apparently, for the three of them and visitors; they stored beluga muktuk and other foods in sealskin pokes, and put the pokes in a sod-covered hole where they stayed cold.

I wandered among the crowd, feeling simultaneously self-conscious about being the only outsider and vastly privileged to be so. I'd met enough people in the previous days to be able to visit among them and to be further introduced to dizzying webs of wives and cousins and uncles. People were busy without being rushed, tired without being weary, happy without being rowdy. Their pleasure and goodwill were palpable things that seemed to flow over that little bit of barrier island and the world it encompassed, and to embrace me within it.

I felt a long way from Cook Inlet, and then I imagined how Arctic hunters, moved to Anchorage, would want to hold on to what they could of this life. For all the years he lived in Anchorage, Percy Blatchford used to regularly return home to Elim. But he had not restricted his village ways to the village; in and around Anchorage, he had carried on the most essential way he knew to live. To my knowledge, no Point Layers had become Anchorage hunters, but they may have, and I could imagine their desires, not only for foods they liked, but for this—and for wanting to share what was so meaningful to them with their children and grandchildren.

I ran into Ben Neakok, an elder who had been on the hunt. "I'm so proud of these baby boomers!" he said. He meant the hunters—in their thirties and forties—who had conducted themselves and the hunt so well and set such an example for the younger hunters coming along behind them. After the year of missed belugas, it was all the more important to keep passing on the lessons and the ways, to remind those of every age who they were and what responsibilities they owned.

It was after midnight when a call went up that it was time for the prayer, and everyone—the children quietly attentive—gathered together near the tent. Charlie Tuckfield spoke about the success of the hunt and how proud he was of everyone. "Nobody got hurt." Then, with lowered head, he led a prayer, thanking God for the good fortune, for the belugas that provide, and for "this food that is good for us." At the end, a cheer went up from the crowd.

And then, people went to their shares, which they marked with a buoy used in the hunt or some other personal item, and began to load them onto tarps in their skiffs or to pack portions into plastic bags, and they boated home through the rising wind and spray. They would return the next day for more, and others would come across to get theirs, and some shares would not be claimed and would be redivided among those who wanted them, or sent along to friends and relatives elsewhere, or put into the ice cellars on the hill for later use.

I caught a spray-drenched passage back to town, very much moved by what I'd seen. I felt—well—almost envious, wishing that I had been a part of it, that it was my lot to live within a value system that so honored community and the food that sustained it. There is nothing in my culture that combines collective effort, food gathering, and spiritual life in so significant a way. I felt like I'd been at some wild combination of bringing in a farm's harvest, Thanksgiving, family reunion, and Christmas gift-giving and -receiving. I knew I was falling into what I've heard called "Indian envy," the romantic notion that white people sometimes get when they so admire some aspect of Native American life—its closeness to nature, its spiritual dimension—that they wish they could be Indians, or Eskimos, too. It's a dangerous thing to do: far too reductive of cultural complexities and, ultimately, short on respect for what makes any people who they are. But I now understood better what the idea meant and why so many Euro-Americans continue to be so attracted to Native American dress, dance, and ceremony. We long for a sense of connectedness to land and tradition—those things most of us left behind in some other, distant place.

I thought as well about the big gulfs that separate the subsistence world from the way most Americans live and get their food, and how far, even from Anchorage, Point Lay and other villages continue to be. Point Lay people know—from TV if nothing else—how other people live, but urban people—people in the "dominant" culture—don't get the same look at the cultures, however ancient and however firmly connected to place, that lie in their shadows. And because they don't, they not only miss out on learning from the broader human experience, but the social and political structures they control continue to misunderstand and undervalue Native life.

The next day was the Fourth of July, and it was, for a long time, a quiet day in Point Lay. The rain blew in sideways, and I bundled into layers of clothes. I had a hard time recalling that just a few days before I'd been sweating in a T-shirt and wishing for shorts. Only a few determined souls, and the researchers seeking more samples, made the boat passage across to Kali. I stopped at Dorcas's to clarify something she'd told me, and she had just finished cooking up a pot of muktuk. I was glad for her offer of a piece and was surprised at just how good it tasted, warm and lightly salted. Then I felt foolish. Of course it was delicious, as fresh as that, in the same way that the salmon I catch are delicious compared to fish bought in a store or kept in a freezer for months; the only muktuk I'd had before had been served from a jar in winter.

"Thank you for trying it," Dorcas said, as though I could not really have liked it, as though too many white people she'd met turned up their noses when offered Native foods.

The annual celebration—a time for all kinds of food, contests, and games—was moved from the ball field into the school gym—and didn't begin until late in the afternoon. I stopped by and watched mothers with babies, small children, larger children, run lengths of the gym to win toys and cans of pop. The researchers were recruited to judge the contest for best "Eskimo donut"—a sort of not-too-sweet frybread bent into donut shape—and everyone lined up for a feast that mixed traditional foods of both kinds: July Fourth foods (hamburgers and hotdogs, potato salad and chips, cake, and fresh watermelon) and Native foods (beluga and bowhead muktuk, dried ugruk, pickled herring, and those Eskimo donuts). Mustard went equally on the hotdogs and the muktuk.

I sat for a while with two women I'd gotten to know a little. One had braved the weather to bring home her share earlier in the day; the other had brought hers home the night before and was happy she had it all put away except for the meat she intended to hang. Julius circled past with a baby on his shoulder, looking entirely different from the stern hunter I'd met at the whale committee meeting in Anchorage. Jim, who had wrangled so well for the researchers, was in and out of the kitchen, carrying boxes and wearing an apron. I visited with other people I'd met during the week, with their children and grandchildren, around our heaping plates of food. Children showed me their prizes, told me their favorite part of beluga was the flukes, ran races with the old people and let the old people win. I was feeling as I had the night before: embraced by a generosity of spirit, privileged to be included.

In the hallway, I studied the trophy case. Among the basketball trophies, stuffed snowy owl, and wooly mammoth tusk sat a jar with a perfectly formed four-inch beluga fetus and, beside that, a plasticized casting of a beluga heart the size of a flattened basketball.

The next day, the weather was sunny, cool, and breezy enough to keep mosquitoes away—a perfect day for taking care of shares. Around town people had them spread on cardboard and plywood for cutting up, and hanging racks began to fill with dark strips.

I visited with Don Neakok as he worked at a plywood table in his backyard, cutting and packaging. He'd already taken care of his meat, which hung

POINT LAY ∾ 225

on a rack behind me. He trimmed the bottom portion of the blubber—where it met the meat—and set that aside as scraps for his dog. Then he cut through the fat layer, leaving about an inch with the skin; the rest of it, about another inch, went into a bucket to be melted down into oil. He cut the muktuk into squares and put the squares into big Ziploc bags for the freezer. "This way I can just take out and cook up what I need." Other people, he said, freeze whole big chunks, but then the whole piece has to be thawed before any of it can be eaten.

I asked how often he generally ate muktuk.

"Anytime we feel like it. We can't eat it all the time, just like you wouldn't eat hamburger all the time—you'd get tired of it. But I eat a lot in winter to keep me warm. The fat keeps me warm."

I ran into Joanne at the office, and she asked if I'd like to help her cut up her share. She may only have been kidding—I thought later—but I was glad to be asked, and we arranged to meet at her brother's after work.

I saw Dorcas again, and she had six white five-gallon buckets (the approved sealed container for airline travel) on her porch, ready to be shipped to relatives and friends in other communities. She said her daughter had been busy—had already shipped out buckets to Barrow and Point Hope. She hoped that every family in the village had gotten its share and taken care of it. "If they're going to live here, they need to do this."

Cutting muktuk and beluga meat was not unlike cutting salmon into fillets and strips for my smokehouse. At her brother's, Joanne's family's share lay on plywood in the yard. Joanne set me up at a piece of plywood atop a barrel and gave me my choice of knife or ulu. (I tried both but, rather than be a clumsy ulu novice, opted for the knife.) Her husband Willard cut on top of another barrel, and Joanne sat on a milk crate to lean over the plywood on the ground, with a large ulu that had been her grandmother's. It had been made from a handsaw, and the hardwood handle was dark with oil absorbed over the years.

With three of us, and with Joanne telling me stories about my friend who had been her teacher and about, before that, being raised by her grandparents, the work went quickly. The blubber had already been cut away and melted into oil, so we only had to chunk the muktuk and pack it into Ziplocs. The fat was as soft as butter, and even the skin offered little resistance—less than salmon skin. My hands were soon slippery with oil. Some of the muktuk we left in slabs to be frozen whole. Whole, the pieces took up less space in the freezer, Joanne said. Then we turned to the meat, cutting away the little bit of gristle and making it into strips to be dried. It was very lean and deep red, already crusted on the outside. I asked Joanne if it would be salted or otherwise treated to prevent it from spoiling as it dried, and she told me it's usually dipped into seawater or lightly salted.

After, we washed up inside and had tea, and then I went back to the researchers' house where, for the first time in days, I was alone. The researchers had gone out again after whales, their forces enlarged with another boat and a couple of hunters. (They would succeed in driving three whales aground and tagging them rather easily and then, in another effort a couple days later, tagging three more, for a total of eight.) Restless, I turned on the TV and surfed through the twenty-five channels, past a religious channel condemning homosexuality, past porno, past a Rocky film. I paused on a beer commercial in which a man on a couch makes a snow igloo fall on the head of the man sitting next to him. Inside the igloo there's an "Eskimo" woman in a fur parka. The man looks her in the face and says, "Nice mukluks." I turned the TV off. I'd seen the commercial before and thought it simply stupid; now I found it embarrassing and deeply offensive.

At the airport the next day, I waited while freight—cases of soda popwas unloaded from the plane. Two of us boarded for the flight to Barrow; the other passenger was a woman headed to a funeral, and her luggage included a box of muktuk. She told me she had buckets packed as well, to share with her family in Kotzebue, but they were in the big freezer where she worked until she could get them on a more direct and cheaper flight. The rest of the outgoing freight consisted of a large box of muktuk going "freight collect" to someone in Barrow. The plane took off, and I looked down fondly on the village that quickly became no more than a dot on a landscape that had, in ten days, turned from dun-colored ground and expanses of sea ice to greening tundra and open water.

I would soon discover just how far Point Lay beluga traveled through the larger Native community. When I visited my fish camp neighbors Fred and Ruth Elvsaas a month later, Fred mentioned that he had muktuk, meat, and oil from Point Lay. He shared his smoked salmon with a Native friend in Anchorage, who had supplied buckets to friends in Point Lay, who had returned a few of those buckets packed with beluga, which he then had shared with more friends, including Fred.

But that was later. First I had to travel through Barrow, Fairbanks, and Anchorage back to Homer. For two travel days, during which I ate in Barrow's

Mexican restaurant, watched "top-of-the-world" tourists board with their pur-
chases of Eskimo yo-yos, stood at phone booths and airline counters, drank a
glass of wine with a friend, slept, and watched part of a tennis match on TV,
my hands kept coming near my face. And each time they did, I smelled—
from the oil that had soaked in while cutting muktuk—the scent of beluga.
It reminded me of where I'd come from and how the people there lived and
that it was possible—even desirable—to love what one killed to eat. For a
long time, through many washings, I smelled beluga oil on my hands, and it
smelled very good to me.

EPILOGUE — WATCHING

Late August 2002

At my fish camp the fireweed blazed to its last, topmost blossoms, and the enormous thorned leaves of the devil's club collapsed into yellow rags. A black bear, having already lipped every watermelonberry off the plant beside the outhouse, returned to my side yard for the last of the summer's strawberries. The north wind carried cold down from the mountains; mornings, to warm the cabin, I fired up the woodstove. Ken was back at work in town, and I lingered by myself with the last batch of smoked fish and the long silences.

The inlet was gray and smelled like dead fish. The smell was subtle, gray itself and quiet and cool, and sad somehow, but not *sad*. The smell took me into myself, back to memories of damp boathouses, to moldering leaves in still forests. It made me want for something I couldn't name, and it reminded me of the circle, of the death that brings new life, season after season. A silver salmon jumped, like a shining blade cutting its way clear, and then fell back beneath the surface.

I sat on the porch of my cabin and watched the patterns made on the water by sunlight and clouds. I was still, always, watching for belugas. Other years, past years, this is when we most often saw them heading south, hundreds of animals rising whitely, fatly, rhythmically, following the shoreline around the point. Another summer had gone, and it was another summer when I didn't see a single beluga from my camp. I didn't sing out to Ken, "belugas!" and wasn't sung out to, and I didn't compare beluga notes with my neighbors. Or I did compare notes. I asked George if he saw any belugas at all, all summer long, and he said he hadn't. I felt bereft.

I wrote the population estimates on a piece of paper so that I could see them lined up against time.

    1994—653
    1995—491
    1996—594
    1997—440
    1998—347
    1999—369
    2000—435
    2001—386

The count from the 2002 June survey hadn't yet been turned into a population estimate, but I'd heard that the surveyors had found about the same numbers of animals in the same places as in recent years. In any case, I knew better than to make too much of any one year's estimate. The only thing the scientists wanted to say about the recent estimates were that, since the last year of unrestricted hunting in 1998, there hadn't been a precipitous drop. The numbers were all within the same statistical range, indicating something like stability.

What I didn't know was that later, when the 2002 estimate was released, it would be a new low of 313. At my camp, I didn't have that new number to add to my string, like another worry bead. I watched the inlet, and then I picked up my cell phone and started making calls.

Jack Sterne, the attorney representing the environmental coalition that had sued for the protections of the Endangered Species Act, was a frustrated man. It had taken a year for the coalition's appeal of the district court ruling to be assigned to an appeals court panel. A look at the three judges' records, then, found them less than sympathetic to endangered species. Reluctantly, Trustees withdrew the appeal.

It was not, Jack told me, that the plaintiffs had changed their minds about the Cook Inlet belugas needing additional protections. They felt as strongly as ever that the small population was vulnerable to a variety of threats and that the law required the whales be listed as endangered. "The reality is that what's right doesn't always happen," Jack said, by way of explaining the decisions of judges as well as the environmental retrenchment. "Anytime you appeal a case, there's a risk of losing. When we looked at the dangers of losing, to the

Endangered Species Act itself, we decided those dangers were too great. Had the decline not abated, we would have had no choice but to continue to push for a listing. But we do have other avenues."

The other avenues were several. First, Jack emphasized, the judge who dismissed the suit said that if, with the cessation of hunting, the decline continued, he would be obligated to insist on a listing. (This is, in fact, an optimistic interpretation of what the judge wrote, which was, "If the [hunting] moratorium fails to control Native American harvesting in the future, ESA listing will be warranted.") In any case, the environmentalists would be closely watching the population counts and the various risks to the belugas and, Jack said, "Should anything happen, we'll demand a listing."

The group also still had a lawsuit in state court, asking that the state list the belugas as endangered under Alaska's own endangered species law. The critical beluga habitat lay in state waters, and the environmentalists thought they might yet force the state to protect that habitat. (They would be disappointed, a few weeks later, when the judge ruled with the state, finding that the fish and game commissioner was "reasonable" in determining that the belugas were *not* endangered.)

A third avenue for gaining beluga protections might be a new, alternative lawsuit, still under consideration by the coalition. One of the requirements for any depleted marine mammal species was a conservation plan, but more than two years after the Cook Inlet belugas were designated as depleted, there was neither a plan nor even a plan for a plan. If it took yet another lawsuit to force the National Marine Fisheries Service to begin one—then that's what the group would have to do.

The law seemed—to me—clear on this. The Marine Mammal Protection Act specifies, "The Secretary shall prepare conservation plans . . . as soon as possible, for any species or stock designated as depleted . . . except that a conservation plan need not be prepared if the Secretary determines that it will not promote the conservation of the species or stock." The purpose of a plan is to conserve and restore the species or stock to its "optimum sustainable population," and plans are to be modeled on the recovery plans required under the Endangered Species Act. "The Secretary shall act expeditiously to implement each conservation plan" and "shall specify in the annual report . . . what measures have been taken to prepare and implement such plans."

As soon as possible. Expeditiously. How much wiggle room was there? A conservation or recovery plan—whatever anyone wanted to call it—was essentially what everyone advocating for the belugas had wanted from the start. Beyond stopping hunting, the kinds of things that needed to be done were easy enough to identify. Protect key habitat areas. Continue monitoring. Fill research holes. Where reasonably possible, prevent human activities from further harming the animals or their habitat. I had seen, from the St. Lawrence recovery plan, what a plan might look like and how one might be implemented. The shaping of a plan could bring people together to work in a cooperative, positive manner.

Several times I'd asked National Marine Fisheries Service people about the delay in putting together a beluga conservation plan, always to be told that a plan would be developed *soon* but that there were other things that had to be finished first. From my porch overlooking the inlet, I again phoned Brad Smith, in the Anchorage office. "It's still in the rotation," Brad told me. He listed the things that had yet to be done before the conservation plan would get its turn. First they needed to finalize the environmental impact statement, which was still only in draft form, nearly two years after it went out for comment. Then they had to finalize the harvest regulations. All that process, Brad said, took longer than anyone expected because the administrative law judge brought in to evaluate the hunting restrictions had taken a year and a half to make his recommendations. Now it was so late that the impact statement may need to go through another draft and an additional comment period before it could be finalized. Finally, after all that, they would be ready to turn to the conservation plan. "It's certainly our intention to prepare a conservation plan," Brad told me. He wanted, he said, to work on a plan, wanted to have goals and objectives, wanted the public to be able to bring their ideas to the table.

"I'm told we're going to be sued," Brad said, with a sound of resignation in his voice.

At my camp, I collected chunks of washed-up cottonwood bark for the smokehouse. A bear had left its pigeon-toed prints and a pile of scat; I squatted to examine the scat and found only grasses and the tough seeds of devil's club berries. It was a poor berry year—too dry at the wrong time—and none of us had found much in the usual blueberry patches.

My neighbor George, before he closed up camp and left for his winter home in Nebraska, was concerned about the swallows. They used to nest by the hundreds in holes all along the sand and clay bluffs, and in the houses we put up for them, but in the last few years they'd gone missing. George said he complained to the fisheries management people, asking why no one paid any attention to any of the odd things happening in the environment, but they didn't have anything to say about it.

Earlier in August, up in Knik Arm and by the Susitna River, the researchers had satellite-tagged eight more belugas. After so many years, so much trial and error, they were getting the technique down. This year they used a newly designed net, slings for holding captured whales between the inflatable boats, and local hunters to help with the tracking.

In 2001 they'd tagged seven belugas, and the signals that located them from August through fall and into winter—one tag kept transmitting until March—proved that Paul and Ringo weren't rogue whales: The whales stayed in the upper inlet. A few traveled south along the west side of the inlet, one as far as Chinitna Bay (across the inlet from Homer), but then returned north. Mostly they hung out in the upper inlet's arms, river mouths, and bays, and later in the winter, offshore areas. The whale that signaled circled throughout the upper inlet and both ice-choked arms until the transmitter went silent in March.

If the belugas stay in the upper inlet in winter, they will be unlike any of Alaska's other belugas, which migrate seasonally over long distances. If they stay, what do they do there? Dive data, reported by the tags, indicates that—compared to summer, when they spend nearly all their time at or near the surface—in winter they spend much more time under water and out of sight. They may be feeding on the bottom or under ice, or they may be finding very little to eat but staying underwater to rest and conserve their energy. Biologists have long thought that there was little marine life in upper Cook Inlet in winter, but the truth is that no one knows what's there because no one has yet designed a research plan to look. There may be flounder there, or marine worms, or other species in enough plenitude to support the belugas, which may live largely off their fat reserves, as some other whale species are known to do.

The mystery of winter whereabouts may be solved—or at least suggested. It may be that the current small beluga population—if not the larger one of the past—stays in the upper inlet year-round, and the reason so few whales are spotted in the winter is that they're simply not at the surface to be seen. One mystery, like one salmon, spawns a thousand more.

At camp the songbirds moved on and left a quietness. I was quiet too, alone and attentive, and the other animals of the place passed around me. On a calm day, a seal, swimming below the surface, left the trace of a wake as it scouted our cove and around the reef. A porcupine with a bum leg pitched to one side as it waddled over the sand; when it saw me, it turned and flared its blond-tipped needles. I knew the skinny fox that trotted along the tideline, and the white-bellied weasel that stretched on the rock wall to study me, and the red squirrel that rattled the alder.

One morning when I was inside, the porch shook, and a brown bear appeared at my window. It stood to place its paws and nose on the glass, but when I clapped my hands, it dropped back down and ran away. I arranged sawhorses on the porch to present minor obstacles, and I left the smeary nose print on the window.

In Anchorage, people were eating muktuk. Under the quota system developed by NMFS, adjusted by the administrative law judge, and negotiated with the Cook Inlet Marine Mammal Council headed by Peter Merryman, two belugas could be taken by hunters in 2002. One was allocated to Tyonek, although the village had yet to take it. The other was for the "Anchorage whaling community," the Eskimo hunters organized by Joel Blatchford. That group had hunted, and the hunt had been successful.

I heard about the hunt first from NMFS's Barbara Mahoney. The hunters had gotten together, under Joel's leadership, and had held a drawing to determine a captain and crew. All hunters, whether they attended the meeting or not, were allowed to enter the lottery, and all names were read aloud so that everyone would know who was participating. (Twenty-eight hunters did.) The winner was a younger man whose family was from Nome and who had lived in Anchorage for a long time. He and his crew welcomed others to join them on the water and at campsites at the Susitna River, and about a dozen people did. "It became a good community effort," Barbara told me over the phone. "Camping together, they got to talk together." They harpooned and shot a large male, and then took every part of it, right down to the bones. The muktuk and meat were cut into small portions for all the participants and to be distributed to others. NMFS personnel arrived partway through the butchering, and the hunters agreeably accommodated their sampling needs.

When I reached Joel on the phone, he was equally pleased with the hunt. He could not, however, keep from gloating that the "Eskimos" had done everything right and well, whereas the Tyonek "Indians" had taken a female the year before and, for the current year, had had no success at all.

Joel hadn't participated in the hunt, but he'd met the returning hunters at the dock, where they'd honored him not just with loads of muktuk but with a flipper. Everyone seemed happy about the hunt and about getting some food, Joel said. "There was people coming down to the dock" with coolers and bags, coming for shares, and getting a part of the whale. He estimated that forty families, maybe more, shared in the one whale. Joel and Dj had helped with the distribution; they cooked and boiled, pickled and jarred, and rendered oil.

Mindful of their concern with toxics and the safety of Native foods, I asked Joel if he and Dj were eating beluga again—or just sharing it with others. Dj took the phone. "We decided we'd eat our food we're used to, even if it means it's not good to eat. You only live once. We haven't had beluga in such a long time, we couldn't help but do the stuff we both used to."

I asked about Joel's dad, Percy. He wasn't doing too well, Joel said. He was living with Joel and Dj and needed a lot of care. So many of the older hunters, like Percy, weren't able to hunt anymore. Joel mentioned one of the main hunters, one who, until the hunting ban, had supported his family with both food and the cash income from muktuk sales. He'd had a heart attack. Joel named two others who had died in recent weeks.

It rained, hard. The rain pounded on the roof and turned the creek into a noisy torrent, and the creek emptied into the inlet in a muddy plume. Inky mushrooms popped up everywhere in the woods; I ate them with pasta.

I called Judy Brady, the executive director of the Alaska Oil and Gas Association, to see how she felt about the current state of beluga protection. She wanted me to be sure to understand that when she spoke to me as a person, about her experience, she wasn't representing AOGA's position. The association's position, from the start, had been that NMFS was responsible for managing the belugas—without needing any new laws, listings, or process—and that the agency had failed to do its job. And AOGA, she said, was as supportive as anyone of having a healthy beluga population—in fact, a healthy Cook Inlet ecosystem—because only in a healthy environment could the industry continue to operate successfully. That is, only then could it function without excessive regulation and burdensome expense.

Whenever I thought of Judy, I pictured her at any number of beluga meetings where, anytime someone would claim that the oil industry was poisoning the belugas, she would clench her jaw, hunch her shoulders, and look like it was all she could do not to explode into a rage. She would testify, again and again, not patiently, that the oil industry had been operating responsibly in the inlet for forty years and that every water quality study that had ever been done had found no pollution attributable to the industry. "For once it's not us!" she protested. I was not an industry booster, but I sometimes found myself with a twinge of sympathy for Judy.

What seemed to bother her most was the uncertainty in the numbers. "To this day," she complained to me, "people don't know if the numbers are right." She'd never thought the inlet's beluga population had been very high to start with, and when she saw what kind of evidence the population estimates were based on—what she characterized as the biologists having done "on the back of an envelope the night before" one of the early meetings, she distrusted all the NMFS figures from then on. "It shook my faith," she said. She'd always assumed that science was, well, more scientific. It was the "flip-floppy realms of science" that frustrated her.

Her answer to the way things had ended up—after what she told me was "the worst process I've ever been involved in"—was that it was satisfactory to AOGA. The depleted designation, the very limited hunting quota, the continuing population monitoring—those were OK. But she was afraid the scientists would try to restore the population to a number that was unrealistically high, and that the population would never get there—would always be "depleted." She did agree that managing the take was essential, and so was continuing to study the animals, including their low (she emphasized) contaminant levels. What annoyed her were the people who kept raising "other issues"—noise, vessel traffic, military activity. "These things are part of the atmosphere of the inlet that the creatures have been living with for a very long time."

Back at the hearing with the administrative law judge, Judy had said she thought a conservation plan for the belugas was a good idea. I wanted to confirm that and find out what she thought such a conservation plan might encompass.

"We changed our mind," she said. "We think if there's a single reason why—and that was the subsistence take—addressing that is sufficient. A conservation plan normally involves habitat—things that are involved in the cause of the depletion. But that's not the case here."

I had wanted, when I started, to learn everything I could about Cook Inlet's belugas. What I'd learned was that most of what was about belugas was really about things other than, or in addition to, belugas.

Dena'ina writer Peter Kalifornsky had taught that everything has a life of its own, but that nothing lives by itself. Cook Inlet's original peopleand traditional people everywhere—understood ecological relationships in a way that our natural and social scientists seem only now to be catching up to. The plankton connects to the salmon and the salmon to the beluga, and the pesticide sprayed in Mexico connects to the river and the air to the beluga, and the old Dena'ina people living in forests connect to hunting platforms and spears that connect to fast boats and rifles to the beluga, and the people eating muktuk connect to those eating beluga burgers who connect to those watching from behind glass walls who connect to those in labs with assays and microscope slides who connect to the woman who reaches out and touches a wild beluga swimming by. The senators and the judges, and the corporations, connect to them all.

At night, the inlet's oil rigs lit up the dark. The new one, a mile from my camp, looked like a whole Coney Island of amusement rides, or the casino-fronts of a Las Vegas strip piled high. By day, a helicopter servicing the rig passed over my cabin at a hundred feet, literally shaking me out of my stillness with the whapping and wash of its rotors. Chartered planes ferried sports fishermen back and forth, back and forth, to and from the rivers behind me.

I sat by my woodstove and thought about extinction. David Quammen, paraphrasing the work of ecologists, wrote that five causal factors account for most extinctions: habitat destruction, habitat fragmentation, overkill, invasive species, and secondary effects cascading through an ecosystem from other extinctions. Quammen, not known to be an alarmist, also wrote that "the consensus among conscientious biologists is that we're headed into another mass extinction," matching the five in our geologic history, the last of which ended the dinosaurs. This one, significantly, can be laid at the feet of humans and their activities.

When I was in Point Lay, waiting for the belugas to arrive, I overheard some of the researchers talking about the Cook Inlet situation. One of the veterinarians asked, "If they go extinct, will it matter?" His was a frank, unsentimental, honest question about the actual biological importance of one small population that was, after all, already isolated from the rest of its kind. The question was, in a sense, a rhetorical one, and no one particularly wanted to debate it; they talked a little about the uniqueness, the history of use, and then let it drop.

But I kept thinking about that question, and I thought about it now. In the big picture of life on Earth, species come and go—albeit usually not as rapidly going as they now are. It could be considered quite "natural" for the Cook Inlet belugas to disappear. As a "remnant," their presence among us may well be judged an accident, a bit of randomness resulting from the way glaciers departed and land divided seas.

I thought about island species and something else that Quammen wrote. Island species live not only on, literally, islands but the equivalent of islands—mountaintops and other geographically isolated territories and, increasingly, fragmented habitats everywhere. They're the species most vulnerable to extinction—and are disappearing with frightening speed. What they have in common are small populations, which may be acted upon, to their great jeopardy, by environmental fluctuation, catastrophe, inbreeding, bad luck, and cascading effects. This point is exactly the one that environmentalists have been trying to make about the Cook Inlet belugas—and that the managers, politicians, and judges have failed to accept.

The dry, beach-scavenged spruce in my fire popped, and I thought about what's natural, and about remnants and risk, and about geologic time. Maybe in a few thousand years another ice age will reassemble this part of the world, and maybe Arctic belugas will come this way again.

Would it matter, really, to lose the Cook Inlet belugas? Without belugas eating hooligan and salmon, there'd be more for other species—including all the people who want a share of Cook Inlet's fish. Without belugas, there would be no need to consider the effects of development projects on them—with that added regulation and expense. There would be no need to monitor dredging activities for nearby whales, or to worry about the effects of seismic testing on them, or to keep boat traffic away from special habitat areas. The state could lease oil and gas tracts wherever it liked. Anchorage is a city, and Cook Inlet supports many industries. Perhaps it was unreasonable to expect to accommodate wild creatures in a place that must meet the needs of hundreds of thousands of people. Some Anchorage residents made that point about the bears that still lived within city boundaries and sometimes wandered into yards: *Hey, this is a city, and cities don't have bears, so forget about them. They don't belong here anymore.*

Would it matter? Some people wouldn't get to hunt belugas, at least not in Cook Inlet, and wouldn't get to eat beluga muktuk and meat, wouldn't get to share it or to pass on traditions that tell them who they are and from where they come. Those people, for the most part, for at least the next generation, weren't going to have much chance to do that anyway.

If you came to Cook Inlet, and you didn't see any belugas, but you didn't know that you ever could have seen belugas in this place, how would you know that you were missing anything? If you were driving the highway and stopped at Beluga Point, would you wonder why it was called Beluga Point— or would you not wonder, would you not even think about it, in the way that we don't think about the origins of all those Salmon Rivers, Bear Creeks, and Eagle Bluffs that dot our nation's maps?

If you lived here, and you didn't live with belugas anymore, would that matter? If it did matter to you, might that be only a selfish and sentimental response? What possible significance do your feelings have to the world's biological health? Anyhow, don't you want that gas to run your car, that port that must be dredged, that boat (or Jet-ski) ride, that silver salmon?

In my querying, I was trying to be my most reasonable, most objective, most disengaged from the situation. They were reasonable questions, I thought. They were modern and practical questions, bottomline business kinds of questions. But they were not all the questions, and not ones that recognized the long view or the power and obligation of our own species. I thought about my time in Tyonek and in Point Lay, and of the values I'd learned in both places. I had seen how villages operated in self-regulatory ways that transferred both knowledge and wisdom across generations, and I had at least heard about how Anchorage hunters had worked together to reconstitute something like the structure and controls of a tribe. I thought about the St. Lawrence belugas, and what people had done there, first nearly to destroy them, then to bring them back. I thought about laws and institutions, and how imperfect they will always be.

In the end, was there any way to justify causing the elimination of species—or subspecies, or stocks, or populations—from this Earth? How arrogant was that?

Do we not have an obligation, not only under the law but—may I say it, *morally*—to treat the Earth and its creatures with respect, which means not destroying them?

Or, to be anthrocentric about it—might the Cook Inlet belugas know or have or be capable of leading us to learn something that may be of great value to us, something that we could not get or learn without them?

Were not all of us, like belugas, also dependent upon clean water and the return, year after year, of salmon and other fish? If we couldn't maintain our house for belugas, could we expect to maintain it for fish, seals, people? Could it be that where go the belugas, there go we?

Did not even *one* whale, harvested by hunters with generational ties to ways of doing and being and shared within a community, fulfill necessary social, cultural, and nutritional needs? Was there not inherent value in belugas and the natural environment that supports them? Was there not something to be said, after all, for spiritual values—for those things that make people feel happy about living in the world?

The tide came in, and the tide went out. In afternoon sun, I sat on a warm rock and faced the water. I was getting closer to what I thought were the most essential questions, and I was, still, watching for belugas.

NOTES

PROLOGUE—WATCHING

20   An account of the dead beluga that washed up on our beach and "deconstructed" over the following days and weeks appears as the last chapter in my book *Fishcamp: Life on an Alaskan Shore* (paperback edition Counterpoint Press, 2000).

23   The Dena'ina names for beluga come from the dictionary compiled by James Kari, formerly with the Alaska Native Language Center, and are mentioned in his "Linguistic Traces of Dena'ina Strategy at the Archaic Periphery" in *Adventures Through Time: Readings in the Anthropology of Cook Inlet Alaska* (Cook Inlet Historical Society, 1996). In the Alutiiq language of the Pacific Eskimos who lived around the inlet's mouth, the name for beluga is *asingaar'naq* ("something that looks fancy or bright"); it appears in *Adventures Through Time,* in Ron Stanek's "Belukha Hunters of Cook Inlet." The Inupiat name for beluga is *sisuaq,* and the Yupik name is *cetuaq.*

CHAPTER 1. OLD TIME

30   Frederica de Laguna briefly described her survey of Kustatan in "Cook Inlet Adventure and Afterthoughts: Alaska 1930," in *Adventures Through Time: Readings in the Anthropology of Cook Inlet Alaska* and in more detail in her now-classic reference, *Archaeology of Cook Inlet.*

31   The archaeological dig I participated in is known as Point West of Halibut Cove, SEL–010.

31   Von Wrangell's account appears in his book, *Inhabitants of the Northwest Coast of America,* translated and edited in 1970 by James W. Van-Stone in *Arctic Anthropology* 6(2), p. 12.

32   *Shem Pete's Alaska: The Territory of the Upper Cook Inlet Dena'ina* was compiled by linguist James Kari and James Fall, an anthropologist with the Alaska Department of Fish and Game, and published in 1987 by the Alaska Native Language Center at the University of Alaska and the CIRI Foundation. Descriptions of beluga hunting appear on pages 61–65.

32   *The Ethnography of the Tanaina* by Cornelius Osgood is number sixteen in the series Yale University Publications in Anthropology. Originally published in 1937, it was reprinted by Human Relations Area Files Press in 1976. His beluga references appear on pages 190 and 194. Aside from noting that belugas were hunted by all coastal Tanaina (the earlier name of Dena'ina) and sometimes preferred to seal, he had little to report from his informants about the significance of belugas.

33   Information about Joseph McGill's and other commercial whaling operations came from issues of *Pacific Fisherman,* volumes 17–27; "A Remarkable Whaling Development" in an unidentified publication found in the Anchorage Museum archives; and Alaska Geographic's *Alaska Whales and Whaling,* "Modern Shore-Based Whaling" by Lael Morgan, 1978, p. 43.

34   "Gunning for White Whales" appeared in *The Alaska Sportsman,* May 1957.

36   The Kenai Days schedule appeared in *The Cook Inlet Courier,* August 6, 1965, and the organizer's quote in the same paper on August 13. The Hulien photo appeared on page one of the *Courier,* July 23, 1965. I found various other mentions to Kenai Days in the *Courier* in 1964 and 1965. In both years the celebration took place in August.

42   Buck Hayden's article "Beluga Hunting Is Weekend Sport at West Foreland" appeared in the *Anchorage News,* May 29, 1966.

42   A history of captive beluga whales is included in Pierre Béland's *Beluga: A Farewell to Whales* (Lyons and Burford, 1996), pp. 142–146.

42   The *National Geographic* article, in the March 1962 issue, was "Three Whales That Flew" by Carleton Ray of the New York Aquarium. The smallest of the portrayed captured whales was 7 feet long and 450 pounds, and the other two were 9 feet and 800 pounds each.

CHAPTER 2. THE WHALE IN THE ROOM

46 The 1979 Murray and Fay paper, "The White Whales or Belukhas, *Delphinapterus leucas,* of Cook Inlet, Alaska," was prepared for the Subcommittee on Small Cetaceans of the Scientific Committee of the International Whaling Commission and refers to unpublished study data. The newspaper article that referenced Fay was about three dead Cook Inlet belugas washing up on a beach ("Whale Toll Grows to 3: Cook Inlet Belugas May Be Special Strain" by Dirk Miller) and appeared in *The Peninsula Clarion,* September 13, 1985.

48 An article in the *Anchorage Daily News,* August 14, 1994, "Beluga Hunting History Remains Fuzzy" by David Hulen, concerned efforts by state and federal agencies to document Cook Inlet beluga hunting by Natives and included the Morris quote. A Greenpeace spokesperson, when asked about the Native hunting, was also quoted: "I'd think as long as it stays at a pretty low level, it's not going to impact the population, and we're not going to have a problem with it." (Greenpeace soon closed its Alaska office.)

49 The proceedings from the three-day beluga conference were edited by Robert Suydam and published by the North Slope Borough in 1996 as "Proceedings of the Alaska Beluga Whale Committee First Conference on the Biology of Beluga Whales, April 5–7, 1995, Anchorage, Alaska."

50 The history of bowhead whaling and cooperative management can be found in Henry P. Huntington's *Wildlife Management and Subsistence Hunting in Alaska* (University of Washington Press, 1992) and *The Bowhead Whale,* edited by John J. Burns et al. (Special Publication #2, The Society for Marine Mammalogy, 1993).

54 *The Anchorage Daily News* article reporting the decline appeared on the front page of the Sunday paper on September 27, 1998, and was written by Natalie Phillips.

57 The scientific papers addressing the status of the Cook Inlet belugas were later published in an issue of *Marine Fisheries Review* devoted to the subject. The issue—62(3) (2000) (not actually published until 2002)—can be found online at http://spo.nwr.noaa.gov/mcontent.htm.

61 At the time, there were hundreds of species (plants as well as animals) listed under the Endangered Species Act, but only five designated as depleted under the Marine Mammal Protection Act—four dolphin populations and the North Pacific fur seal.

63 The report on contaminants in Cook Inlet belugas compared to belugas elsewhere, by Paul Becker of the National Institute of Standards and Technology, is included in the *Marine Fisheries Review* noted above.

CHAPTER 3. THE SCIENTIFIC METHOD

68   The only study of winter range is "Distribution of Cook Inlet Beluga Whales in Winter," published by the Mineral Management Service, U.S. Department of the Interior, 1999. Principal investigators were Donald J. Hansen and Joel D. Hubbard. From mid-February to mid-March of 1997, the period when Cook Inlet sea ice generally is at its maximum, 160 belugas were counted in forty-five hours of aerial surveys. Of the total, 150 were spotted in the (ice-free) central area of Cook Inlet around Kalgin Island, and ten were found outside the inlet, in Yakutat Bay to the east. The 160 likely recounted many of the same whales on different days, as the highest single-day count was fifty.

69   A wealth of information about the use of satellite telemetry to study belugas is found in *Arctic* 54 (3) (September 2001). This issue, published by the Arctic Institute of North America in Calgary, Alberta, consists of a dozen research papers covering recent telemetry applications among Arctic populations of both belugas and narwhals.

79   Descriptions and photos of the 2000 and subsequent Cook Inlet beluga tagging projects, and maps that follow the movements of the tagged whales, can be found on the web at http://nmml.afsc.noaa.gov/CetaceanAssessment/BelugaWhale.html.

81   The National Marine Fisheries Service provided me with various documents detailing the field and analysis methods for conducting their aerial surveys and for determining abundance estimates. Several papers regarding distribution, abundance, and tagging are among those in *Marine Fisheries Review* 62 (3) (2000).

83   The 1979 map of beluga distribution was by Murray and Fay, in "The White Whales or Belukhas of Cook Inlet, Alaska" (the same paper that postulated morphological differentiation of the Cook Inlet stock, based on skull measurements).

85   "Philopatry and Site Tenacity of Belugas Hunted by the Inuit at the Nastapoka Estuary, Eastern Hudson Bay" (L. M. J. Caron and T. G. Smith, 1990) details a study that found that the same belugas (recognized by markings, mainly old bullet holes) returned each summer to the same area and that, each time they left to escape hunters, they quickly returned. The importance of the particular estuary was thought to be for rubbing on the abrasive substrate in warmer water (to help with the molt of old skin).

85   "Historic and Current Use of Lower Cook Inlet, Alaska, by Belugas," by Suzann Speckman and John Piatt as part of a USGS study, appears in *Marine Fisheries Review* 62 (3) (2000).

86   The Abbey quote is from "Down the River with Henry Thoreau," 1982.

CHAPTER 4. BELUGA LOVE

88   The Raffi song "Baby Beluga" is considered his "most popular and beloved." He first recorded it in 1980, and the first book version followed in 1990.

88   The Steinbeck paraphrase is from *The Log from the Sea of Cortez* (Penguin Classic), p. 225.

90   The overall record of captive births has been poor, according to a Scripps-McClatchy newspaper article by Tamyra Wowser, printed in the *Anchorage Daily News* on March 1, 1999. Of seventeen belugas born in North American aquariums between 1972 and 1999, eleven died at or shortly after birth.

94   Barry Lopez's "A Presentation of Whales," about a stranding of sperm whales on the Oregon coast, appears in *Crossing Open Ground* (1988) and in several anthologies.

95   A long list of whale adoption programs can be found at www.acsonline.org, the website of the American Cetacean Society. Beluga whales from the St. Lawrence Estuary can be "adopted" through the St. Lawrence National Institute of Ecotoxicology (www.inesl.org/eng/6/FS6.html).

96   The anecdote about the killer whale studying whale photos appears on page 251 of Roger Payne's *Among Whales* (Scribner's, 1995) and was confirmed for me by John Ford.

96   Ford's *Killer Whales* was published by the University of British Columbia Press in Canada and the University of Washington Press in the United States in 1994. It was revised and updated in 2000. Other catalogs of killer whales include *Transients: Mammal-Hunting Killer Whales of British Columbia, Washington, and Southeastern Alaska* (University of Washington Press, 1999) and *Killer Whales of Southern Alaska* (North Gulf Oceanic Society, 1999.) For the latter, see www.whalesalaska.org.

97   A paper on contaminant levels in J18 and other Puget Sound killer whales was published by Peter Ross, a research scientist with the Canadian Institute of Ocean Sciences, in the *Marine Pollution Bulletin* in its June 2000 issue.

97   Reports on contaminant levels in killer whales appeared widely in the press. The *Anchorage Daily News* on March 3, 2001, reprinted a *Los Angeles Times* article by Marla Cone, "Orcas Threatened by Badly Polluted Food Chain"; the food chain quote, from scientist Peter Ross, appeared therein. The Alaska killer whale situation was reported in the *Anchorage Daily News* on July 22, 2001: "Whales in Sound Imperiled" by Doug O'Harra. *The New*

York Times on October 16, 2001, featured "Struggle to Survive for an 'Urban Whale'" by Carol Kaesuk Yoon.

98 A 1958 Alaska Department of Fish and Game report, commenting upon belugas that had been captured in Alaska for display in California, observed the animals "to be very adaptable to confinement and training." Those belugas were taught to retrieve batons and toot horns, to leap out of water on command, and to tow small boats. The report concluded, "It is remarkable and indicative of a great innate intelligence that the animals have been quick to learn a variety of activities which are altogether unrelated to behavioral patterns displayed in the natural environment."

99 Rachel Carson wrote about a child's engagement with the natural world (and the adult responsibility to nurture it) in *A Sense of Wonder,* published posthumously in 1965.

101 The 1992 attitudinal study is detailed in "International Attitudes to Whales, Whaling and the Use of Whale Products: A Six-Country Study," by Milton M. R. Freeman and Stephen R. Kellert. It appears in *Elephants and Whales: Resources for Whom?* edited by Milton M. R. Freeman and Urs P. Kreuter (Gordon and Breach Science Publishers, 1994). An executive summary of the World Conservation Trust survey can be found at www.iwmc. org/whales/survey107/minke02.htm.

102 The quoted letter came in response to my article, "Two Worlds, One Whale," which appeared in the July-August 2000 issue of *Sierra*. Response letters and my answer to them appeared in the November-December issue.

103 *Whale Watching 2000: Worldwide Tourism Numbers, Expenditures and Expanding Socioeconomic Benefits,* published by the International Fund for Animal Welfare, states that growth of the industry has averaged twelve percent a year, compared to general world tourism of three to four percent, and that the economic impact is about a billion dollars per year.

107 Jim Diehl's unpublished "Elephants in the Arm" detailed his responses to two whale strandings, in both of which he defied authorities to attend to whales. The comparison to elephants remarks on the texture of killer whale skin, which was splitting open in the sun. Diehl published a related piece, "The Death of an Orca: What We Have Learned," in the November 1993 edition of *Eddyline,* the newsletter of the Knik Canoers and Kayakers. *Anchorage Daily News* articles about Cook Inlet killer whale and beluga strandings include those dated October 24, 1988; May 22 and 23, 1991; September 25, 26, and 27, 1993; June 15 and 16, 1994; August 29, 1996; and August 31 and September 1, 1999.

109 The quotes about having fun and repaying the whales come from a profile of Diehl, "Who'll Guard the Whales?" that appeared in *We Alaskans,* the *Anchorage Daily News* Sunday magazine on September 26, 1993. Among Diehl's mentioned accomplishments are a state kayaking championship and the rescue of an unconscious man from a river by kayak—holding the man's sleeve in his teeth while he paddled.

CHAPTER 5. THE GREEN MACHINE

113 The State of Alaska's endangered species list includes only five species (Eskimo curlew, short-tailed albatross, humpback whale, right whale, and blue whale), all of which are also on the federal endangered species list. Alaska also keeps a list of Species of Special Concern, which identifies sixteen species (including the Cook Inlet beluga whale) that are in decline. The point of listing Species of Special Concern, according to the Alaska Department of Fish and Game, is to identify critical habitat, to initiate or increase monitoring or studies, and to recommend management action—to protect species and forestall serious threats to them before those threats become critical.

115 The Center for Biological Diversity opened an Alaska office in July 2002 with an Alaska program coordinator headquartered in Sitka and "a sustained campaign to protect Alaska's species and habitats from [development] threats and help maintain it as our wildest state." *The New Yorker* article about the CBD, "No People Allowed," was by Nicholas Lemann and appeared November 22, 1999.

116 For a thorough and fascinating accounting of the Makah whaling controversy and hunt, see Robert Sullivan's *A Whale Hunt: Two Years on the Olympic Peninsula with the Makah and Their Canoe* (Scribner's, 2000).

118 Other "green decade" laws included the National Environmental Policy Act (1970), the Clean Air Act (1970), the Marine Mammal Protection Act (1972), the Toxic Substances Control Act (1976), the Resource Conservation and Recovery Act (1976), and the Clean Water Act (1977).

120 The John Schoen newspaper column appeared in the *Anchorage Daily News* on November 8, 2001, as half of a point-counterpoint pairing. The other half, by Tadd Owens, the director of the Resource Development Council in Anchorage, argued that hunting restrictions were enough protection for the whales.

129 An article about the work of researcher Peter Scheifele regarding St. Lawrence noise and belugas appeared in *Advance,* February 21, 1997.

129 The noise study, "Acoustic Measurements in Cook Inlet, Alaska, During August 2001" was prepared for NMFS by Greeneridge Sciences, Inc.

Additional discussion of noise (and other anthropogenic) effects on belugas can be found in "Beluga Habitat Associations in Cook Inlet, Alaska," *Marine Fisheries Review* 62 (3) (2000).

135 Barry Lopez quoted anthropologist Cliff Hickey in *Arctic Dreams* (p. 66 of the Bantam paperback edition). They were on Banks Island, in Arctic Canada, to observe musk oxen.

CHAPTER 6. THE OTHER REMNANT

Compared to any other beluga populations, the St. Lawrence belugas have been well studied. I consulted a great many scientific papers and popular articles concerning them—too many to list here—and more are regularly being added to the literature. Short summaries of some of the current work are displayed at www.whales-online.net, which also lists project collaborators, and links and archives can lead the interested reader to the desired level of information.

136 Pierre Béland's book about the St. Lawrence belugas, *Beluga: A Farewell to Whales,* was published by Lyons and Burford in 1996 and has been out of print since 1998. His oft-repeated quote that St. Lawrence belugas "could qualify as hazardous waste" appeared in the *National Geographic* in June 1994, in "Beluga: White Whale of the North" by Kenneth S. Norris, and elsewhere. At the time, Canadian law required permits for the transportation or disposal of anything with more than 50 parts per million (ppm) of PCBs. Of male belugas analyzed, the average ppm was 75.8, with a range from 53.9–89.2; females were somewhat lower, averaging 37.3. The law, of course, was aimed at hazardous materials like transformers, not at wildlife, and dead belugas were never actually disposed of as though they were hazardous waste. They were either buried on beaches or, if taken to a veterinary school for necropsy, trucked away and disposed of with other animal carcasses.

142 The St. Lawrence River for most of its length is actually an estuary. There are tidal movements all the way up to Quebec City, and the tides at Tadoussac rise and fall eleven feet.

150 Michael Kingsley is quoted in a *Smithsonian* article, "The 'Sea Canary' Sings the Blues," by Steve Kemper (November 1999): "Some people's funding depends on low numbers. The motive for keeping belugas endangered is financial."

151 The DFO document is "Population Index Estimate for the Beluga of the St. Lawrence River Estuary in 2000." Its population estimate for 2000, incorporating the new correction factor for animals not visible at the surface, was 952.

It found the population growth rate since 1988 to be 4.4 beluga per year, "which is not significantly different from a zero, or a stable population" and "suggests that this population has been relatively stable over the last twelve years."

153 See Sandra Steingraber's *Living Downstream* (Addison-Wesley, 1997) for a compelling discussion of chemicals in the environment and their relationships to environmental and human health. Steingraber mentions the St. Lawrence belugas in relationship to both local and global pollution problems.

154 Genetic variables are found, for example, in some stocks of Siberian tigers, where low gene variation among animals too closely related has led to poor immunity to disease and to low fertility. This is known as "inbreeding depression."

CHAPTER 7. ADAPTATION

159 The "Whalers of the City" article was written by David Hulen, *Anchorage Daily News* reporter, and published on August 14, 1994. The photographs were taken by *Anchorage Daily News* photographer Erik Hill.

161 The *Voice of the Times* editorial, "Belugas Came By," appeared September 23, 2000. On September 26, the *Voice* published a brief correction, followed on September 29 by a letter from Bart Garber, CEO of the Tyonek Native Corp., expanding on the correction and pointing out that the error was "particularly galling since Tyonek, more than any other community in the Cook Inlet relies upon the beluga for food and depends upon Cook Inlet–based economic activity that would be impacted by an Endangered Species Act listing."

162 Joel's letter was published August 10, 2000.

163 My list of Tyonek's investments came from Bart Garber's letter, cited above.

166 Information regarding tests of subsistence foods following the *Exxon Valdez* oil spill can be found in *Darkened Waters: A Review of the History, Science, and Technology Associated with the Exxon Valdez Oil Spill and Cleanup,* a publication I wrote in 1992 to accompany the Homer Society of Natural History/Pratt Museum exhibit "Darkened Waters: Profile of an Oil Spill." A Native food that tested as high (20,000 parts per billion) as oil-coated mussels for polycyclic aromatic hydrocarbons was (unoiled) salmon sampled from smokehouses. The traditional woodsmoke method of preservation adds hydrocarbons, known carcinogens, to fish and other foods.

168 The *Anchorage Daily News* article, "Dead Belugas Provide Treat for Natives," appeared on September 1, 1999.

168   The study of Cook Inlet seafoods was conducted by the U.S. Environmental Protection Agency between 1997 and 2001. The report is "Human Exposure Evaluation of Chemical Contaminants in Seafoods Collected in the Vicinity of Tyonek, Seldovia, Port Graham and Nanwalek in Cook Inlet, Alaska." It was specifically not prescriptive about what was or was not safe to eat but rather used a "risk assessment modeling approach" and encouraged communities to calculate their own risks depending on consumption patterns.

168   Data on Inuit exposures is included in *Arctic Pollution 2002,* the report from a five-year study by the Arctic Monitoring and Assessment Program (AMAP, an international program). See www.amap.no.

168   The 1999 report that discussed Alaska Native health and the benefits of traditional foods is "Summary of Research-Based Knowledge of Environmental Changes in Alaska," prepared by the Institute of Social and Economic Research at the University of Alaska in collaboration with the Alaska Native Science Commission. A specific purpose of the reader-friendly report was to bring research-based knowledge to Alaska Natives, who can then use it in the context of their traditional knowledge. The report draws heavily on the work of AMAP (mentioned above) and the Canadian Northern Contaminants Program, and it places information into summary form with additional support gathered from workshops on Native foods and other sources.

The Alaska Division of Public Health has also published a report designed for practical decision-making. "Use of Traditional Food in a Healthy Diet in Alaska: Risks in Perspective" is a reasonably comprehensive (144 pages) report published in 1998 and is available from the division's website. It looks most specifically at risks from mercury, cadmium, and PCBs and recommends "the continued unrestricted consumption of traditional subsistence foods in Alaska. . . . Severely limiting the consumption of traditional foods may result in harm by reducing the consumption of food that has health benefits and by increasing the consumption of foods that have potential health risks." It notes as well that what are really needed are global policies to minimize the release of anthropogenic pollutants into the environment.

CHAPTER 8. THE BEACH PEOPLE

176   The account of the establishment of the Tyonek Reservation comes from Donald Craig Mitchell's *Sold American: The Story of Alaska Natives and Their Land, 1867–1959* (University Press of New England, 1997). Mitchell found the quotation in Bureau of Indian Affairs correspondence records.

177   For more on Osgood's *The Ethnography of the Tanaina,* see the note

to Chapter 1. The quotations regarding Tyonek and Tanaina culture appear on pages 191 and 194 in "Culture Changes Among the Tanaina Due to Historic Influences."

178 "Dena'ina Enlightenment" was coined by Alan Boraas and Donita Peter in an anthropological paper, "The True Believer Among the Kenai Peninsula Dena'ina," to describe the cultural changes that occurred when new, Western ideas influenced traditional beliefs in the region. This concept of enlightenment, drawing a parallel to the European Enlightenment, suggests the intellectual vigor with which traditional values were reexamined and adapted. The authors differentiated between enlightenment and assimilation or accommodation—the latter terms suggesting one-directional change. The paper occurs in *Adventures Through Time: Readings in the Anthropology of Cook Inlet, Alaska* (Cook Inlet Historical Society, 1996). Coauthor Donita Peter is from Tyonek.

178 A history of Tyonek's role in funding the organization of Alaska's Natives around land claims issues can be found in Donald Craig Mitchell's *Take My Land, Take My Life: The Story of Congress's Historic Settlement of Alaska Native Land Claims, 1960–1971* (University of Alaska Press, 2001).

182 *The Use of Fish and Wildlife Resources in Tyonek, Alaska,* by James A. Fall, Dan J. Foster, and Ronald T. Stanek, was Technical Paper No. 105 for the Alaska Department of Fish and Game, Subsistence Division, 1984. The report was done in response to requests from the Alaska Boards of Fish and Game for information relating to resource allocation issues and to help identify potential socioeconomic impacts from proposed development in the area. It concluded that a majority of Tyonek households participated in a mixed economy of seasonal wage employment and extensive use of wild fish and game resources and that, "in short, the role of wild resource harvest and use in the ongoing life of the community remained highly significant."

188 *Traditional Ecological Knowledge of Beluga Whales in Cook Inlet, Alaska* was compiled and edited by Henry P. Huntington in March 1999 as a report to the Alaska Beluga Whale Committee and the Cook Inlet Marine Mammal Council. Its preface consists of a strongly worded, six-page statement from the Alaska Beluga Whale Committee about the overhunting and decline of the Cook Inlet belugas, a chronology of its efforts to bring attention to the issue, and a list of recommendations for immediately limiting the harvest through hunter self-regulation and co-management. A version of the report also appears in *Marine Fisheries Review* 62 (3) (2000), the issue devoted to the status of the Cook Inlet beluga.

190 Salmon catch records from the Alaska Department of Fish and Game are reported in the *Draft EIS, Federal Actions Associated with Management and Recovery of Cook Inlet Beluga Whales,* September 2000. Additional discussion of prey species and availability can be found in "Beluga Habitat Associations in Cook Inlet Alaska," in *Marine Fisheries Review* 62 (3) (2000).

191 Henry Huntington's paper, "Using Traditional Ecological Knowledge in Science: Methods and Applications," appeared in *Ecological Applications* 10 (5) (2000). That issue has a special section consisting of numerous papers on TEK applications from around the world.

192 For more on *Shem Pete's Alaska: The Territory of the Upper Cook Inlet Dena'ina,* see the note to Chapter 1. Shem Pete was the principal contributor, but additional place-names and commentary were contributed by three dozen other Dena'ina elders, some from Tyonek and nearly all now deceased.

193 The account of Prince William Sound whaling is in Kaj Birket-Smith's *The Chugach Eskimo* (National Museum, Copenhagen, 1953), pp. 33–37.

194 *A Dena'ina Legacy: The Collected Writings of Peter Kalifornsky,* edited by James Kari and Alan Boraas, was published by the Alaska Native Language Center at the University of Alaska Fairbanks, 1991.

CHAPTER 9. POINT LAY

202 The quote regarding Point Lay's dependence on belugas occurs on page 20 of *Traditional Ecological Knowledge of Beluga Whales: An Indigenous Knowledge Pilot Project in the Chukchi and Northern Bering Seas,* compiled and edited by Henry P. Huntington and Nikolai I. Mymrin and published in 1996. Point Lay was one of five northwest Alaska villages and four Chukotka, Russia, villages where hunters were interviewed. It was also the one place where hunters posed questions of their own, having to do with beluga migration movements and the importance of particular habitats, that they hoped science would help answer.

203 The bowhead census is conducted both visually and with a sophisticated acoustical system that records whales passing at a distance, under ice. I read in the *Arctic Sounder,* a regional newspaper, that noisy belugas traveling with the bowheads sometimes interfered with the acoustical recordings.

203 The North Slope publication that Bill Hess was responsible for was *Uiniq,* or *The Open Lead.* The Winter 1991 issue included "Beluga Hunt!" His book, which incorporated the material in "Beluga Hunt!" into a somewhat different chapter called "Beluga," is *Gift of the Whale: The Inupiat*

Bowhead Hunt, a Sacred Tradition. It was published by Sasquatch Books, Seattle, in 1999. Hess's black and white photos superbly illustrate Inupiat life in whaling villages.

210 The profile came from the Arctic Development Council, a nonprofit that promotes economic development in Alaska's Arctic.

210 *To Keep the Past Alive: The Point Lay Cultural Resource Site Survey* was published in 1985 by the North Slope Borough. Warren and Dorcas Neakok were two of the principal resource experts who participated in a site inventory and provided information about the past.

EPILOGUE—WATCHING

236 Quammen's essay, "Planet of Weeds," was first published in *Harper's* in 1998 and was included in *The Best American Essays 1999.*

ACKNOWLEDGMENTS

This book could not have been written without the cooperation, assistance, and advice of a great many generous people, many of whom appear within these pages. I thank them all, including those who, at their requests or by my decisions to protect personal privacy, go unnamed. I thank as well all those whose published work I drew upon; sources are cited in the notes section above.

In the beginning, Craig Matkin taught me both basic whale biology and something about the passions that whale researchers bring to their work. Dorothy Childers and Scott Highleyman encouraged me to embark on this project as a way of bringing marine conservation issues to a wider audience; each of them have worked tirelessly to protect marine systems and fisheries and to enable coastal people to participate in decision-making. Paul Rauber at *Sierra* encouraged me to struggle with the hardest questions, and gave me a platform for doing that.

Amy Crawford helped mightily with timely and cheerful research assistance.

My agent Elizabeth Wales believed in me and what this book might become, as did Counterpoint editors Jack Shoemaker and Trish Hoard, who allowed me the necessary time. Later, editors Dawn Seferian and Sarah McNally saw me through.

A number of reviewers read parts or the whole of manuscript drafts and offered expert scientific, cultural, and literary advice. These include Robert Suydam, Richard Bailey, Kathy Frost, Mike Payne, Terry Johnson, members of the Point Lay Village Council, and Lisa Whip. I'm particularly indebted to my friend Tom Kizzia for his close reading and helpful suggestions. Any factual or interpretive errors that remain are mine alone.

My partner, Ken Castner, shares fish camp life in the heart of beluga range and, as always, supports my work with enthusiasm.

My parents taught me to love nature and books and never complained when I left New England for the life I needed in Alaska. I was assisted by a number of residency fellowships during the period of research and writing: Ragdale Foundation, Blue Mountain Center, Djerassi Foundation, Escape to Create, Mesa Refuge, and Hedgebrook. The supported time and the invigorating companionship of my fellow residents were invaluable. The Alaska Council on the Arts also greatly honored and assisted me with a 2002 Connie Boochever Fellowship in literature.

I thank you all.

THE MOUNTAINEERS, founded in 1906, is a nonprofit outdoor activity and conservation club, whose mission is "to explore, study, preserve, and enjoy the natural beauty of the outdoors...." Based in Seattle, Washington, the club is now the third-largest such organization in the United States, with seven branches throughout Washington State.

The Mountaineers sponsors both classes and year-round outdoor activities in the Pacific Northwest, which include hiking, mountain climbing, ski-touring, snowshoeing, bicycling, camping, kayaking, nature study, sailing, and adventure travel. The club's conservation division supports environmental causes through educational activities, sponsoring legislation, and presenting informational programs.

All club activities are led by skilled, experienced instructors, who are dedicated to promoting safe and responsible enjoyment and preservation of the outdoors.

If you would like to participate in these organized outdoor activities or the club's programs, consider a membership in The Mountaineers. For information and an application, write or call The Mountaineers, Club Headquarters, 300 Third Avenue West, Seattle, WA 98119; 206-284-6310. You can also visit the club's website at www.mountaineers.org or contact The Mountaineers via email at clubmail@mountaineers.org.

The Mountaineers Books, an active, nonprofit publishing program of the club, produces guidebooks, instructional texts, historical works, natural history, and works on environmental conservation. All books produced by The Mountaineers Books fulfill the club's mission.

Send or call for our catalog of more than 500 outdoor titles:

The Mountaineers Books
1001 SW Klickitat Way, Suite 201
Seattle, WA 98134
800-553-4453
mbooks@mountaineersbooks.org
www.mountaineersbooks.org

Spirited Waters: Soloing South through the Inside Passage
Jennifer Hahn
The gripping account of an unforgettable solo kayaking journey.

Being Caribou
Karsten Heuer
A newlywed couple spends five months wandering with the Arctic caribou and becomes transformed by their adventure.

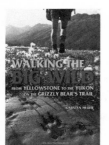

Walking the Big Wild: From Yellowstone to the Yukon on the Grizzly Bear's Trail
Karsten Heuer
Could it be true that wild animals in North America can still find a way to migrate 2,000 miles in one direction? The author follows them to find out.

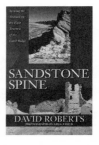

Sandstone Spine: Seeking the Anasazi on the First Traverse of the Comb Ridge
David Roberts
Three friends bound by love of the Southwest's canyonlands undertake the first traverse of the Comb Ridge, in search of the lost civilization of the Anasazi.

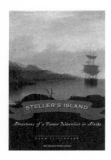

Steller's Island: Adventures of a Pioneer Naturalist in Alaska
Dean Littlepage
History, adventure, and science—the eighteenth-century naturalist, Georg Steller, sailed to the north coast of North America and introduced its biological wonders to the world.

Arctic Wings: Birds of the Arctic National Wildlife Refuge
Manomet Center for Conservation Science
Stunning avian photography and essays by naturalists such as David Allen Sibley celebrate the nesting grounds of nearly 200 bird species from every point on the globe.

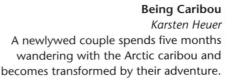

Mountaineers Books has more than 500 outdoor recreation titles in print.
Receive a free catalog at
www.mountaineersbooks.org.